OFFICE OF POPULATION CENSUSES

Birth statistics

Review of the Registrar General
on births and patterns of
family building in England and Wales, 1986

Series FM1 no.15

London: Her Majesty's Stationery Office

ISBN 0 11 691216 2

Her Majesty's Stationery Office

Standing order service

Placing a standing order with HMSO BOOKS enables a customer to receive future editions of this title automatically as published.
This saves the time, trouble and expense of placing individual orders and avoids the problem of knowing when to do so.
For details please write to HMSO BOOKS (PC 13A/1), Publications Centre, PO Box 276, London SW8 5DT and quoting reference X02 02 35.
The standing order service also enables customers to receive automatically as published all material of their choice which additionally saves extensive catalogue research. The scope and selectivity of the service has been extended by new techniques, and there are more than 3,500 classifications to choose from. A special leaflet describing the service in detail may be obtained on request.

Contents

home

List of tables and Appendices

6 Multiple births (*continued*)   England and Wales

Table 6.3   Maternities with multiple births: age of mother,   64
                   legitimacy and type of outcome, 1986

6.4   Legitimate maternities with multiple births: age of   65
                   mother and previous liveborn children, 1986

7 Area of usual residence   England and Wales,
                                                                             England, Wales,
                                                                             standard regions,
                                                                             Greater London,
                                                                             metropolitan counties,
                                                                             regional health authorities

Table 7.1   Live and still births: area of usual residence   66
                   and legitimacy, 1986

7.2   Live births: area of usual residence and age of   67
                   mother, 1986

8 Place of confinement

Table 8.1   Maternities: place of confinement, age of mother   England and Wales   68
                   and previous liveborn children/legitimacy, 1986

8.2   Maternities: place of confinement and area of   England and Wales,   68
                   usual residence, 1986   regional health authorities

9 Birthplace of parents

Table 9.1   Live births: birthplace of mother, 1976 to 1986   England and Wales   69

9.2   Live births: birthplace of mother and area of usual   England and Wales,   70
                   residence, 1986   metropolitan counties,
                                                                             Greater London,
                                                                             London boroughs,
                                                                             selected metropolitan and
                                                                             non-metropolitan districts
                                                                             (where 15% or more of the
                                                                             total live births in 1986 were
                                                                             to mothers born outside the
                                                                             United Kingdom)

9.3   Live births: birthplace of mother and father, 1986   England and Wales   72

9.4   Live births: birthplace of mother and age of mother, 1986 England and Wales   73

9.5   Total period fertility rates by birthplace of mother,   England and Wales   74
                   1981 to 1986

9.6   Live births: birthplace of mother and number of   England and Wales   75
                   previous liveborn children/legitimacy, 1986

10 Cohort analysis   England and Wales

Table 10.1   Age-specific fertility rates: calendar years of birth   76
                   of woman, 1920 to 1971

10.2   Average number of liveborn children by successive   78
                   ages of woman: calendar years of birth of woman,
                   1920 to 1971

Introduction

This volume *Birth statistics* (Series FM1 no.15) relates to births occurring in England and Wales during 1986. Statistics for earlier years, and separate statistics for Scotland and Northern Ireland are published as follows:

for England and Wales - in *Birth statistics* from 1974 onwards, and for 1973 and earlier, in the *Registrar General's Statistical Review of England and Wales, Part II*; and

for Scotland and Northern Ireland - in the *Annual Reports of the Registrars General for Scotland* and *Northern Ireland* respectively.

Quarterly estimates of numbers of birth occurrences, seasonally adjusted fertility rates and detailed fertility statistics for England and Wales are published in *Population Trends* (HMSO).

This volume has been divided into twelve sections, each presenting statistics on particular characteristics of the birth or of the parents (some basic characteristics appear in more than one section - for example, age of mother at birth). In order to economise on printing costs, the time series shown in this volume have been limited to a run of ten years at most. Figures for earlier years are shown in *Birth statistics* (Series FM1 nos. 7 to 12). A volume of historical fertility statistics (Series FM1 no.13) published in early 1987 contains time series of birth statistics back to 1838 (the year following the legislation of 1837 when the registration of births was first made compulsory) and time series of more detailed figures back to 1938 (the year in which the Population (Statistics) Act came into operation).

New tables and changes to existing tables introduced this year

Table 1.7 New table showing mean ages of women at births of different orders regardless of legitimacy.

Table 1.8 and **1.9** Previously described as **Table 1.7** and **1.8.**

Table 10.3 New table showing the average number of first liveborn by successive ages of women by calendar years of birth of woman.

Table 10.5 New table showing percentage distribution of liveborn children at successive ages of women born in selected years.

(See section on birth order regardless of legitimacy for further details).

Birth registration

Birth statistics are compiled annually from the information collected at birth registration for entry into the live birth and stillbirth registers, and from additional confidential particulars collected at the same time under the Population (Statistics) Acts of 1938 and 1960 (see **Appendices A** and **B**).

The details ascertained at birth registration which are relevant to this volume are:

> the child's date and place of birth;
> sex and legitimacy;
> the father's place of birth and
>   occupation (as appropriate); and
> the mother's place of birth and place
>   of usual residence.

The confidential particulars are:

for all births

> the mother's date of birth; and
> the father's date of birth if his
>   name is entered in the register; and

for legitimate births only

> the date of the parents' marriage;
> whether the mother has been married
>   more than once; and
> the number of previous children borne
>   by the mother to the present husband
>   or any other husband, distinguishing
>   the number born alive and the number
>   stillborn.

It should be noted that formal registration began on 1 July 1837 for live births and on 1 July 1927 for stillbirths; it was not until the Population (Statistics) Act, 1938, came into operation on 1 July 1938 that the confidential particulars - excluding the father's date of birth - were ascertained for statistical purposes. (It was also possible to distinguish multiple births on a regular basis as from 1 July 1938.) The Population (Statistics) Act, 1960, with effect from 1 January 1961, added the question on father's date of birth in the case of legitimate births and of illegitimate births where the father's name is entered in the register. The questions relating to father's and mother's place of birth were introduced on 1 April 1969 by the Registration of births, Deaths and Marriages Regulations, 1968. Further details on the production of the Registrar General's statistics can be found in *Population and health statistics in England and Wales* (OPCS, 1980), and the companion volume *Vital registration and marriage in England and Wales* (OPCS, 1977).

Birth order regardless of legitimacy
The sharp increase in the proportions of all births occurring outside marriage in recent years means that it has been necessary to supplement the information about the birth order of legitimate births obtained under the Population Statistics Acts (see above), with estimates for all births of the overall or true birth order regardless of legitimacy. The volume *Period and cohort birth order statistics* Series FM1 no.14 describes how these statistics were estimated and gives detailed analysis of births by true birth order and mother's age for calendar years from 1938-85 and for cohorts of women born in years from 1920 onwards.

Drawing upon the material published in FM1 no.14 with the addition of estimates for 1986, three new tables have been added to this annual volume to give up-to-date summaries of the estimated true birth order statistics. **Table 1.7** gives estimates of the mean ages of women at successive births according to their estimated true birth order; **Table 10.3** gives estimates of the average number of first births (regardless of legitimacy) by successive ages to women born in 1920 and later years; and **Table 10.5** gives the estimated distribution of numbers of children (regardless of legitimacy) by successive ages to women born in 1920 and later years.

Explanatory notes

All figures, unless otherwise indicated, refer to those births which occur in the calendar year and which are registered by 31 January of the following year. Births registered later than this but occurring in the previous year are included in that following year's figures (for the period 1976-86 there were approximately 1,500-2,000 such cases per year).

Maternity/paternity
A maternity/paternity denotes a pregnancy which resulted in the birth of one or more live or still born children.

Stillbirth
A stillbirth is defined in section 41 of the Births and Deaths Registration Act, 1953, as 'a child which has issued forth from its mother after the twenty-eighth week of pregnancy and which did not at any time after being completely expelled from its mother breathe or show other signs of life'.

Total period fertility rate *(Section 1)*
The total period fertility rate (TPFR) is derived by summing the fertility rates for a given year (live births per woman) by single years of age (or, if not available, by five-year age-groups) up to the age by which the childbearing life span of women is effectively finished, taken to be age 50 (see also **Tables 3.1** and **10.1**). It measures the average number of

children which would be born per woman if women experienced the age-specific fertility rates of the calendar year in question throughout their childbearing life span. **Table 1.8** shows TPFRs for years from 1976 to 1986 according to the contributions made by illegitimate and legitimate births of different orders to women in five-year age-groups.

Gross reproduction rate *(Section 1)*
The gross reproduction rate (GRR) is derived by summing female fertility rates (female live births per woman) in the same manner as for the total fertility rate. It measures the average number of daughters born alive per woman that would result if women survived to the end of their reproductive period, and throughout this period were subject to the given age-specific female fertility rates; where these rates are those of the calendar year in question this calculation relates to period fertility (as in the case of the TPFR).

Net reproduction rate *(Section 1)*
The net reproduction rate (NRR) is similar to the GRR, but allows for the effect of mortality - not all women survive to the end of their reproductive period. It measures the average number of daughters born alive per woman that would result if women were subjected, from birth to the end of their reproductive period, to the given age-specific female fertility and mortality rates; where these rates are those of the calendar year in question this calculation relates to period fertility (as in the case of the TPFR).

Legitimacy and sole and joint registration *(Section 1)*
Generally speaking, a legitimate birth is that of a child born to parents who were lawfully married to one another either (a) at the date of the child's birth or (b) when the child was conceived even if they became divorced or the father died before the birth. Only for a legitimate birth will the Registrar of Births enter on Form 309 (see **Appendix A**) confidential particulars relating to the date of the parents' marriage, whether the mother has been married more than once and the number of the mother's previous live and still born children.

If the child is illegitimate, the father's name and other particulars will be entered on the' draft entry ' Form 309 by the Registrar only if the information is provided jointly by both the mother and father in person (unless the mother supplies either a statutory declaration by the father acknowledging paternity or an affiliation order - see footnote to **Table 3.8**).

Information from births draft entries is used to determine whether the mother and father jointly registering an illegitimate birth were usually resident at the same address at the time of registration; **Table 3.10** shows the statistics obtained. Space 10 on the draft entries is used by the registrar of births to record the mother's usual address at the time of the birth. Space 13 is used to record the informant's or informants' address or addresses at the time of the registration of the birth. If there is a sole informant whose usual address is the same as that shown in Space 10, a line is drawn through Space 13. In the case of an illegitimate birth registered by both the father and mother, the father's usual address is always entered in Space 13 even if it is the same as the address recorded in Space 10. The mother's usual address at registration is recorded in Space 13 only if it is different from the father's. The classification of mother's and father's usual addresses shown in **Table 3.1** for jointly registered illegitimate births is therefore defined as follows:

Same address - only one address recorded in Space 13; *Different address* - two different addresses recorded in Space 13.

Seasonality *(Section 2)*
Seasonally adjusted numbers of live births are obtained using the X-11 adjustment package developed by the US Bureau of the Census. Seasonally adjusted TPFRs are based upon these numbers and are estimated using a method due to G. Calot (see Werner, B. A new method for estimating the trend in fertility rates, *Statistical News 60*, HMSO, 1983).

Age of parents *(Section 3)*
The mother's or father's date of birth is recorded and translated into the age at the birthday preceding the date of the child's birth. This age is often termed 'age last birthday'. If the mother's date of birth, or father's date of birth (when applicable) is not given, an age is imputed from the previously processed record with completely stated but otherwise matching particulars. A note of the number of cases dealt with in this way is included with relevant tables.

Previous liveborn children (parity) *(Section 4)*
Information on previous liveborn children is only available for women having a legitimate birth. Sometimes referred to as 'parity' it relates to the number of previous liveborn children by the present or any former husband, as stated at registration. (This use of the term parity should not be confused with those used elsewhere, particularly in medical literature: for example, the number of preceding births, whether live or still, or total number of liveborn children ever born to a woman.) If parity is not given, a value is imputed from the previously processed record with completely stated but otherwise matching particulars. A note of the number of cases dealt with in this way is included in the relevant tables.

Duration of marriage *(Section 5)*
Pre-maritally conceived live births are, by convention, taken to be those births where the calculated duration of marriage is less than 8 months - that is 0-7 completed months. As only month and year of marriage are recorded at registration the calculation relates to the interval in completed months between the middle of the month of marriage and the date of the child's birth. Other durations of marriage are computed similarly. If the date of marriage is not given, a value for the duration of the marriage is imputed from the previously processed record with completely stated but otherwise matching particulars.

For women who have been married more than once, duration of marriage refers to that of the current marriage. Consequently figures relating to all married women show duration of current marriage.

Multiple births *(Section 6)*
Multiple births arising from a single pregnancy are counted as one maternity/paternity, although each child born is reckoned separately in tables relating to births. In tables which show number of previous liveborn children, multiple births are counted as if they had occurred separately, for example, as one first and one second birth.

Area of usual residence *(Section 7)*
Births are assigned to areas according to the usual residence of the mother at the time of the child's birth as stated at registration. If the address of usual residence is outside England and Wales the birth is included in any aggregate for England and Wales as a whole, but excluded from the figures for any individual region or area - in 1986 there were 371 such births. (Prior to 1972 births to women usually resident outside England and Wales were assigned to the area of occurrence.) Institutional premises are treated as a mother's usual place of residence only if no other address is ascertainable or she normally lives there - for example, a member of the resident staff or a permanent hotel resident.

The areas of usual residence shown in this volume are those as constituted after local government reorganisation in England and Wales on 1 April 1974, and after National Health Service re-structuring on 1 April 1982, or as subsequently amended by statutory boundary changes.

Tables 7.1 and **7.2** cover: England and Wales, standard regions, Greater London, Metropolitan counties and regional health authorities.

Basic statistics relating to births (and deaths) for all local authority areas, and for regional and district health authorities are published in *Vital statistics: local and health areas* (from issue VS no.10).

These data were formerly published in *Local authority vital statistics*, Series VS nos. 1-9 (HMSO) and as **Table E** of the *Registrar General's Statistical Review of England and Wales, Part II*.

Place of confinement *(Section 8)*
The place of confinement categories in this volume are detailed below:

NHS hospital A. Hospitals and maternity homes under the National Health Service (other than psychiatric hospitals) with beds allocated to GP maternity but not to consultant obstetrics;

NHS Hospital B. Hospitals and maternity homes under the National Health Service (other than psychiatric hospitals) with beds allocated to consultant obstetrics, which may or may not also have GP maternity beds.

3

Other hospitals. Mainly maternity homes not under the National Health Service;

At home. At the usual place of residence of the mother; and

Elsewhere. Places of confinement which include all psychiatric institutions, homes for unmarried mothers, remand homes, reception centres and private houses (other than mother's usual residence).

Table 8.2 covers: England and Wales and regional health authorities.

Birthplace of mother *(Section 9)*
Information about the place of birth of the parents of children born in England and Wales has been recorded at birth registrations since April 1969. It is important to note, however, when interpreting these data that birthplace does not necessarily equate with ethnic group. In particular, there are an increasing number of women born in Britain from the ethnic minorities (mainly of West Indian origin) in the younger childbearing ages. Any children born to these women will be included in the 'mother born in UK' category although one or both parents would have been from the ethnic minorities. Conversely, the category 'mother born in the New Commonwealth and Pakistan' will include some children born to mothers who, although themselves born in countries of the New Commonwealth and Pakistan, were not of ethnic minority descent. A fuller discussion of the relationship between birthplace and ethnic group is contained in the article 'Estimating the size of the ethnic minority populations in the 1980s', published in *Population Trends 44* (HMSO 1986).

Fertility rates according to mother's country of birth *(Section 9)*
The age-specific fertility rates for women by country of birth shown in **Tables 9.4** and **9.5**, are based on population denominators from the 1981 Census adjusted to agree with 1981 mid year estimates of the female population. The population estimates were brought up-to-date by taking into account annual numbers of deaths of women by age and country of birth and estimates of net migration, obtained from the International Passenger Survey, for each year since 1981.

Birth cohorts *(Section 10)*
Tables 10.1 and **10.2** use a rearrangement of the birth statistics by age of mother which have been compiled since 1938, to present information about the fertility of women according to their period of birth (birth cohorts). **Table 10.3** shows, for women born from 1920 to 1967 the contribution of illegitimate births and legitimate births of different orders to their fertility in each five-year period of their childbearing lives up to the end of 1985. Since analyses of births are only available by calendar year and age of mother at birth, the years of birth shown for the birth cohorts are approximate. For example, women aged 32 giving birth to

children in 1986 could have been born in either 1953 or 1954; for convenience such women have been referred to as the 1953 birth cohort.

Social class *(Section 11)*
For each of the calendar years, samples of live births occurring in those years have been selected for classification by social class. This is achieved by coding father's occupation and employment status and allocating to the appropriate social class. The proportion of birth records sampled in each year were 1 in 10.

For the years 1976-78 the occupation of the father shown on the selected birth record was coded using the *1970 Classification of Occupations*, (HMSO, 1970). For years from 1979 onwards the *Classification of Occupations 1980* (HMSO, 1980) was used; 1979 birth records were dual coded using both classifications, and statistics on both bases appear in the tables in section 11 of this volume.

Occupation codes were allocated as far as possible to the Registrar General's social classes as used in census reports; this procedure is approximate since the questions asked at the time of registration of a birth are less detailed than those in the census schedule.

Broadly speaking the social class categories are:

Non-manual
I	Professional occupations
II	Intermediate occupations (including most managerial and senior administrative occupations)
IIIN	Skilled occupations (non-manual)

Manual
IIIM	Skilled occupations (manual)
IV	Partly skilled occupations
V	Unskilled occupations

Other	Residual groups including, for example, armed forces, students and those whose occupation was inadequately described.

To improve the quality of the sample estimates and to ensure consistency with sub-totals the sample figures have been grossed-up to agree with known totals derived from the 100 per cent processing of birth registrations according to mother's age (see **Table 5.1(a)**). **Appendix tables 3** and **4** give some indication of the 'standard errors' for selected estimated numbers of births and percentages, taking into account the differing sample fractions. The 'standard error' is a conventional measure of the sampling variation that occurs by chance when only a part of the total population - in this instance live births - has been selected. For example, if the estimated number in a particular category was 50.0 thousand (for the 1 in 10 sample for 1976 to 1986) then **Appendix table 3** indicates that the standard error of that estimate would be approximately 0.64 thousand. Statistical theory states that for the type of distribution being considered there is approximately a 95 per cent chance that the true population value - that is, the value if the whole population had been covered rather than 1 in 10 - lies within two standard errors of the estimate. The estimated 95 per cent confidence interval, for this example would be

50.0 ± 1.3 thousand
or
48.7 to 51.3 thousand.

If such an interval were found not to overlap with another similarly calculated interval then the difference between the estimated numbers would be said to be significant at the 5 per cent level or higher. A similar procedure to that explained above also applies to estimated percentages; the appropriate standard errors are given in **Appendix Table 4.**

The median intervals between first and subsequent successive births shown in **Table 11.3** are received from the Department of Health and Social Security in connection with new claims for child benefit payments. The figures are based upon a 4 per cent sample of claims and refer to Great Britain, not to England and Wales.

Table 11.5 shows illegitimate births jointly registered by both parents according to the father's social class.

Conceptions *(Section 12)*
Tables 12.1 to **12.9** bring together records of birth registrations and of abortions under the 1967 Act; they include all the pregnancies of women usually resident in England and Wales which lead to one of the following outcomes (pregnancies which lead to spontaneous abortions are not included).

(i) A maternity at which one or more live or still births occur and are registered in England and Wales.

(ii) A termination of a pregnancy by abortion under the 1967 Act in England and Wales.

Maternities which result in the birth of more than one live or still birth are counted only once. Such multiple birth maternities are classified as 'live' if at least one live birth is included and as 'still' if all the births are stillbirths.

Estimating date of conception
Dates of conception are not directly available from birth registrations and abortion records; such dates are estimated from information available on the records as follows:

Maternities (one or more live births)
38 weeks before date of confinement (the average gestation period, measured between the first day of the last menstrual period and the date of confine ment, is 40 weeks; conception occurs on average 14 days after the first day of the last mentrual period).

Maternities (all stillbirths)
Stated gestation period before date of confinement.

Abortions under the 1967 Act
For conceptions in 1980 and earlier years, date of start of last menstrual period plus 14 days; for conceptions in 1981 and later years date of termination minus stated gestation period plus 14 days (the gestation period is estimated from the first day of the last menstrual period).

Estimating women's ages at conception
Women's ages at conception are estimated from their dates of birth stated on the birth registration or abortion returns together with the estimated dates of conception. For a small number of cases, for which the women's dates of birth were not stated, an age was imputed for the woman by inserting the age stated on the previous comparable record.

Tables 12.5 and **12.7** include conceptions outside marriage which lead to legitimate maternities. In order to maintain consistency with tables elsewhere in the volume, and to avoid erroneous classification of maternities with below average gestation periods, such events have been restricted to those where confinement occurred within 8 months (35 weeks) after marriage. The year and age of woman at conception have, however, been estimated at a date 38 weeks before confinement, as in the case of all other conceptions leading to live births.

Base populations for fertility rates
Throughout this volume fertility rates have been calculated using estimates of the population (see **Appendix table 1**) based on results from the 1981 Census adjusted for esti-

mated under-enumeration. They include residents of England and Wales temporarily outside Great Britain and exclude overseas visitors. Residents of England and Wales temporarily in Scotland are included, and residents of Scotland visiting England and Wales are excluded. The estimates are updated each year by allowing for births, deaths and migration. See *Population Trends* (HMSO, 1983) for further details.

Births to visitors and births overseas

In order to place the birth event numerators for fertility rates on exactly the same basis as the population estimate denominators, births to visitors occurring in England and Wales would have to be excluded from the overall counts and births occurring outside the country to England and Wales residents would have to be included. However, since the Office of Population Censuses and Surveys collects statistics only of births registered in England and Wales, births to residents of England and Wales which are registered elsewhere are excluded from the national statistics and births registered in England and Wales to mothers whose usual residence is elsewhere are included. In 1986 there were 371 live births to visitors from outside the country registered in England and Wales.

In 1986 some 15,000 births occurring outside the United Kingdom to British nationals were voluntarily registered with British Consuls, British High Commissioners or HM Armed Forces registration centres. By far the majority of these, however, were births to people who had emigrated from the United Kingdom (that is, lived outside the UK for at least one year) and were therefore not residents of England and Wales included in the definition of the population. It is estimated that on average around 100 thousand women of childbearing age (15-44) who are usually resident in England and Wales are temporarily absent overseas. However, the great majority of these women are absent for only a short time and it is unlikely that more than a few hundred per year give birth while overseas. During 1986 the numbers of births to residents of England and Wales which were registered in Scotland and Northern Ireland were 189 and 10 respectively.

So far as can be established, therefore, it seems that the number of births to residents of England and Wales occurring outside the country is likely to be of about the same order as the figure for births occurring in England and Wales to visitors from outside the country. The effect on fertility rates of the difference between the definitions used for the birth event numerators and the population denominators can therefore be assumed to be negligible.

Symbols and conventions used

.. not available
: not appropriate
- nil
0 less than half the unit under consideration

Where data are not yet available, cells are left blank.

Additional information

Enquiries about the availability of further national birth statistics should be addressed to the Director and Registrar General, Office of Population Censuses and Surveys (Fertility Statistics Unit), St Catherines House, 10 Kingsway, London, WC2B 6JP. Telephone 01-242 0262 Ext 2162.

Mortality statistics 1985 - perinatal and infant social and biological factors (Series DH3 No.18) contains numbers of live and still births analysed by age, social class and parity for the regional health authorities of England and Wales.

Population and vital statistics 1986 (Series VS No.13) contains birth and death rates in local and health authorities of England and Wales for 1985, including figures of legitimacy and sex of child, death, infant deaths and stillbirths.

Enquiries about the availability of further birth statistics for particular localities should be addressed to the Director and Registrar General, Office of Population Censuses and Surveys (SIS), Room 216S, Titchfield, Fareham, Hants, PO15 5RS. Telephone 0329 42511 Ext 3446.

Fertility trends in England and Wales: 1976-1986

Summary (Table S1)

There were 661 thousand live births in England and Wales during 1986, an increase of nearly 5 thousand (1 per cent) compared with 1985. This was the highest annual total since 1973. However, after allowing for changes in the size and structure of the female population of childbearing age, the total period fertility rate (TPFR) for 1986 was 1.77, which was little changed from the 1985 value of 1.78; this compares with a TPFR of 1.88 at the local peak in 1980. The seasonally adjusted quarterly TPFR is estimated to have reached a peak of 1.80 during the second quarter of 1986, but then to have declined to a level of 1.77 by the fourth quarter of the year. In common with many developed countries, the TPFR for England and Wales has been below the level of 2.1 required for the long-term replacement of the population for over a decade.

The mean age of women at childbirth was 27.0 years in 1986, with the estimated average age of first-time mothers being 24.9 years; this is more than 6 months older than women giving birth during 1976. Illegitimate births as a proportion of all births continued to rise steeply during 1986; 21.4 per cent of all live births in the year occurred outside marriage, compared with 19.2 per cent in 1985 and 9.2 per cent ten years earlier, in 1976.

Table S1 Live birth occurrences, fertility rates and mean ages at maternity   **England and Wales**

Year/Quarter	Number of live births (thousands)	Crude birth rate*	General fertility rate†	Total period fertility rate≠	Mean age at maternity (years)		Illegitimacy ratio††
					Any birth	First birth**	
1964 (max)	876.0	18.5	92.9	2.93	27.2	24.0	72
1976	584.3	11.8	60.4	1.71	26.4	24.3	92
1977 (min)	569.3	11.5	58.1	1.66	26.5	24.4	97
1980	656.2	13.2	64.2	1.88	26.7	24.5	118
1984	636.8	12.8	59.8	1.75	26.9	24.7	173
1985	656.4	13.1	61.0	1.78	27.0	24.8	192
1986	661.0	13.2	60.6	1.77	27.0	24.9	214
1986 March	160.0	13.2	60.7	1.78	27.0	24.9	206
June	169.0	13.4	61.5	1.80	27.1	24.9	204
September	170.8	13.1	60.1	1.76	27.0	24.9	218
December	161.2	13.2	60.5	1.77	27.0	24.9	228

Notes: All quarterly rates are seasonally adjusted.

*   Births per 1,000 population of all ages.
†   Births per 1,000 women aged 15-44.
≠   The total period fertility rate is the average number of children which would be born per woman if women experienced the age-specific fertility rates of the period in question throughout their childbearing lifespan.
** Estimated mean age at first birth regardless of legitimacy.
†† Illegitimate births per 1,000 live births.

Trend in fertility rate (Figure 1)

There were substantial fluctuations in the fertility rate from 1974 to 1986 but throughout the period the rate remained below the level required for long-term stabilisation of the population size (a TPFR of 2.1). During the first part of the period the rate declined by about 5 per cent per year and a minimum TPFR of 1.63 was reached early in 1977. This was followed by an equally rapid three-year period of increase and a peak TPFR of 1.89 was reached in May 1980. The trend was generally downwards (with some periods of stability) during the next four years, until a low point of 1.73 was reached early in 1984. A rising trend then followed during the second to fourth quarters of 1984, and by the end of the year the TPFR had reached 1.80. Fluctuations during 1985 and 1986 were minor and in December 1986 the TPFR was 1.77.

Figure 1. Trend in Total Period Fertility Rate, January 1974 to December 1986

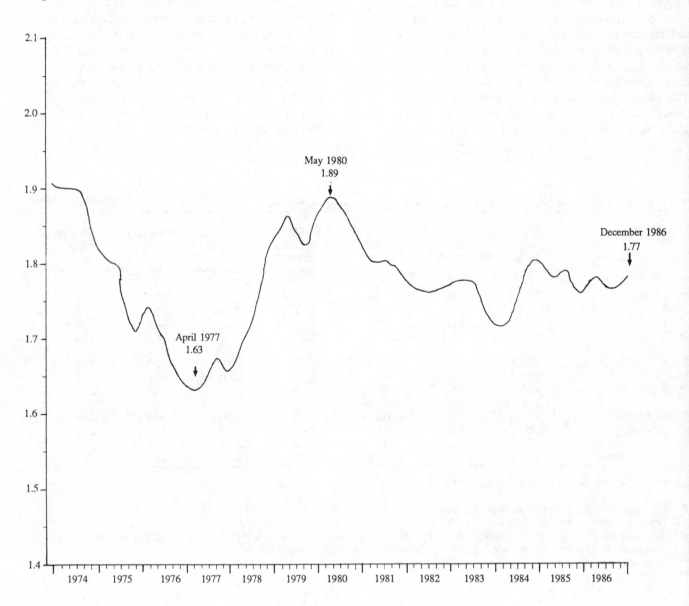

Age-specific fertility rates (Table S2 and Figure 2)

Fertility rates for women in their 20s, the most fertile ages, fell during 1986 compared with 1985 whereas the fertility rates for women in their 30s and for teenage girls increased. The fertility rates for teenage girls rose by 2 per cent in 1986, to 30 births per thousand women aged 15-19; this was a third consecutive annual increase in the teenage fertility rate. The rate for women aged 20-24 fell by 2 per cent in 1986, to 93 births per thousand women of that age (its lowest level since 1941), whilst that for women aged 25-29 fell by 3 per cent from the previous year's level, to 124 births per thousand women. However, the rates for women in their 30s continued to rise in 1986, with increases of 2 per cent from 1985 levels both for women aged 30-34 (to 78 births per thousand women) and for those aged 35-39 (to 25 births per thousand women); both of these rates were at their highest for over a decade. The fertility rate for women aged 40 and over fell very slightly between 1985 and 1986, to equal the 1976 level of 4.8 births per thousand women aged 40-44. **Figure 2** illustrates how these age-specific fertility rates changed between 1976 and 1986; the overall TPFR was only 1.71 in 1976 compared with 1.77 in 1986.

Table S2 Age-specific fertility rates

Year and quarter	Live births (thousands)	Births per 1,000 women in age-group							TPFR
		All ages	Under 20	20-24	25-29	30-34	35-39	40 and over	
1964 (max)	876.0	**92.9**	42.5	181.6	187.3	107.7	49.8	13.7	2.93
1976	584.3	**60.4**	32.2	109.3	118.7	57.2	18.6	4.8	1.71
1977 (min)	569.3	**58.1**	29.4	103.7	117.5	58.6	18.2	4.7	1.66
1980	656.2	**64.2**	30.4	112.7	133.6	70.5	22.3	4.8	1.88
1984	636.8	**59.8**	27.6	95.5	126.2	73.6	23.6	4.9	1.75
1985	656.4	**61.0**	29.5	94.5	127.6	76.4	24.1	5.0	1.78
1986	661.0	**60.6**	30.1	92.7	124.0	78.1	24.6	4.8	1.77

Notes: 1. The rates for women of all ages, under 20 and 40 and over are based upon the female populations aged 15-44, 15-19 and 40-44 respectively.

2. The TPFR (total period fertility rate) is the average number of children which would be born per woman if women experienced the age-specific fertility rates of the period in question throughout their childbearing life span.

Figure 2 Age-specific fertility rates, 1976 and 1986

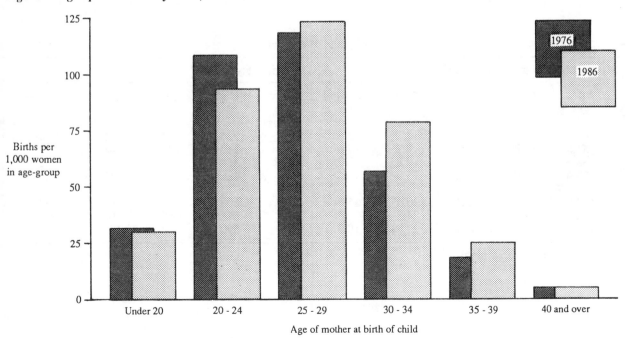

Table S3 Components* of TPFR by legitimacy and birth order

Year and quarter	TPFR	Illegitimate births	Legitimate births						Illegitimacy ratio†
			All	First	Second	Third	Fourth	Fifth or later	
1964 (max)	2.93	0.20	**2.73**	0.94	0.85	0.47	0.23	0.23	72
1976	1.71	0.16	**1.55**	0.63	0.59	0.21	0.07	0.05	92
1977 (min)	1.66	0.16	**1.50**	0.62	0.56	0.20	0.07	0.04	97
1980	1.88	0.21	**1.66**	0.68	0.60	0.25	0.08	0.05	118
1984	1.75	0.29	**1.47**	0.57	0.54	0.23	0.08	0.05	173
1985	1.78	0.33	**1.46**	0.57	0.53	0.23	0.08	0.05	192
1986	1.77	0.37	**1.41**	0.55	0.51	0.22	0.08	0.05	214

* Aggregates of single year of age rates in each category.
† Illegitimate births per 1,000 live births.

Components of TPFR (Table S3)

The contribution to the TPFR made by legitimate live births declined between 1985 and 1986, whilst the contribution made by illegitimate live births continued to increase. The contributions made by first, second and third legitimate births all fell between 1985 and 1986 whereas those made by fourth and later births were unchanged.

Legitimacy (Tables S4 and S5; Figure 3)

The overall increase of 4.6 thousand live births betwween 1985 and 1986 was composed of a rise in the number of children born outside marriage (15.1 thousand more such births, representing a 12 per cent increase over the period) partly offset by a drop in legitimate births (10.5 thousand fewer which represents a 2 per cent decrease). As a result, the illegitimacy ratio rose steeply, from 19.2 per cent of all live births in 1985 to 21.4 per cent in 1986; this was more than double the proportion born outside marriage in 1976.

There were 141 thousand births outside marriage during 1986, more than in any previous year. Increases between

1985 and 1986 in the numbers and proportions of illegitimate births occurred for women in all the fertile age-groups. Sixty-nine per cent of teenage births were illegitimate in 1986, compared with 65 per cent in 1985; only 34 per cent of births to teenage girls occurred outside marriage in 1976. Between 1976 and 1986 the illegitimacy ratio increased most rapidly for women aged 20-24, rising from 9 per cent in 1976 to 28 per cent in 1986.

The proportion of illegitimate births which are jointly registered by both parents (and for whom details of the father are therefore entered in the births register) is often used to indicate the trend in the number of extra-marital births which occur within stable unions. About two-thirds of the illegitimate births occurring in 1986 were jointly registered by both parents, and in nearly three-quarters of these cases both parents gave the same address as their usual place of residence; these figures suggest that at least half of the children born outside marriage during 1986 had parents who were living together in a stable relationship. **Figure 3** illustrates the recent rise in the proportion of births occurring outside marriage, differentiating between births jointly-registered by both parents and those registered by the mother alone.

Table S4 Illegitimate live births and illegitimacy ratios by age of mother

Year	Number of births (thousands)					Illegitimacy ratios*				
	All ages	Under 20	20-24	25-29	30 and over	**All ages**	Under 20	20-24	25-29	30 and over
1964	**63.3**	17.4	20.5	12.1	13.3	**72**	226	74	45	53
1976	**53.8**	19.8	16.6	9.7	7.6	**92**	342	91	44	62
1977	**55.4**	20.1	17.4	9.8	8.2	**97**	368	100	47	62
1980	**77.4**	25.9	26.6	13.5	11.4	**118**	426	132	60	67
1984	**110.5**	33.1	41.1	20.6	15.6	**173**	608	215	95	90
1985	**126.2**	36.9	47.7	24.2	17.5	**192**	648	246	106	98
1986	**141.3**	39.6	54.1	27.7	19.9	**214**	690	282	121	109

* Illegitimate live births per 1,000 live births.

Table S5 Jointly registered illegitimate births by mothers age

Year	Age of mother					
	All ages	Under 20	20-24	25-29	30-34	35 and over
	Jointly registered births as a percentage of all illegitimate births					
1976	**51**	36	52	65	70	68
1985	**65**	57	66	70	72	73
1986	**66**	59	67	70	73	74
	Parents of jointly registered illegitimate births resident at same address as a percentage of all jointly registered illegitimate births					
1976	Not applicable					
1985*	**72**	57	74	79	84	82
1986	**70**	56	71	79	81	80

* Based on births registered in July and November only.

Figure 3 Live births outside marriage as a percentage of total live births: 1976 - 1986

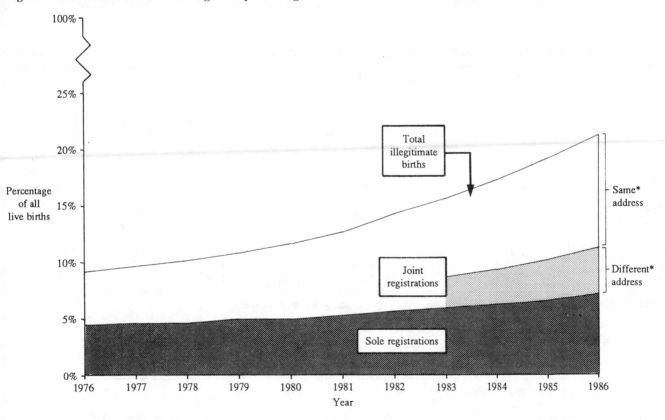

* Estimates of parents' address(es) based on a sample of jointly registered illegitimate births for 1983 to 1985, and all cases for 1986.
  This information is not available for years prior to 1983.

Birth order (Tables S6 and S7; Figure 4)

The fall in the number of legitimate births between 1985 and 1986 (from 530 thousand live births during 1985 to 520 thousand in 1986) was the result of reductions in first, second and third births within marriage; only the number of fourth and higher order legitimate births remained stable over the year. Over the period 1976 to 1986, the numbers of first and second legitimate live births have both fallen (by 5 per cent and 7 per cent respectively), whilst third and fourth or later births within marriage have increased (by 14 per cent and 10 per cent during this time, respectively). This is illustrated in **Figure 4**, where fluctuations in numbers of legitimate live births of different orders can be seen alongside the rising numbers of illegitimate births over the ten-year period to 1986.

Women under 30 years of age had fewer first and second legitimate live births in 1986 than in 1985, whereas the number born to those aged 30 and over increased. Third or later legitimate births were only more frequent among women aged 25-29. During 1986, for the second consecutive year, the number of first legitimate births to women aged 25-29 was higher than the number born to mothers aged 20-24; this had not previously occurred since 1939. Over the period 1976 to 1986, the number of legitimate live births to women aged 30 and over increased: first births by 61 per cent, second births by 41 per cent and third or later legitimate births by 29 per cent. Women aged 30 and over accounted for 19 per cent of all legitimate first births in 1986, compared with only 11 per cent in 1976. Women aged 20-24 had fewer legitimate live births of all orders in 1986 than in 1976; for women aged 25-29, numbers of first and third births were almost the same in the two years, whereas numbers of second births were 14 per cent fewer in 1986 than ten years earlier. Live births to married teenage women during 1986 were roughly half the number born ten years earlier, for all legitimate birth orders.

Information on numbers of births by estimated 'true' birth order (ie according to the number of previous liveborn children, regardless of a mother's marital status at the time of birth) appears in the tabular section of this '1986 Births' volume for the first time this year (see **Tables** Section X and explanatory information in the Introduction p.).

Table S6 Legitimate live births by mother's marriage order and birth order *thousands*

Year	Total legitimate	By mother's marriage order		By birth order*			
		Births in first marriage	Births in second or later marriage	First birth	Second birth	Third birth	Fourth or later births
1964	**812.6**	796.2	16.4	286.1	251.3	138.5	136.8
1976	**530.5**	503.8	26.7	217.2	203.6	71.0	38.8
1977	**513.9**	485.5	28.4	214.6	195.0	68.8	35.5
1980	**578.9**	540.4	38.5	241.0	209.2	86.3	42.4
1984	**526.4**	485.4	41.0	210.4	193.1	80.6	42.2
1985	**530.2**	488.3	41.9	212.0	193.1	82.4	42.7
1986	**519.7**	477.9	41.7	206.9	189.2	80.8	42.7

* Birth order is based on all live births to the mother by her present and any former husband.

Table S7 First, second and third or later legitimate live births by age of mother *thousands*

Year	Age of mother at birth											
	First births*				Second births*				Third or later births*			
	Under 20	20-24	25-29	30 and over	Under 20	20-24	25-29	30 and over	Under 20	20-24	25-29	30 and over
1964	47.4	132.1	73.2	33.4	10.8	84.9	95.8	59.9	1.2	38.6	89.6	145.8
1976	30.2	85.4	77.2	24.3	7.4	62.5	91.8	41.9	0.5	17.7	42.0	49.6
1977	27.9	83.6	75.4	27.7	6.1	57.8	84.9	46.2	0.4	15.8	37.9	50.2
1980	28.2	96.4	81.6	34.8	6.3	60.5	84.6	57.8	0.4	18.0	43.8	66.4
1984	16.9	80.6	77.2	35.8	4.2	52.8	78.3	57.8	0.3	17.0	41.9	63.6
1985	15.8	79.0	79.9	37.3	3.9	50.5	80.0	58.5	0.3	16.7	42.2	64.7
1986	13.8	74.7	79.3	39.2	3.6	47.5	78.9	59.2	0.3	15.8	43.2	64.2

* Birth order is based on all legitimate live births to the mother by her present or any former husband.

Figure 4 Numbers of live births by legitimacy and birth order, 1976 - 1986

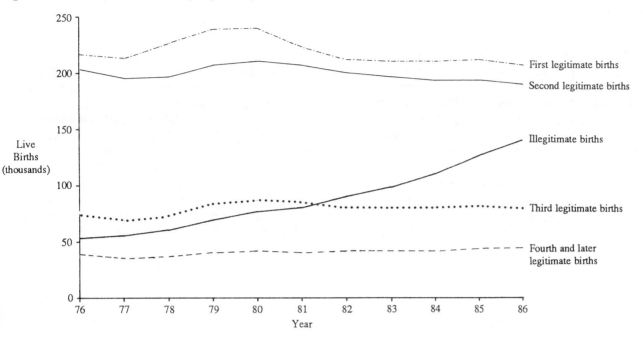

Sex ratio of births and multiple births (Table S8)

There were relatively fewer male live births per thousand female live births in 1986 than either 10 or 20 years earlier; nevertheless, there were still over 5 per cent more males than females born during 1986. The ratio of male to female live births varied little for mothers of different ages.

Over 1 in 100 maternities resulted in a multiple birth during 1986, slightly more than in either 1976 or 1966. There was a marked tendency for the proportion of maternities with multiple births to increase with mother's age; just over 1 in 150 maternities to teenage women involved multiple births in 1986, whereas the proportion for women aged 35 and over was about 1 in 60.

Table S8 Sex ratio of live births and maternities with multiple births

Age of mother	Male live births per 1,000 female live births			Maternities with multiple births per 1,000 maternities		
	1966	1976	1986	1966	1976	1986
All ages	**1,060**	**1,058**	**1,051**	**11.1**	**9.6**	**11.5**
Under 20	1,064	1,058	1,044	6.4	6.2	7.0
20-24	1,057	1,052	1,056	9.0	7.7	9.1
25-29	1,062	1,058	1,050	11.9	10.5	11.6
30-34	1,062	1,067	1,045	14.4	12.4	14.4
35 and over	1,057	1,059	1,059	15.3	12.9	16.9

Seasonal variation in numbers of births (Table S9)

In 1986 the average number of live births per day was highest in September (5 per cent above the annual mean) and lowest in December (6 per cent below the annual mean); this is after taking account of the different compositions of each month with respect to days of the week. This compares with the highest daily average in 1966 occurring in March (8 per cent above the annual mean) and the lowest in November (7 per cent below the annual mean). Over the 20 year period from 1966 to 1986, there was a shift away from births occurring during the winter and early spring (particularly February to April) towards more frequent birth occurrences during the summer and autumn (July to November).

Place of confinement (Table S10)

For almost all maternities in 1986 the place of confinement was an NHS hospital; less than three-quarters of maternities in 1966 took place in NHS hospitals. The proportion of confinements at the mother's own home fell from nearly 1 in 4 in 1966, to 1 in 40 in 1976, and by 1986 accounted for little more than 1 in 100 of all confinements. The proportion of confinements occurring in non-NHS hospitals and in maternity homes also declined over the period, as did those occurring elsewhere (for example, in psychiatric institutions, homes for unmarried mothers, remand homes, reception centres, and private houses other than the mother's usual residence).

Table S9 Monthly variation in numbers of live births

Year	Daily average* number of births as proportion of daily average for whole year												
	Jan	Feb	Mar	Apr	May	June	July	Aug	Sept	Oct	Nov	Dec	Annual average
1966	0.98	1.03	1.08	1.03	1.03	1.01	1.00	0.98	1.01	0.96	0.93	0.95	1.00
1976	0.98	1.01	1.05	1.02	1.03	1.02	1.02	0.99	1.04	0.98	0.94	0.93	1.00
1986	0.97	0.98	1.01	1.00	1.02	1.02	1.03	1.02	1.05	0.99	0.97	0.94	1.00

* Adjusted for variations in proportions of births occurring on different days of the week.

Table S10 Place of confinement

Year	Maternities (thousands)	Percentage distribution of maternities by place of confinement			
		NHS hospitals	Non-NHS hospitals and maternity homes	At home	Elsewhere
1966	863.1	72.4	2.6	23.7	1.2
1976	584.3	96.0	1.4	2.5	0.1
1986	657.3	97.9	1.1	0.9	0.1

* Elsewhere includes psychiatric institutions, homes for unmarried mothers, remand homes, reception centres and private houses (other than mother's usual residence).

Births according to father's social class (Table S11)

Between 1985 and 1986 the number of legitimate births rose by 1.3 thousand for women in Social Classes I and II but fell for women in other social classes. During the period 1976 to 1986, in which the total number of legitimate births fell by 2 per cent, the changes for women in each social class were markedly different: a 14 per cent increase for Social Classes I and II, virtually no change for Social Class III (non-manual) and falls of 12 and 8 per cent for Social Classes III (manual) and IV and V respectively. It should be noted however that marked changes in the social class composition of the population of women of childbearing age contributed to these differing trends (see 'Fertility trends in different social classes' in *Population Trends* No.41).

Legitimate live births to women aged 30 and over rose between 1985 and 1986 for all women except those in Social Classes IV and V. Between 1976 and 1986 such births increased for women in each social class, the rise of 68 per cent for women in Social Classes I and II being the greatest. Jointly registered illegitimate births rose between 1985 and 1986 for women in all social classes. The growth in the numbers of such births between 1976 and 1986 was substantial - 66 thousand (240 per cent) overall - with the greatest numerical increases arising from women in Social Class III (manual) - 26 thousand (200 per cent) and Social Classes IV and V - 23 thousand (270 per cent).

Table S11 Legitimate live births according to social class* of father

Year	All classes (including 'other')	Social class of father			
		I and II	IIIN	IIIM	IV and V
Legitimate live births to women of all ages (thousands)					
1976	530.5	140.6	55.5	204.8	110.3
1977	513.9	142.5	53.2	193.4	106.4
1980	578.9	164.5	61.9	212.2	120.4
1984	526.4	154.8	57.6	185.5	106.3
1985	530.2	158.4	56.2	184.3	105.9
1986	519.7	160.1	55.2	179.5	101.1
Legitimate live births to women aged 30 and over (thousands)					
1977	115.8	43.6	12.7	38.0	18.8
1977	124.1	50.6	13.6	38.7	18.5
1980	159.1	68.3	18.0	46.5	22.3
1984	157.2	69.4	17.8	45.1	21.0
1985	160.6	71.8	17.5	45.2	21.1
1986	162.6	73.4	17.6	46.2	20.6
Jointly registered illegitimate live births to women of all ages (thousands)					
1976	27.4	3.6	1.6	12.7	8.7
1977	29.3	4.3	1.4	12.9	9.9
1980	44.2	5.9	2.7	19.6	14.7
1984	69.9	9.2	4.6	29.3	23.5
1985	81.8	10.7	5.0	34.6	27.4
1986	93.5	13.3	5.8	38.3	31.8

* Definition of the Registrar General's Social Classes

Non-manual
(I   Professional occupations
(II   Intermediate occupations (including most managerial and senior administrative occupations)
(IIIN   Skilled occupations (non-manual)

Manual
(IIIM   Skilled occupations (manual)
(IV   Partly skilled occupations
(V   Unskilled occupations

Other   Residual groups including, for example, Armed Forces, students and those whose occupations were inadequately described.

Birth spacing (Table S12)

The median intervals for women in their first marriage between marriage and the birth of a first child fell a little between 1985 and 1986 for all women except those in Social Classes IV and V; this continued the downward trend observed in 1985. The peak year for median intervals between marriage and first birth was 1978 and between that year and 1986 there were substantial falls for all women except those in Social Classes IV and V. The median intervals between first and second and second and third births also shortened over the same period.

Mean age at childbirth (Table S13)

The mean ages of women at childbirth and at first and second births within marriage continued to rise between 1985 and 1986 for women in all social classes; the overall mean age at first legitimate birth of 26.2 years was the highest for forty years. Mean ages at third births remained unchanged for women in Social Classes I and II and fell for women in Social Class III (non-manual). The increase of 1.3 years between 1976 and 1986 in the mean age of women at their first birth within marriage was slightly less than the increase of 1.3 years in the mean age of women at marriage over the same period; this is consistent with the shortening of the interval from marriage to first birth commented upon in the previous section. Women in Social Classes I and II having a first child in marriage were on average about four years older than women in Social Classes IV and V both in 1976 and in 1986.

However, for second and third births within marriage the increase in mean age for women in Social Classes I and II between 1976 and 1986 was much sharper than for women in Social Classes IV and V. In 1986, for the first time since the statistics were started in 1970, the mean age of women in Social Classes I and II at second births within marriage exceeded thirty years.

Table S12 Median intervals from first marriage to first birth (according to social class* of husband) and between later births

Year	Median intervals in months (women in first marriage)					(All women)	
	First marriage to first legitimate birth					First to second birth†	Second to third birth†
	All social classes (including 'other')	I and II	IIIN	IIIM	IV and V		
1976	29	39	35	26	19	33	42
1978	31	42	39	28	19	34	43
1980	29	41	37	25	18	32	41
1984	29	38	34	27	20	31	40
1985	28	37	33	26	18	32	40
1986	27	36	32	25	19	32	39

* For definition of social classes see footnote to **Table S1**.
† Based on a 4 per cent sample of child benefit returns for Great Britain.

Table S13 Mean age of women at childbirth within marriage according to social class of husband

Social class of husband	Mean ages (in years) at legitimate births											
	All births			First births			Second births			Third births		
	1976	1985	1986	1976	1985	1986	1976	1985	1986	1976	1985	1986
All classes (including 'other')	**26.7**	**27.8**	**27.9**	**24.9**	**26.0**	**26.2**	**26.9**	**27.9**	**28.0**	**28.9**	**29.8**	**29.8**
I and II	28.4	29.7	29.8	26.9	28.0	28.1	28.8	29.8	30.1	30.8	32.1	32.1
IIIN	27.2	28.1	28.3	25.7	26.5	26.8	27.8	28.5	28.6	29.8	30.6	30.4
IIIM	26.1	27.1	27.3	24.1	25.2	25.4	26.0	27.1	27.2	28.3	29.0	29.3
IV and V	25.5	26.1	26.3	23.1	24.0	24.2	25.3	25.9	26.0	27.5	27.7	27.9

* For definition of social classes see footnote to **Table S1**.

Average family size (Table S14; Figure 5)

Average completed family size reached a peak at about 2.4 children per woman for women born in the mid 1930s and has since been declining. **Figure 5**, supplemented by the statistics for selected cohorts in **Table S14**, illustrates the trends that are present. The average completed family size seems likely to decline below 2.1 - the level at which the population replaces itself in the long term - for women born in the early 1950s and later. The decline in the family size achieved by the age of thirty fell sharply from 1.86 for women born in 1942 to 1.50 for women born in 1952 and 1.38 for women born in 1957. Although the subsequent rate of childbearing in their early thirties increased substantially for women born in 1952 compared with earlier cohorts, the final average completed family size for this cohort seemed unlikely to be much above 2.0, even assuming a further increase in childbearing at aged 35 and over. The average number of children achieved by the age of 25 dropped even further for women born in 1962 compared with those born in the 1950s. For the 1962 cohort the level of childbearing between the fertile ages 20 to 24 - 0.48 children per woman - was little more than half the average number achieved at those ages by women born twenty years earlier in 1942.

Table S14 Family building of women born in selected years

Women's year of birth	Mean number of children per woman achieved by successive ages reached before the end of 1986					
	20	25	30	35	40	45*
1922	0.07	0.61	1.33	1.76	1.98	2.05
1927	0.08	0.72	1.43	1.91	2.15	2.20
1932	0.11	0.78	1.59	2.11	2.30	2.33
1937	0.12	0.93	1.83	2.25	2.37	2.39
1942	0.18	1.07	1.86	2.16	2.26	2.28
1946†	0.22	1.04	1.74	2.05	2.16	
1952	0.25	0.86	1.50	1.87		
1957	0.19	0.74	1.38			
1962	0.15	0.63				
1967	0.14					

	Increments to average family size between given ages					
	15-20	21-25	26-30	31-35	36-40	41-45
1922	0.07	0.54	0.72	0.43	0.23	0.07
1927	0.08	0.64	0.70	0.48	0.24	0.05
1932	0.11	0.68	0.81	0.52	0.19	0.02
1937	0.12	0.80	0.90	0.42	0.12	0.02
1952	0.18	0.90	0.79	0.30	0.10	0.02
1946†	0.22	0.82	0.69	0.31	0.11	
1952	0.25	0.62	0.64	0.37		
1957	0.19	0.55	0.64			
1962	0.15	0.48				
1967	0.14					

* Includes births at ages 45 and over achieved up to the end of 1986.

† Figures for women born in 1946 are included in place of those for 1947 as the latter are affected by the method of estimation.

Figure 5. Average number of children born to women by successive ages, by woman's year of birth: 1920-1967

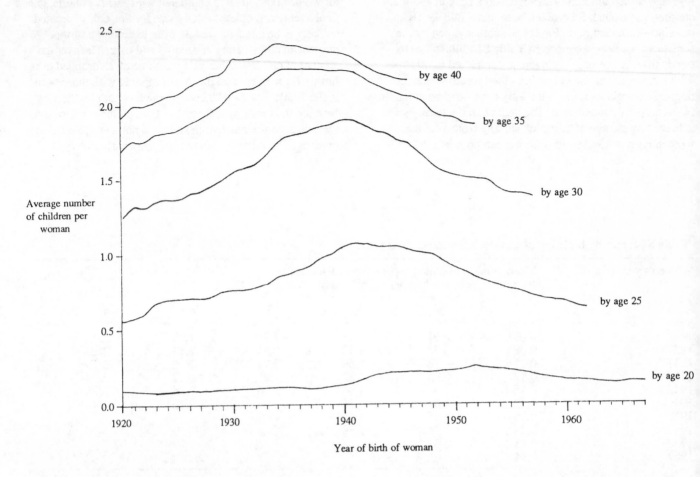

Births by birthplace of mother (Table S15)

There were about 82 thousand births in England and Wales in 1986 to women born outside the United Kingdom. This represented 12.3 per cent of all live births during 1986, the same proportion as in 1985 but slightly below that recorded in 1981. The number of births to women born in the New Commonwealth and Pakistan (NCWP) remained virtually unchanged from last year at just below 53 thousand or 8.0 per cent of all live births. Again, this represented a slight fall from the figures recorded in 1981.

It is important to note, however, that birthplace does not necessarily equate with ethnic group (see note on page 10). So, for example, although births to Caribbean-born women have gradually fallen over the last ten years, it is likely that there has been an increasing number of births to UK-born women of West Indian origin during the same period. Conversely, however, births to NCWP-born women will include some to mothers who although themselves born in countries of the NCWP, were not of ethnic minority descent.

TPFRs for women born outside the United Kingdom have generally fallen since 1981 although they remain higher than those for UK-born women. The TPFR for women born in Pakistan or Bangladesh was still much higher than for other immigrant groups. This reflects both the higher rates recorded in these particular countries and also the interrupted childbearing patterns of these most recently arrived migrant groups. In contrast, fertility rates for the relatively long established Caribbean-born group have now fallen to virtually the same level as those for UK-born women.

The proportion of births occurring outside marriage to women born in the Caribbean Commonwealth has remained at around 50 per cent over the last ten years. In marked contrast illegitimacy ratios for women born in the Indian sub-continent have remained extremely low; below 2 per cent for women born in India and below 1 per cent for women born in Pakistan and Bangladesh. During the same period, the proportion of births occurring outside marriage for UK-born women has more than doubled; from around 9 per cent in 1976 to almost 23 per cent in 1986.

Table S15 Live births, total period fertility rates by country of birth of mother

Country of birth of mother	All live births										
	Thousands			Percentages			TPFR*		Illegitimacy ratio†		
	1976	1981	1986	1976	1981	1986	1981	1986	1976	1981	1986
All birthplaces	**584.3**	**634.5**	**661.0**	**100.0**	**100.0**	**100.0**	**1.80**	**1.77**	**92**	**128**	**214**
United Kingdom	511.2	551.4	579.3	87.5	86.9	87.6	1.7	1.7	92	134	229
Outside United Kingdom	72.4	82.8	81.6	12.4	13.1	12.3	2.5	2.4	95	88	103
New Commonwealth and Pakistan	42.0	53.2	52.7	7.2	8.4	8.0	2.9	2.9	104	84	84
India	12.0	12.4	10.6	2.1	2.0	1.6	3.1	2.9	11	12	17
Pakistan and Bangladesh	9.6	16.4	18.3	1.6	2.6	2.8	6.5	5.6	7	5	6
East Africa	4.2	6.6	7.1	0.7	1.0	1.1	2.1	2.0	27	24	34
Rest of Africa	2.5	3.5	3.7	0.4	0.6	0.6	3.4	2.8	105	130	221
Caribbean	7.2	6.2	4.7	1.2	1.0	0.7	2.0	1.8	484	500	483
Other	6.5	8.0	8.3	1.1	1.3	1.3	2.0	2.0	49	63	99
Rest of the World	30.4	29.7	28.9	5.2	4.7	4.4	2.0	1.9	84	94	137

* Not available for 1976.
† Illegitimate births per 1,000 live births.

International comparison of fertility rates (Tables S16 and S17)

Although there were substantial declines in the TPFRs between 1965 and the present for all the countries of Europe, North America and Australia shown in **Table S15** there were considerable differences in the trends in different countries at different periods during the last twenty years, and by the mid 1980s distinct groupings of relatively high, medium and low fertility countries had developed. In many of the countries shown in the table the TPFR fell sharply from 1965 to 1975. The fall of 42 per cent in the TPFR in West Germany to a level of 1.45 was the greatest in this period of those for the countries shown but the proportional falls in the United Kingdom, Canada and the USA were not far short of this; in these countries, however, the TPFRs started and ended the period at a substantially higher level than in West Germany. Notable exceptions to the pattern of rapidly declining fertility between 1965 and 1975 were the Irish Republic, Italy and Spain where the falls were all less than 20 per cent.

The net changes in TPFRs between 1975 and 1985 or 1986 in the United Kingdom, France, Sweden and the United States were relatively small. In contrast, in the Irish Republic, Italy and Spain fertility started to fall sharply during the period and in West Germany fertility continued to fall sharply as it had in the previous decade. By the mid 1980s, therefore, the TPFR in West Germany of about 1.3 was substantially lower than in the United Kingdom, France, Sweden, Australia and the USA where the levels were about 1.8.

Other countries of relatively low fertility in the mid 1980s were Denmark, where the TPFR had recovered by 1986 to 1.5 from a low point of under 1.4 reached in 1983, and Italy where fertility fell below 1.5 in 1984. The TPFR in the Irish Republic fell to 2.43 in 1986 and for the first time was lower than that of 2.46 for Northern Ireland.

The fertility rates for women of different ages, shown in **Table S16** for the most recent year available for each country differed markedly even betweeen countries with similar overall TPFRs. For teenage women the fertility rate

Table S16 International comparison of TPFRs

Country	Year									
	1965	1970	1975	1980	1981	1982	1983	1984	1985	1986
United Kingdom	2.86	2.44	1.81	1.89	1.81	1.78	1.77	1.77	1.80	1.78
Great Britain	2.86	2.41	1.77	1.87	1.78	1.75	1.75	1.75	1.78	1.77
England	2.84	2.41	1.77	1.87	1.78	1.75	1.75	1.75	1.78	1.77
Wales	2.82	2.44	1.84	1.95	1.86	1.84	1.82	1.81	1.84	1.82
Scotland	3.00	2.57	1.90	1.84	1.84	1.74	1.70	1.68	1.71	1.68
Northern Ireland	3.58	3.25	2.62	2.70	2.55	2.53	2.45	2.44	2.44	2.46
Irish Republic	4.03	3.87	3.40	3.23	3.07	2.96	2.74	2.58	2.49	2.43
France	2.83	2.47	1.93	1.94	1.94	1.91	1.79	1.81	1.82	1.84
West Germany	2.51	2.02	1.45	1.44	1.44	1.41	1.33	1.29	1.28	-
Italy	2.67	2.42	2.21	1.69	1.62	1.59	1.52	1.46	-	-
Denmark	2.61	1.95	1.92	1.55	1.44	1.43	1.38	1.40	1.45	1.48
Spain	3.08	2.84	2.79	2.16	1.99	1.87	1.71	1.65	-	-
Sweden	2.42	1.94	1.78	1.68	1.63	1.62	1.61	1.65	1.73	1.79
Australia	2.97	2.85	2.14	1.90	1.94	1.94	1.93	1.85	-	-
Canada	3.14	2.33	1.89	1.75	1.70	1.69	1.68	1.69	1.67	-
United States of America	2.93	2.48	1.77	1.84	1.82	1.83	1.80	1.81	1.84	1.81

Sources: for non-United Kingdom figures (a) Council of Europe, Strasbourg

(b) National publications of Australia, Canada and United States of America

Note: For more recent years, some figures are provisional.

varied between only 9 to 14 births per 1,000 girls aged 15 to 19 in West Germany, Denmark, Sweden and France up to 51 births per 1,000 in the USA. The teenage fertility rate for the UK of 30 briths per 1,000 girls aged 15-19 was between these two extremes. Fertility rates for women in their twenties were lowest in West Germany and highest in Northern Ireland and Spain (although the latest available figures for Spain were somewhat out-of-date and more recent rates were probably much lower).

The sharp decline in the fertility rate at ages 20-24 up to 1986 seen in the United Kingdom had also occurred in several other countries over the previous ten to fifteen years. In the Irish Republic, in particular, the decline of 36 per cent in the fertility rate for women aged 20-24 from 134 births per 1,000 in 1976 to 86 births per 1,000 in 1986 was more than twice as great as the equivalent fall in the United Kingdom, from 111 to 93 births per 1,000. The trend towards older average ages at childbearing, illustrated in the United Kingdom by the rising rate of fertility for women aged 30-34, was also present in several other European countries and, to a lesser extent in the USA. With the

exceptions of Northern Ireland and the Irish Republic, where fertility rates at ages 30-34 are still inflated by high order births, the highest rate of fertility in the age-group in the mid 1980s in the countries considered was found in Sweden. In that country the fertility rate for women aged 30-034 had risen by 45 per cent from 62 births per 1,000 in 1976 to 90 births per 1,000 in 1986; the equivalent increase in the United Kingdom was 37 per cent from 57 to 78 births per 1,000 women aged 30-34.

The illegitimacy ratio continued to increase during the 1980s in all the countries considered. Particularly high proportions of births occurred outside marriage in Denmark and Sweden and in the latter case the proportion almost reached 50 per cent in 1986. Similar levels of the illegitimacy ratio, around 20 per cent, were present in the United Kingdom, France, Canada and the USA. Low, but increasing, proportions of births outside marriage occurred in the early 1980s in Spain and Italy, predominantly Catholic countries, but in the Irish Republic the illegitimacy ratio reached 10 per cent in 1986, a value reached in the United Kingdom only as recently as 1978.

Table S17 International comparison of age-specific fertility rates and illegitimacy ratios

Country	Latest year for which data are available	Illegitimacy ratio*	Births per 1,000 women in age-group						
			All ages†	Under 20†	20-24	25-29	30-34	35-39	40 and over†
United Kingdom	1986	210	**61**	30	93	125	78	25	5
Great Britain	1986	213	**60**	30	93	124	77	24	5
England	1986	214	**61**	30	92	124	78	25	5
Wales	1986	211	**62**	36	103	127	73	22	4
Scotland	1986	206	**59**	31	91	120	70	20	4
Northern Ireland	1986	127	**84**	30	122	164	112	52	12
Irish Republic	1986	96	**71**	17	86	149	134	72	22
France	1985	196	**64**	12	97	143	79	28	6
West Germany	1985	94	**44**	9	58	102	64	23	3
Italy	1984	50	**48**	14	79	103	65	26	5
Denmark	1986	430	**49**	10	75	120	68	20	3
Spain	1980	39	**74**	25	116	148	92	45	16
Sweden	1986	484	**58**	11	83	136	90	32	6
Australia	1984	148	**65**	23	94	141	81	25	5
Canada	1985	194	**61**	24	85	125	75	22	3
United States of America	1985	220	**66**	51	109	110	68	24	4

* Illegitimate births per 1,000 live births.
† The rates for women aged all ages, under 20 and 40 and over are based upon the female populations 15-44, 15-19 and 40-44 respectively.

Sources: (a) Council of Europe, Strasbourg
          (b) EUROSTAT, Luxembourg
          (c) National publications of Australia, Canada and United States of America.

Note: For some countries figures are provisional.

21

Trends in conceptions to women resident in England and Wales: 1975-85

Outcome of conceptions - Table S18

It is estimated that 797 thousand conceptions occurred to women resident in England and Wales during 1985 compared with 790 thousand in 1984. Of these, 36 per cent occurred outside marriage compared with 33 per cent in 1984 and 23 per cent ten years earlier in 1975. Eighteen per cent of conceptions during 1985 were legally terminated by abortion under the 1967 Act. Of the 119 thousand conceptions to teenage girls which occurred during 1985, 85 per cent occurred outside marriage and 34 per cent were legally terminated. Fifty six per cent of the total of 9.4 thousand conceptions during 1985 to girls under the age of 16 were legally terminated.

Between 1975 and 1985, the proportion of conceptions outside marriage to women of all ages which were legally terminated changed very little; the 1985 figure was 37 per cent compared with 39 per cent in 1975. However, the proportion of conceptions outside marriage which led to a legitimate maternity, following the mother's marriage whilst pregnant, fell steeply from 26 per cent in 1975 to 15 per cent in 1985. In contrast, the proportion of such conceptions which led to births to parents who whilst not married to each other, registered the birth in joint names, rose from 17 per cent in 1975 to 32 per cent in 1985. For a birth occurring outside marriage the name of the father may normally only be entered in the register if both the father and mother register the birth together in person. Such cases of 'joint' registration are taken to indicate that the parents are likely to be brining up the child within a stable non-marital union. About three-quarters of parents jointly registering births outside marriage give the same address of usual residence.

For teenage girls the trend in conceptions outside marriage was similar to that for women of all ages. Of the 101 thousand unmarried teenage girls who became pregnant during 1985 (excluding those whose pregnancy ended in spontaneous abortion), 39 per cent had a legal abortion, 13 per cent married the father before giving birth to the child, 29 per cent gave birth to the child outside marriage and registered the birth jointly with the father and 20 per cent gave birth to the child outside marriage and registered the birth in her name alone.

Table S18 Outcome of conceptions inside and outside marriage

Residents of England and Wales

	All ages			Under 20			Under 16		
Age of woman at conception/year of conception	1975	1984	1985	1975	1984	1985	1975	1984	1985
All conceptions									
Base number (thousands)	**693.3**	**790.1**	**797.2**	**112.0**	**118.2**	**119.3**	**9.2**	**9.6**	**9.4**
Percentage conceived:									
Outside marriage	23	33	36	68	83	85	100	100	100
Inside marriage	77	67	64	32	17	15	0	0	0
Percentage leading to:									
Maternity	85	83	82	74	67	66	48	44	44
Legal abortion*	15	17	18	26	33	34	52	56	56
Conceptions outside marriage:									
Base number (thousands)	**160.6**	**263.4**	**283.5**	**76.1**	**97.9**	**101.0**	**9.1**	**9.6**	**9.4**
Percentage leading to:									
Illegitimate maternity	34	47	48	31	46	48	38	41	42
(of which: Sole†)	17	17	17	20	19	20	27	24	24
(of which: Joint†)	17	30	32	11	27	29	10	17	18
Legitimate maternity	26	16	15	31	14	13	10	3	2
Legal abortion*	39	37	37	38	40	39	52	56	56
Conceptions inside marriage:									
Base number (thousands)	**532.8**	**526.8**	**513.7**	**35.9**	**20.4**	**18.3**	**0.0**	**0.0**	**0.0**
Percentage leading to:									
Maternity	92	93	93	97	96	96	0	0	0
Legal abortion*	8	7	7	3	4	4	0	0	0

* Legal terminations under 1967 Abortion Act.
† An illegitimate birth may be registered by the mother alone (sole registration) or by the mother and father together (joint registration).

22

Numbers and rates of conceptions - Tables S19 and S20

The estimated increase of 7 thousand (about 1 per cent) in the total number of conceptions inside and outside marriage between 1984 and 1985 is matched almost exactly by the rise in the number terminated by legal abortion; the number of conceptions leading to maternities remained almost unchanged. The number of conceptions outside marriage rose between 1984 and 1985, by 8 per cent for those leading to maternities and by 7 per cent for those leading to legal abortion. In contrast, numbers of conceptions inside marriage fell, by 2 per cent for those leading to maternities and by 1 per cent for those legally terminated.

Table S19 Numbers of conceptions inside and outside marriage

Residents of England and Wales

Age of woman at conception/outcome of conception	All conceptions (thousands)			Conceptions outside marriage (thousands)			Conception inside marriage (thousands)		
	1975	1984	1985	1975	1984	1985	1975	1984	1985
All ages									
All	**693.3**	**790.1**	**797.2**	**160.6**	**263.4**	**283.5**	**532.8**	**526.8**	**513.7**
Maternities	**587.0**	**653.8**	**654.3**	**97.1**	**165.3**	**178.6**	**489.8**	**488.5**	**475.8**
Legal abortions*	**106.4**	**136.3**	**142.9**	**63.4**	**98.0**	**105.0**	**43.0**	**38.3**	**37.9**
Under 20									
All	112.0	118.2	119.3	76.1	97.9	101.0	35.9	20.4	18.3
Maternities	82.3	78.8	78.9	47.5	59.2	61.4	34.8	19.6	17.6
Legal abortions*	29.7	39.5	40.3	28.6	38.7	39.6	1.1	0.8	0.7
20-24									
All	221.8	249.1	249.2	45.5	90.4	99.8	176.3	158.6	149.4
Maternities	196.6	210.6	207.2	26.8	58.1	64.0	169.8	152.5	143.2
Legal abortions*	25.1	38.5	42.0	18.7	32.4	35.8	6.4	6.1	6.2
25-29									
All	227.9	238.6	242.6	22.3	42.6	48.0	205.5	196.0	194.7
Maternities	207.5	214.7	216.5	13.4	28.3	31.7	194.1	186.4	184.8
Legal abortions*	20.4	23.9	26.2	9.0	14.3	16.2	11.4	9.7	9.9
30-34									
All	88.3	126.0	127.8	10.2	20.4	22.1	78.1	105.7	105.7
Maternities	73.2	109.0	110.6	6.0	13.2	14.5	67.2	95.8	96.1
Legal abortions*	15.1	17.0	17.2	4.2	7.1	7.6	10.9	9.8	95.9
35-39									
All	33.5	48.5	48.8	4.9	9.9	10.4	28.5	38.6	38.4
Maternities	22.5	35.6	36.1	2.8	5.6	6.0	19.7	30.0	30.1
Legal abortions*	11.0	12.9	12.7	2.2	4.3	4.4	8.8	8.6	8.3
40 and over									
All	10.0	9.7	9.6	1.5	2.2	2.3	8.5	7.5	7.3
Maternities	4.9	5.1	5.1	0.7	0.9	0.9	4.2	4.2	4.2
Legal abortions*	5.1	4.5	4.5	0.8	1.3	1.4	4.3	3.2	3.1

* Legal terminations under 1967 Abortion Act.

Trends in conceptions outside and inside marriage are most usefully described by the conception rates shown in **Table S20.** These rates take into account, not only the numbers of conceptions shown in **Table S19**, but also changes in the size of the population of women of childbearing age and in its composition by age and marital status.

The overall rate of conceptions per 1,000 women aged 15-44 remained virtually unchanged between 1984 and 1985. Conception rates for teenage girls and for women aged 30-

34 increased whereas those for women in their twenties and for women aged 35 and over fell. For all women aged under 35 the rate of conceptions legally terminated by abortion rose between 1984 and 1985, the largest rise of 7 per cent occurring for women aged 20-24.

The rate of conceptions outside marriage per 1,000 unmarried women aged 15-44 rose a little, by 2 per cent, between 1984 and 1985 whereas the rate of conceptions inside marriage per 1,000 married women aged 15-44 fell by 2 per cent; this pattern was repeated in most age-groups.

Table S20 Rates of conceptions inside and outside marriage

Residents of
England and Wales

Age of woman at conception/outcome of conception	All conceptions (per 1,000 women)†			Conceptions outside marriage (per 1,000 unmarried women)†			Conceptions inside marriage (per 1,000 married women)†		
	1975	1984	1985	1975	1984	1985	1975	1984	1985
All ages									
All	**72.4**	**74.2**	**74.1**	**50.8**	**57.5**	**60.0**	**83.0**	**86.7**	**85.0**
Maternities	**61.3**	**61.4**	**60.8**	**30.7**	**36.1**	**37.8**	**76.3**	**80.4**	**78.8**
Legal abortions*	**11.1**	**12.8**	**13.3**	**20.0**	**21.4**	**22.2**	**6.7**	**6.3**	**6.3**
Under 20									
All	64.2	59.9	61.7	47.4	51.2	53.8	256.8	322.7	326.7
Maternities	47.2	39.9	40.8	29.6	31.0	32.7	249.0	310.3	314.0
Legal abortions*	17.0	20.0	20.9	17.8	20.3	21.1	7.9	12.5	12.7
20-24									
All	133.0	124.2	121.4	63.2	70.9	73.7	186.2	217.5	214.0
Maternities	118.0	105.0	100.9	37.2	45.5	47.2	179.4	209.1	205.1
Legal abortions*	15.1	19.2	20.5	26.0	25.4	26.4	6.8	8.4	8.9
25-29									
All	122.9	138.1	136.1	69.7	80.7	82.8	134.0	163.4	161.8
Maternities	111.9	124.3	121.5	41.7	53.7	54.7	126.6	155.3	153.6
Legal abortions*	11.0	13.8	14.7	28.0	27.0	28.1	7.4	8.1	8.2
30-34									
All	57.9	75.6	77.4	55.1	61.2	63.6	58.3	79.2	81.1
Maternities	48.8	65.4	67.0	32.5	39.7	41.9	50.2	71.8	73.7
Legal abortions*	9.9	10.2	10.4	22.6	21.5	21.8	8.2	7.4	7.4
35-39									
All	23.6	26.7	26.5	30.4	33.4	33.0	22.8	25.4	25.1
Maternities	15.9	19.6	19.6	17.0	18.9	19.1	15.7	19.7	19.7
Legal abortion*	7.8	7.1	6.9	13.4	14.5	13.9	7.0	5.7	5.4
40 and over									
All	7.2	6.6	6.4	8.9	9.2	9.2	7.2	6.1	5.8
Maternities	3.5	3.5	3.4	4.1	3.7	3.8	3.5	3.5	3.3
Legal abortions*	3.7	3.1	3.0	4.8	5.5	5.4	3.5	2.7	2.5

* Legal terminations under 1967 Abortion Act.
† Rates for women of all ages, under 20 and 40 and over are based upon the populations of women aged 15-44, 15-19 and 40-44 respectively.

Conceptions to teenage girls - Tables S21 and S22

Numbers of conceptions to girls aged 13 or under and those aged 15 fell during 1985 compared with 1984 whereas the number to girls aged 14 rose. The overall number of conceptions to girls aged under 16 is estimated to have fallen by 243 in 1985 following a rise of 280 between 1983 and 1984. However, the number of girls aged 13-15 years fell by 30 thousand between 1984 and 1985 and the 1985 rate of conceptions per 1,000 girls aged 13-15 remained at 8.6 the same level as in 1984. The 1984 and 1985 rates were both slightly higher than the 1983 rate of 8.3 conceptions per thousand girls aged 13-15.

At ages 16 to 19 both numbers and rates of conceptions increased between 1984 and 1985; the increases were greatest for girls aged 17 and 18 at the date of conception. In spite of the upward trend since 1983 in the rate of conceptions for teenage girls, the conception rate for all girls aged under 20 was still lower in 1985 than it had been in 1975. Although the rates at each single year of age up to 15 increased slightly between 1975 and 1985, the rates at each single year of age from 16 to 19 fell.

Table S21   Number and rates of conceptions to teenage girls, by outcome of conception

Residents of England and Wales

Age	Outcome of conception/year of conception								
	All conceptions			Maternities			Legal abortions†		
	1975	1984	1985	1975	1984	1985	1975	1984	1985
*Number of conceptions**									
Under 14	401	378	325	159	151	139	242	227	186
14	1,919	2,018	2,063	8737	794	836	1,082	1,224	1,227
15	6,861	7,253	7,018	3,398	3,333	3,194	3,463	3,920	3,824
Under 16	9,181	9,649	9,406	4,394	4,278	4,169	4,787	5,371	5,237
16	15,278	15,995	16,146	9,447	8,842	9,107	5,831	7,153	7,039
17	23,349	24,209	24,619	16,747	15,642	15,922	6,602	8,567	8,697
18	29,952	31,382	31,939	23,555	22,302	22,235	6,397	9,080	9,704
19	34,216	36,993	37,157	28,177	27,691	27,489	6,039	9,302	9,668
Under 20	111,976	118,228	119,267	82,320	78,755	78,922	29,656	39,473	40,345
Conception rates per 1,000 women≠									
Under 14	1.0	1.0	0.9	0.4	0.4	0.4	0.6	0.6	0.5
14	5.0	5.5	5.5	2.2	2.2	2.2	2.8	3.3	3.8
15	18.8	19.1	19.1	9.3	8.8	8.7	9.5	10.3	10.4
Under 16	8.1	8.6	8.6	3.9	3.8	3.9	4.2	4.8	4.8
16	42.8	41.9	42.4	26.5	23.2	23.9	16.3	18.7	18.5
17	66.9	61.4	64.2	48.0	39.6	41.5	18.9	21.7	22.7
18	88.0	77.9	80.7	69.2	55.3	56.2	18.8	22.5	24.5
19	102.5	89.3	91.7	84.4	66.9	67.9	18.1	22.5	23.9
Under 20	64.1	59.9	61.7	47.2	39.9	40.8	17.0	20.0	20.9

* The exact numbers of conceptions shown are subject to errors arising from the estimation of women's ages at conception.
† Legal terminations under 1967 Abortion Act.
≠ Rates for women aged under 14, under 16 and under 20 are based on the populations of women aged 13, 13-15 and 15-19 respectively.

Table S22 gives a comparison of the estimated numbers and rates of conceptions to girls aged under 16 and under 20 during each quarter of 1983, 1984 and 1985. The figures are relevant to the assessment of the trend in numbers of conceptions to girls aged under 16 between December 1984, when the Appeal Court ruled that the guidelines laid down for doctors giving contraceptive advice to girls aged under 16 required them to obtain parental consent, and October 1985 when the Appeal Court ruling was overturned by the House of Lords. The figures show that the estimated number of conceptions to girls aged under 16 during the period January to September 1985 was 7,017 compared with 7,221 during the same period of 1984 and 6,982 during the same period of 1983.

When the decline in the population of girls aged 13-15 is taken into account, the estimated rates of conceptions per 1,000 girls aged 13-15 were almost unchanged in each quarter of 1985 compared with the equivalent quarter of 1984. An increase in the March quarter rate was matched by a fall in the September quarter rate, so that the overall rate for the January to September period was unchanged between 1984 and 1985 at 6.5 conceptions per 1,000 girls aged 13-15. The equivalent rate for the first nine months of 1983 was 6.2.

In contrast to the stability in the rate of conceptions at ages under 16 during the first three quarters of 1985, the rate of conceptions for all teenage women increased in each quarter compared with the equivalent quarter of 1984. Over the nine months period as a whole the increase was 4 per cent. This difference in the trend in rates for the under 16 and under 20 age-groups was also evident between the first nine months of 1983 and the equivalent months of 1984. Between these two periods conception rates rose both for girls aged under 16 and for all teenages, but whereas for women aged under 20 the rate rose by 7 per cent, for girls aged under 16 the rate rose by only 4 per cent.

In summary, the estimated quarterly conceptions figures show that although the numbers of conceptions to girls aged under 16 fell during the period from January to September of 1985 compared with the same period of 1984, there were fewer girls in the age-group and the rate of conceptions remained unchanged. In contrast to this stability in the conception rate during the nine month period for girls aged under 16, conception rates for girls aged 16 to 19 increased. However, a similar contrast had previously been seen between 1983 and 1984 when conception rates for girls aged under 16 rose much less than those for girls aged 16-19.

Table S22 Quarterly numbers and rates of conceptions to teenage girls, by outcome of conception

Year/quarter of conception	Number of conceptions*			Conception rates per 1,000 women†		
	Total	Leading to:		Total	Leading to:	
		Maternities	Legal abortions≠		Maternities	Legal abortions≠
Conceptions at ages under 20						
1983						
March	**28,249**	18,749	9,500	14.1	9.3	4.7
June	**27,614**	18,339	9,275	13.8	9.1	4.6
September	**27,361**	18,303	9,058	13.6	9.1	4.5
December	**29,127**	19,606	9,521	14.5	9.8	4.7
1984						
March	**30,027**	19,974	10,053	15.2	10.1	5.1
June	**28,911**	18,996	9,915	14.7	9.6	5.0
September	**28,840**	19,138	9,702	14.6	9.7	4.9
December	**30,450**	20,647	9,803	15.4	10.5	5.0
1985						
March	**30,154**	19,872	10,282	15.6	10.3	5.3
June	**29,299**	19,278	10,021	15.2	10.0	5.2
September	**29,551**	19,447	10,104	15.3	10.1	5.2
December	**30,263**	20,325	9,938	15.7	10.5	5.1
Conceptions at ages under 16						
1983						
March	**2,352**	998	1,354	2.1	0.9	1.2
June	**2,293**	979	1,314	2.0	0.9	1.2
September	**2,337**	1,011	1,326	2.1	0.9	1.2
December	**2,387**	1,058	1,329	2.1	0.9	1.2
1984						
March	**2,316**	975	1,341	2.1	0.9	1.2
June	**2,462**	1,098	1,364	2.2	1.0	1.2
September	**2,443**	1,059	1,384	2.2	0.9	1.2
December	**2,428**	1,146	1,282	2.2	1.0	1.1
1985						
March	**2,343**	1,053	1,290	2.2	1.0	1.2
June	**2,388**	1,064	1,324	2.2	1.0	1.2
September	**2,286**	964	1,322	2.1	0.9	1.2
December	**2,389**	1,088	1,301	2.2	1.0	1.2

* The exact numbers of conceptions shown are subject to errors arising from the estimation of women's ages at conception.
† Rates for women aged under 16 and under 20 are based on the populations of women aged 13-15 and 15-19 respectively.
≠ Legal terminations under 1967 Abortion Act.

Corrections

Birth statistics, Historical, Series FM1 no.13. Tables 7.2(a) and 7.2(b).

The live births, numbers and rates, shown in the tables below replace those published in Birth Statistics, Historical, Series FM1 no.13.The figures have been corrected for areas (as constituted after local government reorganisation in England and Wales on 1 April 1974) to compare with those published for 1974 and later years.

TABLE 7.2 Live births: area of usual residence and age of mother, 1971-1973
(a) numbers

Area of usual residence	All ages 1971	1972	1973	20-24 1971	1972	1973	30-34 1971	1972	1973	40 and over 1971	1972	1973
England and Wales	783,155	725,440	675,953	285,835	249,267	223,837	109,481	98,600	91,687	12,715	10,997	9,267
Outside England and Wales	-	613	559	-	183	184	-	92	101	-	11	9
England	740,099	684,907	637,827	269,693	234,693	210,600	103,825	93,239	86,688	12,086	10,467	8,762
Wales	43,056	39,920	37,567	16,142	14,391	13,053	5,656	5,269	4,898	629	519	496
Standard regions												
Northern	50,103	45,478	41,867	19,250	16,600	14,756	6,745	5,836	5,123	830	674	518
Yorkshire and Humberside	81,547	74,182	68,084	31,164	26,444	23,410	10,598	9,351	8,459	1,392	1,273	1,033
East Midlands	60,890	56,276	53,420	22,746	19,934	18,286	7,912	7,065	6,805	975	821	721
East Anglia	26,664	25,683	25,165	10,249	9,271	8,772	3,467	3,135	3,184	374	301	302
South East	261,839	243,986	227,172	91,274	79,282	70,731	39,273	35,889	33,602	4,107	3,461	2,977
South West	61,711	58,203	55,828	23,404	20,782	19,587	7,997	7,250	7,096	803	777	613
West Midlands	88,280	80,882	74,917	31,237	27,516	24,561	12,516	11,082	10,403	1,674	1,433	1,241
North West	109,065	100,217	91,374	40,369	34,864	30,497	15,317	13,631	12,016	1,931	1,727	1,357
Greater London	113,068	103,526	95,033	38,590	33,044	29,181	17,808	16,135	15,040	2,026	1,687	1,441

Area of usual residence	15-19 1971	1972	1973	25-29 1971	1972	1973	35-39 1971	1972	1973
England and Wales	82,721	79,153	73,297	247,242	247,658	243,762	45,161	39,765	34,103
Outside England and Wales	-	75	65	-	217	157	-	35	43
England	77,443	73,944	68,392	234,263	234,919	231,133	42,789	37,645	32,252
Wales	5,278	5,134	4,840	12,979	12,522	12,472	2,372	2,085	1,808
Standard regions									
Northern	5,646	5,580	5,257	14,760	14,363	14,224	2,872	2,425	1,989
Yorkshire and Humberside	9,743	9,294	8,575	24,023	23,804	23,229	4,627	4,016	3,378
East Midlands	6,804	6,625	6,101	19,164	19,011	19,103	3,289	2,820	2,404
East Anglia	2,723	2,731	2,514	8,481	9,030	9,267	1,370	1,215	1,126
South East	23,650	22,079	20,164	88,070	89,480	87,831	15,465	13,795	11,867
South West	6,674	6,395	5,902	19,706	20,146	20,210	3,127	2,853	2,420
West Midlands	9,626	9,268	8,561	27,839	26,870	26,084	5,388	4,713	4,067
North West	12,577	11,972	11,318	32,220	32,215	31,185	6,651	5,808	5,001
Greater London	10,662	9,845	9,047	36,694	36,325	34,710	7,288	6,490	5,614

Note: Prior to 1972 women usually resident outside England and Wales were included in the region of registration. Births to mothers usually resident outside England and Wales for 1972 and later years are included in the total for England and Wales.

(b) rates per 1,000 women in age-group

Area of usual residence	1971	1972	1973	1971	1972	1973	1971	1972	1973	1971	1972	1973
	All ages			20-24			30-34			40 and over		
England and Wales	83.5	77.0	71.3	152.9	140.5	130.3	77.0	69.2	63.0	8.7	7.6	6.5
Outside England and Wales	-	-	-	-	-	-	-	-	-	-	-	-
England	83.4	76.9	71.1	152.3	139.8	129.6	77.2	69.1	62.9	8.7	7.7	6.5
Wales	84.7	78.0	72.8	163.5	151.2	140.2	74.4	69.2	63.0	7.8	6.5	6.3
Standard regions												
Northern	83.5	75.9	69.6	166.5	150.4	136.3	74.9	65.9	57.6	8.5	7.0	5.5
Yorkshire and Humberside	88.4	80.3	73.2	168.9	150.8	137.1	75.9	67.5	60.2	9.6	8.9	7.3
East Midlands	87.5	80.0	74.7	167.6	153.0	143.6	74.9	65.7	61.4	8.9	7.6	6.7
East Anglia	84.0	79.2	76.1	161.9	149.5	143.8	71.8	63.2	61.7	7.6	6.2	6.2
South East	78.1	72.7	67.4	132.5	122.8	114.4	77.0	70.2	64.4	8.0	6.8	6.0
South West	82.5	76.7	72.7	161.6	148.0	142.5	72.2	64.2	60.6	6.9	6.7	5.4
West Midlands	88.7	81.1	74.9	162.8	151.4	139.6	81.8	72.1	66.4	10.7	9.3	8.2
North West	87.9	80.6	73.2	164.4	149.2	134.9	81.3	72.7	63.3	9.9	9.0	7.1
Greater London	75.2	69.8	64.5	114.9	108.7	102.6	79.2	72.4	66.7	9.0	7.7	6.7
	15-19			25-29			35-39					
England and Wales	50.7	48.1	43.9	153.2	141.8	134.0	32.7	28.8	24.5			
Outside England and Wales	-	-	-	-	-	-	-	-	-			
England	50.3	47.6	43.4	153.2	142.0	134.1	32.8	28.9	24.5			
Wales	57.0	55.0	51.5	153.6	136.6	129.2	31.3	27.7	23.8			
Standard regions												
Northern	50.4	49.4	45.9	156.4	141.2	134.2	31.8	27.1	22.1			
Yorkshire and Humberside	59.2	56.0	51.0	157.6	143.9	134.0	33.9	29.5	24.6			
East Midlands	57.0	54.6	49.0	156.2	143.7	137.0	32.0	27.2	22.8			
East Anglia	50.1	49.7	45.2	152.0	145.9	141.5	29.4	25.7	23.1			
South East	42.5	39.3	35.4	147.8	138.8	131.2	31.6	28.3	24.1			
South West	48.1	45.7	41.8	155.9	145.1	138.4	28.4	25.8	21.6			
West Midlands	55.5	53.1	48.6	159.5	144.5	136.4	36.8	32.1	27.4			
North West	57.1	53.8	50.1	155.5	143.8	134.2	36.4	31.8	27.2			
Greater London	45.4	42.0	38.1	133.9	122.7	113.9	35.0	31.4	27.1			

TABLE 1.1 Live births: legitimacy and sex, 1976-1986
a. numbers

England and Wales

Year	All			Legitimate			Illegitimate		
	Total	Males	Females	Total	Males	Females	Total	Males	Females
1976	584,270	300,313	283,957	530,504	272,682	257,822	53,766	27,631	26,135
1977	569,259	292,957	276,302	513,880	264,490	249,390	55,379	28,467	26,912
1978	596,418	307,088	289,330	535,781	275,826	259,955	60,637	31,262	29,375
1979	638,028	328,308	309,720	568,561	292,422	276,139	69,467	35,886	33,581
1980	656,234	335,954	320,280	578,862	296,234	282,628	77,372	39,720	37,652
1981	634,492	325,711	308,781	553,509	284,004	269,505	80,983	41,707	39,276
1982	625,931	321,352	304,579	536,074	275,408	260,666	89,857	45,944	43,913
1983	629,134	323,192	305,942	529,923	272,080	257,843	99,211	51,112	48,099
1984	636,818	326,039	310,779	526,353	269,655	256,698	110,465	56,384	54,081
1985	656,417	336,835	319,582	530,167	271,886	258,281	126,250	64,949	61,301
1986	661,018	338,852	322,166	519,673	266,517	253,156	141,345	72,335	69,010

TABLE 1.1 Live births: legitimacy and sex, 1976-1986
b. rates

England and Wales

Year	Crude birth rate: All births per 1,000 population of all ages	General fertility rate: all births per 1,000 women aged 15-44	Legitimate births per 1,000 married women aged 15-44	Illegitimate births per 1,000 single, widowed and divorced women aged 15-44	Illegitimate births per 1,000 all births	Sex ratio: male births per 1,000 female births		
						All	Legit-imate	Illegit-imate
1976	11.8	60.4	83.0	16.4	92.0	1,058	1,058	1,057
1977	11.5	58.1	80.8	16.1	97.3	1,060	1,061	1,058
1978	12.1	60.1	84.7	16.8	101.7	1,061	1,061	1,064
1979	12.9	63.3	90.2	18.4	108.9	1,060	1,059	1,069
1980	13.2	64.2	92.2	19.6	117.9	1,049	1,048	1,055
1981	12.8	61.3	88.8	19.7	127.6	1,055	1,054	1,062
1982	12.6	59.9	86.9	21.0	143.6	1,055	1,057	1,046
1983	12.7	59.7	86.8	22.4	157.7	1,056	1,055	1,063
1984	12.8	59.8	86.7	24.1	173.5	1,049	1,050	1,043
1985	13.1	61.0	87.8	26.7	192.3	1,054	1,053	1,060
1986	13.2	60.6	86.3	28.9	213.8	1,052	1,053	1,048

TABLE 1.2 Stillbirths: legitimacy and sex, 1976-1986

England and Wales

Year	Numbers									Rates			
	All			Legitimate			Illegitimate			Stillbirths per 1,000 live and still births	Sex ratio: male births per 1,000 female births		
	Total	Males	Females	Total	Males	Females	Total	Males	Females		All	Legit-imate	Illegit-imate
1976	5,709	2,950	2,759	5,022	2,571	2,451	687	379	308	9.7	1,069	1,049	1,231
1977	5,405	2,813	2,592	4,706	2,462	2,244	699	351	348	9.4	1,085	1,097	1,009
1978	5,108	2,634	2,474	4,409	2,265	2,144	699	369	330	8.5	1,065	1,056	1,118
1979	5,125	2,656	2,469	4,410	2,283	2,127	715	373	342	8.0	1,076	1,073	1,091
1980	4,773	2,483	2,290	4,077	2,117	1,960	696	366	330	7.2	1,084	1,080	1,109
1981	4,207	2,186	2,021	3,510	1,817	1,693	697	369	328	6.6	1,082	1,073	1,125
1982	3,939	2,092	1,847	3,282	1,743	1,539	657	349	308	6.3	1,133	1,133	1,133
1983	3,631	1,960	1,671	2,913	1,594	1,319	718	366	352	5.7	1,173	1,208	1,040
1984	3,643	1,967	1,676	2,825	1,533	1,292	818	434	384	5.7	1,174	1,187	1,130
1985	3,645	1,983	1,662	2,773	1,514	1,259	872	469	403	5.5	1,193	1,203	1,164
1986	3,549	1,904	1,645	2,600	1,412	1,188	949	492	457	5.3	1,157	1,189	1,077

TABLE 1.3 Natural change in population, 1976-1986 England and Wales

Year	Numbers			Rates per 1,000 population of all ages		
	Live births	Deaths	Natural change: live births minus deaths	Live births (crude birth rate)	Deaths (crude death rate)	Natural change
1976	584,270	598,516	-14,246	11.8	12.1	-0.3
1977	569,259	575,928	-6,669	11.5	11.6	-0.1
1978	596,418	585,901	10,517	12.1	11.9	0.2
1979	638,028	593,019	45,009	12.9	12.0	0.9
1980	656,234	581,385	74,849	13.2	11.7	1.5
1981	634,492	577,890	56,602	12.8	11.6	1.1
1982	625,931	581,861	44,070	12.6	11.7	0.9
1983	629,134	579,608	49,526	12.7	11.7	1.0
1984	636,818	566,881	69,937	12.8	11.4	1.4
1985	656,417	590,734	65,686	13.1	11.8	1.3
1986	661,018	581,203	79,815	13.2	11.6	1.6

TABLE 1.4 TPFR, GRR and NRR, 1976-1986 England and Wales

Year	Total period fertility rate (TPFR)	Gross reproduction rate (GRR)	Net reproduction rate (NRR)
1976	1.71	0.83	0.81
1977	1.66	0.81	0.79
1978	1.73	0.84	0.82
1979	1.84	0.89	0.88
1980	1.88	0.91	0.90
1981	1.80	0.87	0.85
1982	1.76	0.86	0.84
1983	1.76	0.86	0.84
1984	1.75	0.86	0.84
1985	1.78	0.87	0.86
1986	1.77	0.86	0.85

TABLE 1.5 Marriages, 1976-1986 England and Wales

Year	Number of marriages			Marriage rates				
	All	Bachelors	Spinsters	Crude marriage rate - all persons marrying per 1,000 population of all ages	Males marrying per 1,000 single, widowed and divorced males aged 16 and over	Females marrying per 1,000 single, widowed and divorced females aged 16 and over	Bachelors marrying per 1,000 single males aged 16 and over	Spinsters marrying per 1,000 single females aged 16 and over
1976	358,567	274,431	276,544	14.5	66.0	51.2	62.8	76.9
1977	356,954	269,046	272,215	14.4	63.9	49.8	60.1	73.9
1978	368,258	273,719	276,385	14.9	64.0	50.2	59.6	73.0
1979	368,853	273,986	277,166	14.9	62.2	49.2	58.0	71.5
1980	370,022	274,140	277,826	14.9	60.4	48.1	56.3	69.6
1981	351,973	259,106	263,368	14.2	55.7	44.7	51.7	64.0
1982	342,166	250,999	255,171	13.8	52.5	42.5	48.7	60.4
1983	344,334	251,845	256,214	13.9	51.2	41.8	47.5	59.1
1984	349,186	255,469	260,359	14.0	50.5	41.6	47.1	58.9
1985	346,389	253,296	258,089	13.9	48.7	40.5	45.6	57.1
1986	347,924	252,953	256,767	13.9	47.7	39.9	44.6	55.7

TABLE 1.6 Mean age of women at marriage and at live birth, 1976-1986 England and Wales

Year	Mean age at marriage		Mean ages at live birth		Legitimate births				
	All brides	Spinsters	All births	Illegitimate births	All birth orders	First birth	Second birth	Third birth	Fourth birth
1976	26.5	22.8	26.4	23.3	26.7	24.9	26.9	28.9	30.7
1977	26.6	22.9	26.5	23.4	26.8	25.0	27.1	29.1	30.9
1978	26.7	22.9	26.6	23.4	27.0	25.1	27.2	29.3	31.0
1979	26.6	22.9	26.7	23.4	27.1	25.2	27.4	29.4	31.0
1980	26.7	23.0	26.7	23.5	27.1	25.2	27.4	29.5	31.1
1981	26.9	23.1	26.8	23.5	27.3	25.4	27.5	29.6	31.1
1982	27.0	23.3	26.8	23.5	27.4	25.5	27.5	29.6	31.2
1983	27.1	23.4	26.9	23.6	27.5	25.6	27.6	29.7	31.2
1984	27.3	23.6	26.9	23.7	27.6	25.8	27.8	29.7	31.2
1985	27.5	23.8	27.0	23.7	27.8	26.0	27.9	29.8	31.2
1986	27.8	24.1	27.0	23.8	27.9	26.2	28.0	29.8	31.2

Note: Mean ages at live birth for 1981 are based on a 10 per cent sample.

TABLE 1.7   Mean ages of women at births of different   **England and Wales**
             orders*, 1976-1986

Year	Mean age at live birth				
	All births	All births			
		First	Second	Third	Fourth
1976	26.4	24.3	26.6	28.6	30.1
1977	26.5	24.4	26.8	28.8	30.3
1978	26.6	24.5	26.9	28.9	30.4
1979	26.7	24.5	27.0	29.1	30.4
1980	26.7	24.5	27.0	29.2	30.4
1981	26.8	24.5	27.1	29.3	30.5
1982	26.8	24.6	27.1	29.3	30.5
1983	26.9	24.7	27.2	29.4	30.4
1984	26.9	24.7	27.3	29.4	30.3
1985	27.0	24.8	27.4	29.4	30.3
1986	27.0	24.9	27.4	29.5	30.3

Note: Mean ages at birth for 1981 are based on a 10 per cent sample.
* Includes legitimate and illegitimate children (see Introduction).

TABLE 1.8   **Proportion of total first marriages with a birth**   **England and Wales**
                  within 8 months of marriage, 1975-1985

Year of marriage	Percentages of marriages with a birth within 8 months according to woman's age at marriage				
	Under 45	Under 20	20-24	25-29	30-44
1975	13.0	23.8	8.1	7.4	7.4
1976	12.2	22.6	7.6	7.3	6.7
1977	12.4	22.9	7.8	7.5	7.7
1978	13.3	24.4	8.7	8.5	8.5
1979	14.1	26.1	9.5	8.8	9.6
1980	14.0	25.5	9.8	9.6	10.7
1981	13.2	25.3	9.7	8.6	8.5
1982	13.5	26.2	9.9	9.3	10.7
1983	13.1	25.5	10.0	9.3	11.3
1984	13.0	26.0	10.4	9.4	10.8
1985	13.4	26.8	10.9	10.4	11.0

Notes: 1. The rates are based on the total number of live births occurring to women within a eight-month period - that is, 0-7 completed
           months - following their first marriage in year x; this period spans the calendar year x and x+1 (see Introduction).
     2. Figures for 1980 (partly) and 1981 are based on a 10 per cent sample.

TABLE 1.9 Components of total period fertility rates, 1976-1986   England and Wales

Left panel:

Year	All live births	Illegitimate live births	Legitimate live births All	First	Second	Third	Fourth	Fifth and later
All ages of mother at birth								
1976	1.71	0.16	1.55	0.63	0.59	0.21	0.07	0.05
1977	1.66	0.16	1.50	0.62	0.56	0.20	0.07	0.04
1978	1.73	0.17	1.56	0.65	0.57	0.22	0.07	0.04
1979	1.84	0.19	1.64	0.69	0.60	0.24	0.08	0.04
1980	1.88	0.21	1.66	0.68	0.60	0.25	0.08	0.05
1981	1.80	0.22	1.58	0.63	0.59	0.24	0.08	0.05
1982	1.76	0.24	1.52	0.59	0.57	0.24	0.08	0.04
1983	1.76	0.26	1.49	0.58	0.55	0.23	0.08	0.05
1984	1.75	0.29	1.47	0.57	0.54	0.23	0.08	0.05
1985	1.78	0.33	1.46	0.57	0.53	0.23	0.08	0.05
1986	1.77	0.37	1.41	0.55	0.51	0.22	0.08	0.05
Under 20								
1976	0.17	0.06	0.11	0.09	0.02	0.00		
1977	0.15	0.05	0.10	0.08	0.02	0.00		
1978	0.15	0.06	0.09	0.08	0.02	0.00		
1979	0.15	0.06	0.09	0.07	0.02	0.00		
1980	0.15	0.07	0.09	0.07	0.02	0.00		
1981	0.14	0.07	0.08	0.06	0.02	0.00		
1982	0.14	0.07	0.07	0.05	0.01	0.00		
1983	0.13	0.07	0.06	0.05	0.01	0.00		
1984	0.14	0.08	0.05	0.04	0.01	0.00		
1985	0.14	0.09	0.05	0.04	0.01	0.00		
1986	0.15	0.10	0.05	0.04	0.01	0.00		
20-24								
1976	0.55	0.05	0.50	0.26	0.19	0.04	0.01	0.00
1977	0.52	0.05	0.47	0.25	0.17	0.04	0.01	0.00
1978	0.54	0.06	0.48	0.26	0.17	0.04	0.01	0.00
1979	0.56	0.07	0.49	0.27	0.17	0.04	0.01	0.00
1980	0.57	0.07	0.49	0.27	0.17	0.04	0.01	0.00
1981	0.53	0.08	0.45	0.24	0.16	0.04	0.01	0.00
1982	0.51	0.09	0.43	0.22	0.16	0.04	0.01	0.00
1983	0.50	0.09	0.40	0.21	0.14	0.04	0.01	0.00
1984	0.48	0.10	0.38	0.20	0.13	0.04	0.01	0.00
1985	0.47	0.12	0.36	0.19	0.12	0.03	0.01	0.00
1986	0.46	0.13	0.33	0.18	0.12	0.03	0.01	0.00

Right panel:

Year	All live births	Illegitimate live births	Legitimate live births All	First	Second	Third	Fourth	Fifth and later
25-29								
1976	0.60	0.03	0.57	0.21	0.25	0.08	0.02	0.01
1977	0.59	0.03	0.56	0.22	0.24	0.08	0.02	0.01
1978	0.61	0.03	0.58	0.23	0.24	0.08	0.02	0.01
1979	0.66	0.04	0.62	0.24	0.25	0.09	0.03	0.01
1980	0.67	0.04	0.63	0.24	0.25	0.09	0.03	0.01
1981	0.65	0.04	0.60	0.23	0.25	0.09	0.03	0.01
1982	0.63	0.05	0.58	0.22	0.24	0.09	0.03	0.01
1983	0.63	0.05	0.58	0.22	0.23	0.09	0.03	0.01
1984	0.63	0.06	0.57	0.22	0.23	0.09	0.03	0.01
1985	0.64	0.07	0.57	0.22	0.22	0.09	0.03	0.01
1986	0.62	0.07	0.54	0.21	0.21	0.08	0.02	0.01
1976	0.28	0.02	0.27	0.06	0.11	0.06	0.02	0.01
1977	0.28	0.02	0.27	0.06	0.11	0.06	0.02	0.01
1978	0.31	0.02	0.29	0.07	0.12	0.07	0.02	0.01
1979	0.34	0.02	0.32	0.08	0.13	0.08	0.03	0.01
1980	0.35	0.02	0.33	0.08	0.13	0.08	0.03	0.01
1981	0.35	0.02	0.33	0.08	0.13	0.08	0.03	0.01
1982	0.35	0.02	0.33	0.08	0.13	0.08	0.03	0.01
1983	0.36	0.03	0.33	0.08	0.13	0.08	0.03	0.02
1984	0.37	0.03	0.34	0.09	0.14	0.08	0.03	0.02
1985	0.38	0.03	0.35	0.09	0.14	0.08	0.03	0.02
1986	0.39	0.04	0.35	0.09	0.14	0.08	0.03	0.02
35 and over								
1976	0.12	0.01	0.11	0.02	0.03	0.02	0.02	0.02
1977	0.11	0.01	0.10	0.02	0.03	0.02	0.02	0.02
1978	0.12	0.01	0.11	0.02	0.03	0.03	0.02	0.02
1979	0.13	0.01	0.12	0.02	0.03	0.03	0.02	0.02
1980	0.13	0.01	0.12	0.02	0.03	0.03	0.02	0.02
1981	0.13	0.01	0.12	0.02	0.03	0.03	0.02	0.02
1982	0.13	0.01	0.12	0.02	0.03	0.03	0.02	0.02
1983	0.14	0.01	0.12	0.02	0.03	0.03	0.02	0.02
1984	0.14	0.02	0.12	0.02	0.04	0.03	0.02	0.02
1985	0.15	0.02	0.13	0.02	0.04	0.03	0.02	0.02
1986	0.15	0.02	0.13	0.02	0.04	0.03	0.02	0.02

Notes: 1. Age-standardised rates are calculated by summing rates for each single year of age. The value for all live births is the total period fertility rate (TPFR) - see Introduction.
2. Figures for 1981 are based on a 10 per cent sample.

TABLE 2.1 Live births and total period fertility rates: **England and Wales**
quarter of occurrence, 1976-1986

Year	Total	Quarter of occurrence ended				Total	Quarter ended			
		31 March	30 June	30 September	31 December		31 March	30 June	30 September	31 December
	a. Number (thousands)					b. Total period fertility rates (TPFR)				
	Live births					Actual TPFR				
1976	584.3	151.3	150.7	147.2	135.1	1.71	1.77	1.76	1.72	1.58
1977	569.3	140.4	144.9	146.6	137.4	1.66	1.64	1.69	1.71	1.60
1978	596.4	142.4	149.3	154.6	150.2	1.73	1.65	1.73	1.79	1.74
1979	638.0	156.2	164.8	162.1	154.9	1.84	1.80	1.90	1.87	1.78
1980	656.2	162.3	168.1	168.3	157.4	1.88	1.86	1.92	1.92	1.79
1981	634.5	156.2	160.8	164.3	153.1	1.80	1.78	1.83	1.86	1.73
1982	625.9	153.4	157.0	162.1	153.4	1.76	1.73	1.77	1.82	1.72
1983	629.1	152.4	161.3	163.4	151.9	1.76	1.71	1.80	1.82	1.69
1984	636.8	153.5	157.7	167.1	158.4	1.75	1.70	1.74	1.84	1.74
1985	656.4	160.4	165.3	172.3	158.5	1.78	1.75	1.80	1.87	1.71
1986	661.0	160.0	169.0	170.8	161.2	1.77	1.72	1.82	1.83	1.72
	Seasonally adjusted live births					Seasonally adjusted TPFR				
1976	Same	149.7	147.9	143.8	140.9	Same	1.76	1.73	1.68	1.65
1977	as	141.3	142.0	142.9	143.2	as	1.65	1.65	1.66	1.66
1978	above	143.6	146.3	150.8	156.2	above	1.67	1.70	1.75	1.81
1979		158.0	161.6	158.1	160.4		1.83	1.86	1.82	1.84
1980		163.5	165.0	163.4	162.2		1.88	1.89	1.87	1.85
1981		159.8	158.1	159.0	157.6		1.82	1.80	1.80	1.78
1982		157.2	154.8	156.5	157.5		1.78	1.75	1.76	1.77
1983		156.6	159.4	157.3	156.2		1.75	1.78	1.75	1.74
1984		156.0	156.0	160.9	162.6		1.73	1.72	1.77	1.78
1985		165.0	163.6	165.6	162.4		1.80	1.78	1.80	1.76
1986		164.8	167.4	163.9	165.2		1.78	1.80	1.76	1.77

TABLE 2.2 Stillbirths: quarter of occurrence, 1976-1986   **England and Wales**

Year	Total	Quarter of occurrence ended			
		31 March	30 June	30 September	31 December
1976	5,709	1,577	1,405	1,404	1,323
1977	5,405	1,416	1,324	1,377	1,288
1978	5,108	1,301	1,273	1,284	1,250
1979	5,125	1,368	1,263	1,281	1,213
1980	4,773	1,230	1,263	1,185	1,095
1981	4,207	1,042	1,083	1,049	1,033
1982	3,939	1,020	955	1,023	941
1983	3,631	880	938	900	913
1984	3,643	879	932	955	877
1985	3,645	891	922	983	849
1986	3,549	888	909	909	843

TABLE 2.3 Live births and total period fertility rates: month of occurrence, 1976-1986 — England and Wales

Year	Total	January	February	March	April	May	June	July	August	September	October	November	December
a) Numbers (thousands)													
Live births													
1976	**584.3**	48.6	48.3	54.3	49.3	50.9	50.4	50.0	48.3	49.0	46.9	43.7	44.5
1977	**569.3**	46.9	43.7	49.7	46.3	50.7	47.8	48.8	48.4	49.4	48.2	44.5	44.7
1978	**596.4**	46.6	44.3	51.5	48.8	51.1	49.4	50.6	51.3	52.7	51.6	48.4	50.2
1979	**638.0**	51.4	48.6	56.2	53.4	56.8	54.5	55.6	53.7	52.9	53.7	50.8	50.5
1980	**656.2**	54.4	51.5	56.4	55.5	57.8	54.7	57.9	54.8	55.6	55.4	50.5	51.6
1981	**634.5**	52.7	48.5	55.0	52.8	54.7	53.4	56.5	54.2	53.6	53.2	49.9	50.0
1982	**625.9**	51.5	47.7	54.3	52.2	53.8	51.0	54.5	53.4	54.2	53.0	49.4	51.0
1983	**629.1**	51.2	47.6	53.6	52.6	54.8	54.0	55.4	53.8	54.3	51.5	49.7	50.7
1984	**636.8**	51.3	48.9	53.3	50.1	54.3	53.4	55.9	55.8	55.4	55.3	52.5	50.6
1985	**656.4**	54.7	49.6	56.0	53.3	57.5	54.5	58.2	57.1	57.0	55.8	51.9	50.7
1986	**661.0**	53.6	49.6	56.7	55.2	58.2	55.7	56.7	57.4	56.7	55.9	51.1	54.2
Seasonally adjusted live births													
1976		48.8	50.3	50.6	49.0	48.9	49.9	48.1	48.0	47.8	47.1	47.1	46.8
1977		47.9	47.0	46.4	46.1	48.6	47.3	47.2	47.7	48.0	48.5	47.6	47.1
1978	*Same*	47.5	47.9	48.3	49.0	48.6	48.8	49.1	50.5	51.3	51.5	51.5	53.2
1979	*as*	52.1	52.7	53.2	53.6	53.9	54.1	53.7	52.6	51.8	53.0	53.8	53.5
1980	*above*	55.0	54.1	54.4	55.2	55.1	54.7	55.1	54.2	54.1	53.4	53.9	53.9
1981		53.4	53.2	53.2	52.6	52.6	52.9	53.4	53.7	51.9	52.6	53.0	52.0
1982		52.4	52.4	52.3	52.4	52.1	50.3	51.7	52.5	52.4	52.7	52.1	52.8
1983		52.4	52.5	51.7	53.1	53.0	53.3	52.8	52.1	52.3	51.4	52.1	52.7
1984		52.3	52.0	51.7	51.2	52.0	52.9	53.4	53.6	53.9	54.6	54.9	53.1
1985		55.3	54.9	54.8	54.2	55.0	54.4	55.1	55.0	55.4	55.0	54.4	53.0
1986		54.1	54.9	55.7	56.0	55.9	55.6	53.5	55.6	54.7	54.9	54.0	56.3
b) Total period fertility rates (TPFR)													
Actual TPFR													
1976	**1.71**	1.71	1.70	1.91	1.73	1.79	1.77	1.75	1.70	1.72	1.64	1.53	1.56
1977	**1.66**	1.64	1.53	1.74	1.62	1.77	1.67	1.71	1.69	1.72	1.68	1.55	1.56
1978	**1.73**	1.62	1.54	1.79	1.70	1.78	1.72	1.76	1.78	1.83	1.79	1.68	1.74
1979	**1.84**	1.78	1.68	1.95	1.85	1.97	1.89	1.92	1.85	1.83	1.85	1.75	1.74
1980	**1.88**	1.87	1.77	1.94	1.91	1.99	1.88	1.99	1.88	1.90	1.89	1.73	1.76
1981	**1.80**	1.80	1.65	1.88	1.80	1.86	1.82	1.92	1.84	1.82	1.81	1.69	1.70
1982	**1.76**	1.75	1.61	1.84	1.77	1.82	1.72	1.84	1.80	1.83	1.79	1.67	1.72
1983	**1.76**	1.72	1.60	1.80	1.76	1.84	1.81	1.85	1.80	1.81	1.72	1.66	1.69
1984	**1.75**	1.71	1.63	1.77	1.66	1.80	1.77	1.85	1.84	1.83	1.82	1.73	1.66
1985	**1.78**	1.80	1.63	1.84	1.74	1.88	1.78	1.90	1.86	1.85	1.81	1.68	1.64
1986	**1.77**	1.74	1.60	1.83	1.78	1.87	1.79	1.82	1.84	1.82	1.79	1.64	1.74
Seasonally adjusted TPFR													
1976		1.72	1.77	1.78	1.72	1.72	1.75	1.69	1.68	1.68	1.65	1.65	1.64
1977		1.68	1.65	1.63	1.61	1.70	1.65	1.65	1.66	1.68	1.69	1.66	1.64
1978	*Same*	1.65	1.67	1.68	1.70	1.69	1.70	1.71	1.75	1.78	1.79	1.79	1.84
1979	*as*	1.81	1.83	1.84	1.86	1.87	1.87	1.86	1.82	1.79	1.83	1.86	1.84
1980	*above*	1.89	1.86	1.87	1.90	1.89	1.88	1.89	1.86	1.85	1.86	1.84	1.84
1981		1.82	1.81	1.81	1.79	1.79	1.80	1.82	1.83	1.76	1.79	1.80	1.76
1982		1.78	1.78	1.77	1.77	1.76	1.70	1.75	1.77	1.77	1.78	1.75	1.78
1983		1.76	1.77	1.74	1.78	1.78	1.78	1.77	1.74	1.75	1.72	1.74	1.75
1984		1.74	1.73	1.72	1.70	1.72	1.75	1.76	1.77	1.78	1.80	1.81	1.74
1985		1.81	1.80	1.79	1.77	1.80	1.77	1.80	1.79	1.80	1.79	1.77	1.72
1986		1.75	1.78	1.80	1.81	1.80	1.79	1.72	1.79	1.76	1.76	1.73	1.80

TABLE 2.4   Maternities, live and still births: quarter and month of occurrence, legitimacy and sex, 1986   **England and Wales**

Month of occurrence	Maternities	Live births			Stillbirths		Live births		Stillbirths	
		Total	Legit-imate	Illegit-imate	Legit-imate	Illegit-imate	Male	Female	Male	Female
Annual total	657,308	661,018	519,673	141,345	2,600	949	338,852	322,166	1,904	1,645
March quarter	159,140	159,983	127,022	32,961	659	229	82,226	77,757	485	403
June quarter	168,099	169,050	134,634	34,416	664	245	86,785	82,265	481	428
September quarter	169,876	170,778	133,529	37,249	664	245	87,385	83,393	489	420
December quarter	160,193	161,207	124,488	36,719	613	230	82,456	78,751	449	394
January	53,348	53,636	42,584	11,052	222	78	27,540	26,096	165	135
February	49,374	49,630	39,234	10,396	215	82	25,496	24,134	157	140
March	56,418	56,717	45,204	11,513	222	69	29,190	27,527	163	128
April	54,876	55,180	44,072	11,108	224	92	28,231	26,949	169	147
May	57,858	58,191	46,521	11,670	211	74	29,796	28,395	146	139
June	55,365	55,679	44,041	11,638	229	79	28,758	26,921	166	142
July	56,395	56,700	44,636	12,064	243	77	29,028	27,672	161	159
August	57,139	57,421	44,808	12,613	204	83	29,394	28,027	153	134
September	56,342	56,657	44,085	12,572	217	85	28,963	27,694	175	127
October	55,461	55,887	43,417	12,470	205	74	28,588	27,299	145	134
November	50,814	51,072	39,254	11,817	197	84	26,157	24,914	155	126
December	53,918	54,249	41,817	12,432	211	72	27,711	26,538	149	134

TABLE 2.5   Live birth occurrences in 1986: month of occurrence and of registration   **England and Wales**

Quarter/month of occurrence in 1986	Month of registration in 1986*												Registra-tion in January 1987	1986/1987 Total
	January	February	March	April	May	June	July	August	September	October	November	December		
Annual total	28,730	48,456	49,683	61,493	55,352	56,752	58,848	52,747	59,268	58,766	49,288	49,688	31,947	661,018
Quarters ending:														
March	28,730	46,735	49,610	32,625	2,065	80	28	23	22	28	18	13	6	159,983
June	-	11	4	28,851	53,274	56,669	28,282	1,787	81	30	27	18	16	169,050
September	-	25	8	1	4	2	30,534	50,936	59,165	28,232	1,758	71	42	170,778
December	-	1,685	61	16	9	1	4	1	-	30,476	47,485	49,586	31,883	161,207
Months:														
January	28,730	22,246	2,516	85	15	8	6	6	6	8	8	2	-	53,636
February	-	24,487	22,512	2,534	43	14	8	4	7	10	3	5	3	49,630
March	-	2	24,582	30,006	2,007	58	14	13	9	10	7	6	3	56,717
April	-	6	1	28,848	24,244	1,987	50	13	7	5	10	2	7	55,180
May	-	2	1	3	29,030	26,792	2,263	56	16	9	7	9	3	58,191
June	-	3	2	-	-	27,890	25,969	1,718	58	16	10	7	6	55,679
July	-	5	-	-	1	1	30,533	23,781	2,290	68	11	6	4	56,700
August	-	5	6	-	2	-	-	27,155	28,150	2,035	48	8	12	57,421
September	-	15	2	1	1	1	1	-	28,725	26,129	1,699	57	26	56,657
October	-	17	5	4	3	-	-	1	-	30,474	22,991	2,306	86	55,887
November	-	47	7	2	4	-	1	-	-	2	24,492	23,912	2,604	51,071
December	-	1,621	49	10	2	1	3	-	-	-	2	23,368	29,193	54,249

* The figures refer to those births which occurred in 1986 and were registered by 31 January 1987, births registered later than this date will be added to the occurrences for 1987; the above figures similarly include those births which occurred in 1985 but were registered later than 31 January 1986.

TABLE 3.1 Live births: age of mother and legitimacy, 1976-1986
a. numbers

England and Wales

Year	Age of mother at birth							
	All ages	Under 20	20-24	25-29	30-34	35-39	40-44	45 and over
All live births								
1976	584,270	57,943	182,210	220,712	90,791	26,117	5,999	498
1977	569,259	54,477	174,544	207,916	100,807	25,527	5,534	454
1978	596,418	55,984	182,580	210,598	113,077	27,937	5,719	523
1979	638,028	59,143	193,209	222,102	125,664	31,394	5,978	538
1980	656,234	60,754	201,541	223,438	129,908	33,893	6,075	625
1981	634,492	56,570	194,500	215,760	126,590	34,210	6,170	690
1982	625,931	55,435	192,322	211,905	120,758	38,992	5,886	633
1983	629,134	54,059	191,852	214,078	120,996	41,277	6,210	662
1984	636,818	54,508	191,455	218,031	122,774	42,921	6,576	553
1985	656,417	56,929	193,958	227,486	126,185	44,393	6,882	584
1986	661,018	57,406	192,064	229,035	129,487	45,465	7,033	528
Legitimate								
1976	530,504	38,124	165,579	211,035	86,058	23,866	5,393	449
1977	513,880	34,426	157,168	198,158	95,527	23,311	4,882	408
1978	535,781	34,341	162,879	200,167	107,188	25,604	5,123	479
1979	568,561	35,138	170,338	209,796	118,773	28,716	5,311	489
1980	578,862	34,894	174,934	209,976	122,320	30,846	5,314	578
1981	553,509	30,140	165,690	201,460	118,720	31,480	5,340	680
1982	536,074	26,696	159,911	195,839	112,625	35,310	5,118	575
1983	529,923	23,636	155,209	196,162	111,722	37,160	5,422	612
1984	526,353	21,373	150,371	197,401	112,660	38,350	5,691	507
1985	530,167	20,057	146,262	203,272	114,862	39,293	5,883	538
1986	519,673	17,793	137,985	201,323	116,369	39,753	5,959	491
Illegitimate								
1976	53,766	19,819	16,631	9,677	4,733	2,251	606	49
1977	55,379	20,051	17,376	9,758	5,280	2,216	652	46
1978	60,637	21,643	19,701	10,431	5,889	2,333	596	44
1979	69,467	24,005	22,871	12,306	6,891	2,678	667	49
1980	77,372	25,860	26,607	13,462	7,588	3,047	761	47
1981	80,983	26,430	28,810	14,300	7,870	2,730	840	20
1982	89,857	28,739	32,411	16,066	8,133	3,682	768	58
1983	99,211	30,423	36,643	17,916	9,274	4,117	788	50
1984	110,465	33,135	41,084	20,630	10,114	4,571	885	46
1985	126,250	36,872	47,696	24,214	11,323	5,100	999	46
1986	141,345	39,613	54,079	27,712	13,118	5,712	1,074	37

Note: 1981 births for age-groups are based on a 10 per cent sample.

TABLE 3.1 Live births: age of mother and legitimacy, 1976-1986
b. rates

Year	Age of mother at birth							
	All ages	Under 20	20-24	25-29	30-34	35-39	40-44	45 and over
	All live births per 1,000 women							
1976	60.4	32.2	109.3	118.7	57.2	18.6	4.4	0.3
1977	58.1	29.4	103.7	117.5	58.6	18.2	4.1	0.3
1978	60.1	29.4	106.9	122.6	63.1	19.5	4.2	0.4
1979	63.3	30.3	111.3	131.2	69.0	21.3	4.3	0.4
1980	64.2	30.4	112.7	133.6	70.5	22.3	4.3	0.5
1981	61.3	28.1	105.3	129.1	68.6	21.7	4.4	0.5
1982	59.9	27.4	101.6	126.4	69.1	22.8	4.2	0.5
1983	59.7	26.9	98.5	126.4	71.5	23.1	4.4	0.5
1984	59.8	27.6	95.5	126.2	73.6	23.6	4.5	0.4
1985	61.0	29.5	94.5	127.6	76.4	24.1	4.6	0.4
1986	60.6	30.1	92.7	124.0	78.1	24.6	4.5	0.4
	Legitimate live births per 1,000 married women							
1976	83.0	294.6	179.1	138.6	62.0	19.3	4.5	0.4
1977	80.8	293.5	174.4	138.9	64.0	18.9	4.1	0.3
1978	84.7	315.3	187.1	147.2	69.4	20.5	4.3	0.4
1979	90.2	332.4	201.7	159.3	76.3	22.5	4.4	0.4
1980	92.2	340.4	210.8	164.6	78.4	23.6	4.4	0.5
1981	88.8	324.8	204.3	161.5	76.9	23.3	4.5	0.6
1982	86.9	331.2	204.5	160.0	78.2	24.3	4.3	0.5
1983	86.8	329.7	205.8	162.6	81.4	24.7	4.5	0.5
1984	86.7	338.7	206.2	164.5	84.4	25.2	4.6	0.4
1985	87.8	358.8	209.5	168.9	88.1	25.7	4.7	0.5
1986	86.3	360.9	209.8	167.2	90.1	26.2	4.6	0.4
	Illegitimate live births per 1,000 single, widowed and divorced women							
1976	16.4	11.9	22.4	28.7	23.6	13.5	3.5	0.2
1977	16.1	11.6	22.2	28.5	23.2	12.7	3.7	0.2
1978	16.8	12.1	23.5	29.1	23.7	12.6	3.3	0.2
1979	18.4	13.0	25.7	32.7	26.1	13.6	3.5	0.2
1980	19.6	13.7	27.8	33.9	26.8	14.5	3.8	0.2
1981	19.7	13.7	27.8	33.7	26.0	11.9	4.1	0.1
1982	21.0	14.8	29.2	35.4	26.4	14.4	3.6	0.3
1983	22.4	15.7	30.7	36.8	29.0	14.7	3.5	0.2
1984	24.1	17.3	32.2	39.1	30.4	15.4	3.8	0.2
1985	26.7	19.7	35.2	41.8	32.6	16.2	4.0	0.2
1986	28.9	21.3	38.2	43.1	35.8	17.2	4.0	0.2

Notes: 1. 1981 births for age-groups are based on a 10 per cent sample.
2. The rates for women of all ages, under 20 and 45 and over are based upon the population of women aged 15-44, 15-19 and 45-49 respectively.

D

TABLE 3.2 **Maternities, live and still births: age of mother, legitimacy and sex, 1986**

Age of mother at birth	Maternities			Births			
	Total	Legitimate	Illegitimate	Live		Still	
				Total	Female only	Total	Female only
All ages	657,308	516,380	140,928	661,018	322,166	3,549	1,645
11	-	-	-	-	-	-	-
12	1	-	1	1	-	-	-
13	31	-	31	31	10	-	-
14	194	-	194	190	82	4	-
15	1,151	4	1,147	1,144	578	9	5
16	4,323	446	3,877	4,303	2,033	35	20
17	10,700	2,028	8,672	10,678	5,233	72	30
18	17,429	5,247	12,182	17,449	8,522	108	51
19	23,565	10,049	13,516	23,610	11,637	139	68
Under 20	57,394	17,774	39,620	57,406	28,095	367	174
20	28,600	15,662	12,938	28,650	13,903	153	80
21	33,814	21,660	12,154	33,883	16,509	208	95
22	39,045	28,188	10,857	39,151	19,007	223	91
23	43,393	33,746	9,647	43,591	21,270	197	89
24	46,573	38,212	8,361	46,789	22,709	236	118
20-24	191,425	137,468	53,957	192,064	93,398	1,017	473
25	48,786	41,477	7,309	49,020	23,809	252	109
26	47,920	41,854	6,066	48,226	23,669	223	128
27	46,859	41,393	5,466	47,169	22,907	223	118
28	44,032	39,322	4,710	44,356	21,689	209	109
29	39,982	35,965	4,017	40,264	19,559	191	75
25-29	227,579	200,011	27,568	229,035	111,633	1,098	539
30	35,408	31,883	3,525	35,694	17,488	186	95
31	29,618	26,647	2,971	29,850	14,636	170	73
32	25,573	23,034	2,539	25,804	12,585	125	49
33	21,166	18,970	2,196	21,373	10,428	105	40
34	16,592	14,800	1,792	16,766	8,186	94	45
30-34	128,357	115,334	13,023	129,487	63,323	680	302
35	13,929	12,343	1,586	14,072	6,805	94	37
36	10,855	9,524	1,331	10,949	5,339	67	24
37	8,395	7,268	1,127	8,495	4,079	59	28
38	6,713	5,818	895	6,775	3,236	57	26
39	5,119	4,408	711	5,174	2,562	38	16
35-39	45,011	39,361	5,650	45,465	22,021	315	131
40	3,002	2,555	447	3,018	1,482	24	8
41	1,855	1,549	306	1,863	894	16	7
42	1,127	963	164	1,132	580	8	3
43	656	560	96	656	302	8	2
44	369	310	59	364	176	7	3
40-44	7,009	5,937	1,072	7,033	3,434	63	23
45	205	183	22	205	99	1	1
46	123	114	9	120	59	3	-
47	59	56	3	60	35	-	-
48	44	44	-	42	19	2	1
49	32	29	3	32	15	1	-
45-49	463	426	37	459	227	7	2
50	23	23	-	22	14	1	-
51	12	11	1	12	4	-	-
52	16	16	-	16	8	-	-
53	4	4	-	4	2	-	-
54	7	7	-	7	2	-	-
55	8	8	-	8	5	1	1
50-55	70	69	1	69	35	2	1

The following cases in which the mother's age was not stated have been included in the above table (for method of distribution see Introduction).

	1,387	1,017	370	1,348	635	56	31

England and Wales

Legitimate births				Illegitimate births				Age of mother at birth
Live		Still		Live		Still		
Total	Female only	Total	Female only	Total	Female only	Total	Female only	
519,673	253,156	2,600	1,188	141,345	68,010	949	457	All ages
-	-	-	-	-	-	-	-	11
-	-	-	-	1	-	-	-	12
-	-	-	-	31	10	-	-	13
-	-	-	-	190	82	4	-	14
4	-	-	-	1,140	578	9	5	15
445	217	5	4	3,858	1,816	30	16	16
2,016	953	17	6	8,662	4,280	55	24	17
5,269	2,552	26	16	12,180	5,970	82	35	18
10,059	4,940	59	28	13,551	6,697	80	40	19
17,793	8,662	107	54	39,613	19,433	260	120	Under 20
15,703	7,661	61	26	12,947	6,242	92	54	20
21,715	10,616	122	53	12,168	5,893	86	42	21
28,258	13,682	158	62	10,893	5,325	65	29	22
33,922	16,636	139	66	9,669	4,634	58	23	23
38,387	18,624	188	90	8,402	4,085	48	28	24
137,985	67,219	668	297	54,079	26,179	349	176	20-24
41,667	20,257	207	92	7,353	3,552	45	17	25
42,131	20,700	180	103	6,095	2,969	43	25	26
41,669	20,152	184	96	5,500	2,755	39	22	27
39,624	19,283	174	92	4,732	2,406	35	17	28
36,232	17,604	162	60	4,032	1,955	29	15	29
201,323	97,996	907	443	27,712	13,637	191	96	25-29
32,142	15,740	163	83	3,552	1,748	23	12	30
26,855	13,182	140	58	2,995	1,454	30	15	31
23,252	11,342	105	39	2,552	1,243	20	10	32
19,160	9,353	91	33	2,213	1,075	14	7	33
14,960	7,304	82	40	1,806	882	12	5	34
116,369	56,921	581	253	13,118	6,402	99	49	30-34
12,471	6,012	81	34	1,601	793	13	3	35
9,607	4,664	60	23	1,342	675	7	1	36
7,348	3,524	54	26	1,147	555	5	2	37
5,872	2,796	51	24	903	440	6	2	38
4,455	2,198	32	11	719	364	6	5	39
39,753	19,194	278	118	5,712	2,827	37	13	35-39
2,566	1,269	22	7	452	213	2	1	40
1,558	740	9	5	305	154	7	2	41
970	491	6	3	162	89	2	-	42
559	267	8	2	97	35	-	-	43
306	150	6	3	58	26	1	-	44
5,959	2,917	51	20	1,074	517	12	3	40-44
183	92	1	1	22	7	-	-	45
112	55	2	-	8	4	1	-	46
57	34	-	-	3	1	-	-	47
42	19	2	1	-	-	-	-	48
29	13	1	-	3	2	-	-	49
423	213	6	2	36	14	1	-	45-49
22	14	1	-	-	-	-	-	50
11	3	-	-	1	1	-	-	51
16	8	-	-	-	-	-	-	52
4	2	-	-	-	-	-	-	53
7	2	-	-	-	-	-	-	54
8	5	1	1	-	-	-	-	55
68	34	2	1	1	1	-	-	50-55

The following cases in which the mother's age was not stated have been included in the above table (for method of distribution see Introduction).

| 1,007 | 481 | 26 | 15 | 341 | 154 | 30 | 16 | |

TABLE 3.3   Legitimate live births: age of father, 1976-1986   **England and Wales**

Year   Age of father at birth

	All ages	Under 20	20-24	25-29	30-34	35-39	40-44	45-49	50-54	55-59	60-64	65 and over
	Numbers											
1976	**530,504**	11,590	105,601	211,337	126,916	47,741	17,884	6,455	2,058	673	200	89
1977	**513,880**	10,094	98,817	194,267	137,245	46,737	17,637	6,150	2,007	629	217	80
1978	**535,781**	9,858	101,503	195,588	149,465	50,894	18,897	6,392	2,193	714	184	93
1979	**568,561**	10,126	105,683	202,153	163,048	57,077	20,251	6,921	2,221	795	192	94
1980	**578,862**	9,889	108,836	202,446	166,174	60,084	20,984	6,967	2,368	756	259	99
1981	**553,509**	7,970	102,130	191,030	160,250	60,290	21,030	7,020	2,660	760	280	120
1982	**536,074**	7,126	96,046	185,471	150,346	66,064	20,212	7,147	2,489	809	271	93
1983	**529,923**	6,192	90,466	184,214	148,058	68,833	20,635	7,581	2,689	872	256	99
1984	**526,353**	5,371	86,263	183,174	147,749	70,512	21,593	7,705	2,657	929	304	96
1985	**530,167**	4,941	83,152	184,986	149,651	72,904	22,470	7,947	2,658	1,019	327	112
1986	**519,673**	4,466	76,895	180,926	149,531	72,745	23,146	7,646	2,817	1,087	332	112
	Rates: legitimate live births per 1,000 married men in the age-group											
1976	**42.4**	413.9	189.6	159.4	94.8	38.7	14.8	5.2	1.6	0.6	0.2	0.0
1977	**41.2**	407.0	184.4	158.0	95.7	38.2	14.6	5.0	1.6	0.5	0.2	0.0
1978	**43.2**	436.2	198.2	168.3	101.4	41.2	15.6	5.3	1.8	0.6	0.2	0.0
1979	**46.0**	458.2	213.5	180.0	110.0	45.2	16.6	5.8	1.8	0.6	0.2	0.0
1980	**47.0**	462.1	224.8	186.3	112.6	46.6	17.2	5.9	2.0	0.6	0.3	0.0
1981	**45.2**	408.7	219.3	180.8	110.4	45.5	17.6	6.0	2.3	0.6	0.3	0.1
1982	**44.2**	439.9	223.9	180.8	111.7	46.6	17.1	6.2	2.1	0.7	0.3	0.0
1983	**44.0**	430.0	227.7	183.8	115.4	47.3	17.2	6.5	2.3	0.8	0.2	0.0
1984	**43.8**	429.7	228.0	185.3	118.5	48.1	17.6	6.6	2.4	0.8	0.3	0.0
1985	**44.3**	445.1	235.5	189.8	122.9	49.7	18.0	6.8	2.4	0.9	0.3	0.1
1986	**43.7**	451.1	238.7	189.3	124.7	50.2	17.9	6.7	2.5	1.0	0.3	0.1

Note: 1. 1981 births for five-year age-groups are based on a 10 per cent sample.

TABLE 3.4   Paternities, live and still births: age of father, legitimacy and sex, 1986   England and Wales

Age of father at birth	Legitimate paternities	Legitimate births				Illegitimate births registered* on joint information of parents			
		Live		Still		Live		Still	
		Total	Male only	Total	Male only	Total	Male only	Total	Male only
All ages	516,380	519,673	266,517	2,600	1,412	93,523	47,929	465	238
11	-	-	-	-	-	-	-	-	-
12	-	-	-	-	-	-	-	-	-
13	-	-	-	-	-	2	-	-	-
14	-	-	-	-	-	7	3	-	-
15	-	-	-	-	-	72	44	-	-
16	31	30	16	1	1	414	209	2	-
17	252	248	130	4	2	1,402	725	13	8
18	1,172	1,170	611	10	4	3,100	1,582	17	8
19	3,012	3,018	1,570	15	6	4,995	2,580	36	16
Under 20	4,467	4,466	2,327	30	13	9,992	5,143	68	32
20	5,728	5,748	2,909	22	13	6,399	3,260	28	11
21	9,827	9,862	5,039	56	25	7,237	3,644	32	20
22	14,908	14,941	7,713	86	54	7,252	3,717	46	19
23	20,342	20,420	10,485	104	53	6,744	3,453	24	13
24	25,839	25,924	13,299	117	63	6,508	3,368	32	21
20-24	76,644	76,895	39,445	385	208	34,140	17,442	162	84
25	30,573	30,719	15,684	141	80	5,749	2,950	21	13
26	34,644	34,817	17,827	157	79	5,012	2,648	34	16
27	37,216	37,420	19,346	188	93	4,566	2,372	26	16
28	38,914	39,145	20,018	181	93	4,022	1,997	18	8
29	38,597	38,825	19,919	178	94	3,721	1,973	12	7
25-29	179,944	180,926	92,794	845	439	23,070	11,940	111	60
30	36,273	36,569	18,773	168	97	3,221	1,645	13	3
31	33,050	33,300	17,129	157	91	2,788	1,405	12	7
32	30,006	30,225	15,326	151	83	2,514	1,281	7	2
33	26,550	26,773	13,773	117	66	2,321	1,143	8	5
34	22,476	22,664	11,651	112	55	2,041	1,045	9	2
30-34	148,355	149,531	76,652	705	392	12,885	6,519	49	19
35	19,324	19,467	10,012	116	64	1,823	931	8	3
36	16,496	16,616	8,489	89	49	1,631	807	12	8
37	13,916	14,029	7,243	73	39	1,471	773	8	5
38	11,929	12,058	6,233	60	33	1,440	736	7	5
39	10,486	10,575	5,444	80	43	1,322	669	4	2
35-39	72,151	72,745	37,421	418	228	7,687	3,916	39	23
40	6,958	7,012	3,557	41	27	933	498	5	3
41	5,477	5,535	2,875	27	14	808	397	4	3
42	4,470	4,520	2,283	26	18	671	335	5	1
43	3,467	3,498	1,783	14	5	539	288	2	1
44	2,554	2,581	1,338	12	6	453	233	1	1
40-44	22,926	23,146	11,836	120	70	3,404	1,751	17	9
45	2,000	2,009	1,031	21	15	403	215	5	3
46	1,835	1,851	936	12	6	336	176	1	-
47	1,459	1,469	720	11	8	294	143	1	-
48	1,209	1,209	645	9	7	264	152	2	2
49	1,097	1,108	557	8	5	194	85	2	1
45-49	7,600	7,646	3,889	61	41	1,491	771	11	6
50-54	2,795	2,817	1,406	21	11	570	295	6	3
55-59	1,056	1,057	521	11	8	192	102	2	2
60-64	331	332	175	3	2	70	37	-	-
65-69	82	82	36	1	-	14	6	-	-
70-74	21	22	11	-	-	6	5	-	-
75 and over	8	8	4	-	-	2	2	-	-

The following births in which the age of the father was not stated have been included in the above table (for method of distribution see Introduction)

	549	537	276	19	7	546	274	7	1

* The figures in these columns should be treated with reserve because they do not include 47,822 live births and 484 stillbirths registered without any information on the child's father.

TABLE 3.5 Legitimate paternities, live and still birth rates: age of father and sex, 1986 — England and Wales

| Age of father | Estimated number of married men (thousands) | Legitimate paternities per 1,000 married men | Legitimate births per 1,000 married men | | | |
| | | | Live | | Still | |
			Total	Male only	Total	Male only
All ages	11,885.8	43.4	43.7	22.4	0.22	0.12
Under 20	9.9	451.2	451.1	235.1	3.03	1.31
20–24	322.1	238.0	238.7	122.5	1.20	0.65
25–29	955.7	188.3	189.3	97.1	0.88	0.46
30–34	1,199.6	123.7	124.7	63.9	0.59	0.33
35–39	1,450.4	49.7	50.2	25.8	0.29	0.16
40–44	1,292.6	17.7	17.9	9.2	0.09	0.05
45–49	1,146.2	6.6	6.7	3.4	0.05	0.04
50–54	1,108.5	2.5	2.5	1.3	0.02	0.01
55–59	1,101.1	1.0	1.0	0.5	0.01	0.01
60–64	1,067.2	0.3	0.3	0.2	0.00	0.00
65 and over	2,232.7	0.0	0.1	0.0	0.00	0.00

TABLE 3.6 Legitimate live births: age of mother and father, 1986 — England and Wales

| Age of father at birth | Age of mother at birth | | | | | | | | |
	All ages	Under 20	20–24	25–29	30–34	35–39	40–44	45–49	50 and over
All ages	519,673	17,793	137,985	201,323	116,369	39,753	5,959	423	68
Under 20	4,466	2,890	1,389	150	26	9	2	–	–
20–24	76,895	10,801	54,091	10,425	1,287	251	40	–	–
25–29	180,926	3,126	62,157	100,828	12,926	1,697	188	4	–
30–34	149,531	674	14,670	67,695	59,156	6,830	491	15	–
35–39	72,745	180	3,867	16,233	32,255	18,902	1,279	29	–
40–44	23,146	80	1,169	4,088	7,277	8,218	2,249	63	2
45–49	7,646	28	403	1,233	2,190	2,474	1,134	180	4
50–54	2,817	5	143	465	851	846	387	87	33
55–59	1,057	7	50	147	296	378	122	35	22
60–64	332	1	31	42	83	119	45	6	5
65 and over	112	1	15	17	22	29	22	4	2

TABLE 3.7 Legitimate stillbirths: age of mother and father, 1986 — England and Wales

| Age of father at birth | Age of mother at birth | | | | | | | | |
	All ages	Under 20	20–24	25–29	30–34	35–39	40–44	45–49	50 and over
All ages	2,600	107	668	907	581	278	51	6	2
Under 20	30	21	7	2	–	–	–	–	–
20–24	385	61	252	57	9	5	1	–	–
25–29	845	21	298	435	74	16	1	–	–
30–34	705	3	79	299	273	47	4	–	–
35–39	418	–	24	86	164	132	11	1	–
40–44	120	–	4	20	31	50	15	–	–
45–49	61	–	3	5	22	20	7	3	1
50–54	21	1	1	2	6	3	7	1	–
55–59	11	–	–	1	1	3	4	1	1
60–64	3	–	–	–	–	2	1	–	–
65 and over	1	–	–	–	1	–	–	–	–

TABLE 3.8 Jointly registered illegitimate live births: age of mother and father in combination, 1986

England and Wales

Age of father at birth	Age of mother at birth							
	All ages	Under 20	20-24	25-29	30-34	35-39	40-44	45 and over
	(i) Total illegitimate live births							
All ages	141,345	39,613	54,079	27,712	13,118	5,712	1,074	37
	(ii) Sole registered							
All ages	47,822	16,379	17,922	8,246	3,479	1,479	306	11
	(iii) Jointly registered							
All ages	93,523	23,234	36,157	19,466	9,639	4,233	768	26
Under 20	9,992	7,739	1,883	283	73	13	1	-
20-24	34,140	11,975	17,620	3,495	784	238	27	1
25-29	23,070	2,508	10,663	7,111	2,113	611	62	2
30-34	12,885	610	3,520	4,802	2,908	920	121	4
35-39	7,687	254	1,553	2,266	2,204	1,228	176	6
40-44	3,404	89	572	966	915	693	165	4
45-49	1,491	46	225	377	396	324	118	5
50-54	570	9	90	119	160	130	60	2
55-59	192	3	20	35	57	53	22	2
60 and over	92	1	11	12	29	23	16	-

Note: The figures for jointly registered illegitimate births include a small number of cases registered by the mother alone for which the father's name was included in the birth register. During 1986 there were 787 such birth registrations; in 689 cases the mother supplied a statutory declaration by the father acknowledging paternity, and in the other 98 cases the mother supplied an affiliation order.

TABLE 3.9 Illegitimate live births according to registration by mother or by both parents, 1976-1986 **England and Wales**

Year		All ages	Under 20	20-24	25-29	30-34	35 and over	All ages	Under 20	20-24	25-29	30-34	35 and over
		a. Number (thousands)						b. Percentage sole/joint in each age-group					
1976	Total	53.8	19.8	16.6	9.7	4.7	2.9						
	Sole	26.4	12.6	8.0	3.4	1.4	0.9	49.0	63.7	48.0	35.2	29.9	31.8
	Joint	27.4	7.2	8.6	6.3	3.3	2.0	51.0	36.3	52.0	64.8	70.1	68.2
1977	Total	55.4	20.1	17.4	9.8	5.3	2.9						
	Sole	26.1	12.2	8.1	3.3	1.6	0.9	47.1	60.8	46.4	34.2	29.5	31.1
	Joint	29.3	7.8	9.3	6.4	3.7	2.0	52.9	39.2	53.6	65.8	70.5	68.9
1978	Total	60.6	21.6	19.7	10.4	5.9	3.0						
	Sole	27.8	12.8	8.8	3.6	1.7	0.9	45.9	59.0	44.9	34.1	29.2	31.4
	Joint	32.8	8.9	10.9	6.9	4.2	2.0	54.1	41.0	55.1	65.9	70.8	68.6
1979	Total	69.5	24.0	22.9	12.3	6.9	3.4						
	Sole	31.1	13.7	10.1	4.2	2.0	1.1	44.8	57.1	44.3	33.9	29.4	31.8
	Joint	38.3	10.3	12.7	8.1	4.9	2.3	55.2	42.9	55.7	66.1	70.6	68.2
1980	Total	77.4	25.9	26.6	13.5	7.6	3.9						
	Sole	33.2	14.0	11.3	4.5	2.2	1.1	42.9	54.3	42.6	33.5	28.7	29.6
	Joint	44.2	11.8	15.3	8.9	5.4	2.7	57.1	45.7	57.4	66.5	71.3	70.4
1981	Total	81.0	26.4	28.8	14.3	7.9	3.6						
	Sole	33.8	13.7	12.0	4.8	2.3	1.1	41.8	51.7	41.6	33.4	29.7	29.9
	Joint	47.1	12.8	16.8	9.5	5.5	2.5	58.2	48.3	58.4	66.6	70.3	70.1
1982	Total	89.9	28.7	32.4	16.1	8.1	4.5						
	Sole	36.5	14.5	13.0	5.4	2.3	1.3	40.6	50.3	40.1	33.5	28.3	29.5
	Joint	53.4	14.3	19.4	10.7	5.8	3.2	59.4	49.7	59.9	66.5	71.7	70.5
1983	Total	99.2	30.4	36.6	17.9	9.3	5.0						
	Sole	38.4	14.4	14.1	5.8	2.7	1.5	38.7	47.2	38.5	32.5	28.6	30.3
	Joint	60.8	16.1	22.6	12.1	6.6	3.5	61.3	52.8	61.5	67.5	71.4	69.7
1984	Total	110.5	33.1	41.1	20.6	10.1	5.5						
	Sole	40.6	14.9	14.9	6.4	2.8	1.6	36.7	45.1	36.2	30.9	27.9	28.8
	Joint	69.9	18.2	26.2	14.2	7.3	3.9	63.3	54.9	63.8	69.1	72.1	71.2
1985	Total	126.2	36.9	47.7	24.2	11.3	6.1						
	Sole	44.5	15.9	16.4	7.4	3.1	1.6	35.2	43.0	34.5	30.4	27.8	26.7
	Joint	81.8	21.0	31.3	16.9	8.2	4.5	64.8	57.0	65.5	69.6	72.2	73.3
1986	Total	141.3	39.6	54.1	27.7	13.1	6.8						
	Sole	47.8	16.4	17.9	8.2	3.5	1.8	33.8	41.3	33.1	29.8	26.5	26.3
	Joint	93.5	23.2	36.2	19.5	9.6	5.0	66.2	58.7	66.9	70.2	73.5	73.7

Note: Figures for jointly registered illegitimate live births include a small number of cases registered by the mother alone for which the father's name was included in the birth register.

TABLE 3.10 Jointly registered illegitimate births according to whether parents gave same or different addresses of usual residence at registration: age of mother, 1983-1986

England and Wales

Year	Addresses of mother and father	Age of mother											
		All ages	Under 20	20-24	25-29	30-34	35 and over	All ages	Under 20	20-24	25-29	30-34	35 and over
		a. Numbers of jointly registered illegitimate births						b. Percentage same/different addresses in each age-group					
1983*	Total	10,157	2,679	3,755	1,999	1,124	571						
	Same	7,427	1,513	2,860	1,661	924	457	73.1	56.5	76.2	83.1	82.2	80.0
	Different	2,730	1,166	895	338	200	114	26.9	43.5	23.8	16.9	17.8	20.0
1984*	Total	12,216	2,771	4,803	2,587	1,302	732						
	Same	8,843	1,550	3,505	2,098	1,066	609	72.4	55.9	73.0	81.1	85.0	83.2
	Different	3,373	1,221	1,298	489	236	123	27.6	44.1	27.0	18.9	15.0	16.8
1985*	Total	14,234	3,646	5,380	3,019	1,379	787						
	Same	10,274	2,084	3,971	2,394	1,162	649	72.2	57.2	73.8	79.3	84.3	82.5
	Different	3,960	1,562	1,409	625	217	138	27.8	42.8	26.2	20.7	15.7	17.5
1986	Total	93,523	23,234	36,157	19,466	9,639	5,027						
	Same	65,844	12,908	25,760	15,300	7,849	4,027	70.4	55.6	71.2	78.6	81.4	80.1
	Different	27,679	10,326	10,397	4,166	1,790	1,000	29.6	44.4	28.8	21.4	18.6	19.9

* Births registered in July and November of each year.

**TABLE 4.1   Legitimate live births: previous liveborn children
and age of mother (five-year age-groups), 1976-1986
a. all married women**

Year	Number of previous liveborn children						Year	Number of previous liveborn children					
	Total	0	1	2	3	4 or more		Total	0	1	2	3	4 or more
	All ages of mother at birth							**25-29**					
1976	530,504	217,211	203,576	70,967	23,569	15,181	1976	211,035	77,219	91,836	29,783	8,591	3,606
1977	513,880	214,573	195,035	68,796	21,935	13,541	1977	198,158	75,384	84,896	27,320	7,492	3,066
1978	535,781	226,586	198,088	74,173	23,358	13,576	1978	200,167	78,588	82,745	28,112	7,747	2,975
1979	568,561	238,890	206,667	82,742	25,963	14,299	1979	209,796	82,260	84,739	31,137	8,475	3,185
1980	578,862	240,975	209,164	86,336	27,537	14,850	1980	209,976	81,554	84,580	31,461	8,988	3,393
1981	553,520	224,290	205,690	82,400	26,160	14,980	1981	201,460	77,200	82,750	29,480	8,660	3,380
1982	536,074	211,862	200,681	81,431	27,123	14,977	1982	195,839	73,585	80,633	29,194	8,882	3,545
1983	529,923	211,753	195,630	80,728	26,646	15,166	1983	196,162	75,876	78,657	29,291	8,788	3,550
1984	526,353	210,421	193,093	80,643	26,860	15,336	1984	197,401	77,208	78,280	29,323	8,895	3,695
1985	530,167	212,017	193,058	82,403	26,865	15,824	1985	203,272	79,906	80,043	30,546	8,977	3,800
1986	519,673	206,942	189,186	80,842	26,920	15,783	1986	201,323	79,255	78,858	30,243	9,123	3,844
	Under 20							**30-34**					
1976	38,124	30,223	7,381	486	31	3	1976	86,058	19,727	34,679	19,506	7,503	4,643
1977	34,426	27,907	6,138	365	14	2	1977	95,527	23,106	39,027	21,446	7,628	4,320
1978	34,341	28,078	5,913	333	16	1	1978	107,188	26,262	42,400	24,574	8,534	4,418
1979	35,138	28,581	6,189	349	16	3	1979	118,773	28,306	47,805	28,298	9,599	4,765
1980	34,894	28,189	6,307	386	12	-	1980	122,320	28,907	48,205	30,052	10,063	5,093
1981	30,140	23,650	6,090	390	10	-	1981	118,720	27,800	47,680	28,720	9,430	5,090
1982	26,696	21,071	5,231	377	17	-	1982	112,625	26,272	45,255	26,592	9,454	5,052
1983	23,636	18,723	4,577	319	16	1	1983	111,722	27,264	44,807	25,364	8,983	5,304
1984	21,373	16,865	4,204	290	14	-	1984	112,660	28,261	44,946	25,196	8,907	5,350
1985	20,057	15,811	3,941	287	17	1	1985	114,862	29,477	45,225	25,690	8,894	5,576
1986	17,793	13,837	3,641	285	29	1	1986	116,369	30,754	45,543	25,565	8,907	5,600
	20-24							**35 and over**					
1976	165,579	85,448	62,478	14,363	2,779	511	1976	29,708	4,594	7,202	6,829	4,665	6,418
1977	157,168	83,565	57,822	12,922	2,414	445	1977	28,601	4,611	7,152	6,743	4,387	5,708
1978	162,879	88,446	58,101	13,459	2,414	459	1978	31,206	5,212	7,929	7,695	4,647	5,723
1979	170,338	94,158	58,928	14,214	2,635	403	1979	34,516	5,585	9,006	8,744	5,238	5,943
1980	174,934	96,393	60,501	14,830	2,772	438	1980	36,738	5,932	9,571	9,607	5,702	5,926
1981	165,690	89,460	59,040	14,070	2,640	480	1981	37,500	6,180	10,130	9,740	5,410	6,030
1982	159,911	84,438	58,064	14,248	2,707	454	1982	41,003	6,496	11,498	11,020	6,063	5,926
1983	155,209	82,829	55,380	13,915	2,668	417	1983	43,194	7,061	12,209	11,839	6,191	5,894
1984	150,371	80,585	52,782	13,867	2,694	443	1984	44,548	7,502	12,881	11,967	6,350	5,848
1985	146,262	78,992	50,526	13,587	2,706	451	1985	45,714	7,831	13,323	12,293	6,271	5,996
1986	137,985	74,695	47,519	12,708	2,591	472	1986	46,203	8,401	13,625	12,041	6,270	5,866

Note: 1981 births for age-groups and for number of previous liveborn children are based on a 10 per cent sample.

TABLE 4.1 Legitimate live births: previous liveborn children and age of mother (five-year age-groups), 1976-1986
b. women married once only

England and Wales

Year	Number of previous liveborn children						Year	Number of previous liveborn children					
	Total	0	1	2	3	4 or more		Total	0	1	2	3	4 or more
	All ages of mother at birth							25-29					
1976	503,816	211,178	195,118	64,393	20,251	12,876	1976	200,564	74,381	88,207	27,368	7,538	3,070
1977	485,521	207,824	185,980	61,866	18,535	11,316	1977	187,401	72,297	81,144	24,844	6,498	2,618
1978	504,036	218,644	188,135	66,350	19,621	11,286	1978	188,735	75,014	78,946	25,506	6,718	2,551
1979	531,693	229,694	194,982	73,585	21,699	11,733	1979	196,871	78,275	80,356	28,095	7,359	2,786
1980	540,375	231,270	197,102	76,755	23,080	12,168	1980	196,740	77,373	80,075	28,523	7,815	2,954
1981	514,760	214,840	192,730	73,080	21,850	12,250	1981	188,020	73,460	77,720	26,360	7,530	2,950
1982	497,183	202,166	188,118	71,976	22,556	12,367	1982	182,493	69,355	76,031	26,314	7,714	3,079
1983	490,198	201,487	182,694	71,126	22,266	12,625	1983	182,691	71,485	74,042	26,377	7,681	3,106
1984	485,364	199,827	179,788	70,871	22,157	12,721	1984	183,809	72,770	73,628	26,467	7,706	3,238
1985	488,303	200,955	179,509	72,457	22,270	13,112	1985	189,675	75,516	75,272	27,703	7,873	3,311
1986	477,934	195,906	175,382	71,149	22,353	13,144	1986	188,114	75,083	74,236	27,455	7,968	3,372
	Under 20							30-34					
1976	38,033	30,173	7,348	481	29	2	1976	77,343	17,958	32,072	17,188	6,277	3,848
1977	34,328	27,844	6,111	359	13	1	1977	85,721	20,972	36,047	18,891	6,294	3,517
1978	34,279	28,034	5,901	327	16	1	1978	95,616	23,717	39,801	21,547	7,027	3,524
1979	35,082	28,544	6,172	349	16	1	1979	105,038	25,164	43,475	24,718	7,875	3,806
1980	34,831	28,146	6,289	384	12	-	1980	107,747	25,562	43,675	26,135	8,293	4,082
1981	30,050	23,580	6,070	390	-	-	1981	104,650	24,370	43,050	25,220	7,930	4,090
1982	26,668	21,052	5,224	376	16	-	1982	98,288	23,031	40,465	22,954	7,677	4,161
1983	23,586	18,687	4,565	318	15	1	1983	97,166	23,671	39,903	21,847	7,353	4,392
1984	21,344	16,850	4,193	288	13	-	1984	97,665	24,528	39,852	21,577	7,232	4,476
1985	20,021	15,786	3,933	285	16	1	1985	99,477	25,421	40,135	22,028	7,255	4,638
1986	17,744	13,813	3,625	281	25	-	1986	100,959	26,663	40,204	22,076	7,308	4,708
	20-24							35 and over					
1976	162,724	84,631	61,261	13,737	2,617	478	1976	25,152	4,035	6,230	5,619	3,790	5,478
1977	154,194	82,700	56,533	12,308	2,249	404	1977	23,877	4,011	6,145	5,464	3,481	4,786
1978	159,635	87,424	56,724	12,815	2,248	424	1978	25,771	4,455	6,763	6,155	3,612	4,786
1979	166,805	92,996	57,480	13,509	2,459	361	1979	27,897	4,715	7,499	6,914	3,990	4,779
1980	171,274	95,154	59,049	14,091	2,591	389	1980	29,783	5,035	8,014	7,622	4,369	4,743
1981	162,090	88,260	57,540	13,430	2,460	400	1981	29,960	5,170	8,340	7,680	3,930	4,820
1982	156,887	83,411	56,902	13,603	2,547	424	1982	32,847	5,317	9,496	8,729	4,602	4,703
1983	152,352	81,910	54,211	13,317	2,526	388	1983	34,403	5,734	9,973	9,267	4,691	4,738
1984	147,579	79,716	51,662	13,277	2,515	409	1984	34,967	5,963	10,453	9,262	4,691	4,598
1985	143,522	78,091	49,492	12,998	2,521	420	1985	35,608	6,141	10,677	9,443	4,605	4,742
1986	135,359	73,777	46,500	12,190	2,463	429	1986	35,758	6,570	10,817	9,147	4,589	4,635

Note: 1981 births for age-groups and for number of previous liveborn children are based on a 10 per cent sample.

TABLE 4.1 Legitimate live births: previous liveborn children and age of mother (five-year age-groups), 1976-1986   **England and Wales**
c. remarried women

All ages of mother at birth

Year	Total	0	1	2	3	4 or more
1976	26,666	6,033	8,458	6,547	3,318	2,305
1977	28,359	6,749	9,055	6,930	3,400	2,225
1978	31,745	7,942	9,953	7,823	3,737	2,290
1979	36,868	9,196	11,685	9,157	4,264	2,556
1980	38,487	9,705	12,062	9,581	4,457	2,682
1981	38,750	9,450	12,960	9,320	4,300	2,720
1982	38,891	9,696	12,563	9,455	4,567	2,610
1983	39,725	10,266	12,936	9,602	4,380	2,541
1984	40,989	10,594	13,305	9,772	4,703	2,615
1985	41,864	11,062	13,549	9,946	4,595	2,712
1986	41,739	11,036	13,804	9,693	4,567	2,639

Under 20

Year	Total	0	1	2	3	4 or more
1976	91	50	33	5	2	1
1977	98	63	27	6	1	1
1978	62	44	12	6	-	-
1979	56	37	17	-	-	2
1980	63	43	18	2	-	-
1981	90	60	20	-	10	-
1982	28	19	7	1	1	-
1983	50	36	12	1	1	-
1984	29	15	11	2	1	-
1985	36	25	8	2	1	-
1986	49	24	16	4	4	1

20-24

Year	Total	0	1	2	3	4 or more
1976	2,855	817	1,217	626	162	33
1977	2,974	865	1,289	614	165	41
1978	3,244	1,022	1,377	644	166	35
1979	3,533	1,162	1,448	705	176	42
1980	3,660	1,239	1,452	739	181	49
1981	3,600	1,200	1,490	640	180	80
1982	3,024	1,027	1,162	645	160	30
1983	2,857	919	1,169	598	142	29
1984	2,792	869	1,120	590	179	34
1985	2,740	901	1,034	589	185	31
1986	2,626	918	1,019	518	128	43

25-29

Year	Total	0	1	2	3	4 or more
1976	10,471	2,838	3,629	2,415	1,053	536
1977	10,757	3,087	3,752	2,476	994	448
1978	11,432	3,574	3,799	2,606	1,029	424
1979	12,925	3,985	4,383	3,042	1,116	399
1980	13,236	4,181	4,505	2,938	1,173	439
1981	13,440	3,740	5,020	3,120	1,130	430
1982	13,346	4,230	4,602	2,880	1,168	466
1983	13,471	4,391	4,615	2,914	1,107	444
1984	13,592	4,438	4,652	2,856	1,189	457
1985	13,597	4,390	4,771	2,843	1,104	489
1986	13,209	4,172	4,622	2,788	1,155	472

30-34

Year	Total	0	1	2	3	4 or more
1976	8,715	1,769	2,607	2,318	1,226	795
1977	9,806	2,134	2,980	2,555	1,334	803
1978	11,572	2,545	3,599	3,027	1,507	894
1979	13,735	3,142	4,330	3,580	1,724	959
1980	14,573	3,345	4,530	3,917	1,770	1,011
1981	14,070	3,440	4,630	3,500	1,500	1,010
1982	14,337	3,241	4,790	3,638	1,777	891
1983	14,556	3,593	4,904	3,517	1,630	912
1984	14,995	3,733	5,094	3,619	1,675	874
1985	15,385	4,056	5,090	3,662	1,639	938
1986	15,410	4,091	5,339	3,489	1,599	892

35 and over

Year	Total	0	1	2	3	4 or more
1976	4,556	559	972	1,210	875	940
1977	4,724	600	1,007	1,297	906	932
1978	5,435	757	1,166	1,540	1,035	987
1979	6,619	870	1,507	1,830	1,248	1,164
1980	6,955	897	1,557	1,985	1,333	1,183
1981	7,550	1,010	1,800	2,050	1,480	1,210
1982	8,156	1,179	2,002	2,291	1,461	1,223
1983	8,791	1,327	2,236	2,572	1,500	1,156
1984	9,581	1,539	2,428	2,705	1,659	1,250
1985	10,106	1,690	2,646	2,850	1,666	1,254
1986	10,445	1,831	2,808	2,894	1,681	1,231

Note: 1981 births for age-groups and for number of previous liveborn children are based on a 10 per cent sample.

TABLE 4.2 **Legitimate live births: previous liveborn children and age of mother (single years of age), 1986**
a. all married women

England and Wales

Number of previous liveborn children

Age of mother at birth	Total	0	1	2	3	4	5	6	7	8	9	10-14	15 and over
All ages	519,673	206,942	189,186	80,842	26,920	8,978	3,774	1,663	728	333	168	136	3
Under 16	4	4	-	-	-	-	-	-	-	-	-	-	-
16	445	425	19	-	1	-	-	-	-	-	-	-	-
17	2,016	1,819	188	8	1	-	-	-	-	-	-	-	-
18	5,269	4,314	908	41	6	-	-	-	-	-	-	-	-
19	10,059	7,275	2,526	236	21	1	-	-	-	-	-	-	-
Under 20	17,793	13,837	3,641	285	29	1	-	-	-	-	-	-	-
20	15,703	10,045	4,900	698	57	2	1	-	-	-	-	-	-
21	21,715	12,814	7,179	1,498	206	15	2	-	-	1	-	-	-
22	28,258	15,763	9,573	2,458	407	55	1	1	-	-	-	-	-
23	33,922	17,574	11,947	3,529	748	111	10	3	-	-	-	-	-
24	38,387	18,499	13,920	4,525	1,173	235	29	5	-	-	1	-	-
20-24	137,985	74,695	47,519	12,708	2,591	418	43	9	-	1	1	-	-
25	41,667	18,812	15,570	5,381	1,482	357	51	11	2	-	1	-	-
26	42,131	17,567	16,284	5,966	1,711	476	98	23	4	-	1	1	-
27	41,669	16,426	16,395	6,212	1,852	590	153	30	9	1	-	1	-
28	39,624	14,426	15,891	6,302	2,035	674	220	63	11	2	-	-	-
29	36,232	12,024	14,718	6,382	2,043	701	253	80	24	4	3	-	-
25-29	201,323	79,255	78,858	30,243	9,123	2,798	775	207	50	7	5	2	-
30	32,142	9,905	12,875	6,227	2,017	688	289	93	38	4	6	-	-
31	26,855	7,500	10,850	5,536	1,866	634	290	125	38	11	4	1	-
32	23,252	5,856	9,142	5,251	1,850	624	324	134	45	13	11	2	-
33	19,160	4,242	7,381	4,672	1,711	637	301	110	68	27	9	2	-
34	14,960	3,251	5,295	3,879	1,463	542	311	126	53	25	8	7	-
30-34	116,369	30,754	45,543	25,565	8,907	3,125	1,515	588	242	80	38	12	-
35	12,471	2,568	4,179	3,236	1,463	512	296	126	52	24	7	8	-
36	9,607	1,825	3,072	2,631	1,165	474	200	127	68	27	9	9	-
37	7,348	1,348	2,188	1,984	1,005	410	204	106	54	24	13	12	-
38	5,872	1,036	1,719	1,524	880	316	184	107	50	26	15	15	-
39	4,455	739	1,163	1,170	713	326	173	92	35	26	7	11	-
35-39	39,753	7,516	12,321	10,545	5,226	2,038	1,057	558	259	127	51	55	-
40	2,566	393	613	664	424	210	118	69	34	15	16	8	2
41	1,558	231	306	379	259	163	92	58	36	17	12	5	-
42	970	141	205	236	156	96	46	36	22	19	3	9	1
43	559	66	102	118	90	51	46	37	19	14	9	7	-
44	306	27	38	50	61	28	27	26	18	16	8	7	-
40-44	5,959	858	1,264	1,447	990	548	329	226	129	81	48	36	3
45	183	19	16	24	22	17	18	30	16	9	6	6	-
46	112	4	14	12	12	11	13	12	10	9	8	7	-
47	57	1	3	5	10	8	4	7	7	3	2	7	-
48	42	1	4	2	4	4	6	7	4	5	-	5	-
49 and over	97	1	3	6	6	10	14	19	12	11	9	6	-
45 and over	491	27	40	49	54	50	55	75	48	37	25	31	-

Notes: 1. 1,007 cases in which age of mother at birth, and 184 cases in which the number of previous liveborn children was not stated, have been included with the stated cases (for method of distribution see Introduction).
2. The distribution of legitimate live births in the '10-14' and '15 and over' categories is given below:

Number of previous liveborn children

10	11	12	13	14	15	16	17	18
71	40	14	7	4	1	1	0	1

TABLE 4.2 Legitimate live births: previous liveborn children
and age of mother (single years of age), 1986
b. women married once only

England and Wales

Age of mother at birth	Number of previous liveborn children												
	Total	0	1	2	3	4	5	6	7	8	9	10-14	15 and over
All ages	477,934	195,906	175,382	71,149	22,353	7,317	3,146	1,447	646	303	152	130	3
Under 16	4	4	-	-	-	-	-	-	-	-	-	-	-
16	445	425	19	-	1	-	-	-	-	-	-	-	-
17	2,012	1,815	188	8	1	-	-	-	-	-	-	-	-
18	5,255	4,308	903	39	5	-	-	-	-	-	-	-	-
19	10,028	7,261	2,515	234	18	-	-	-	-	-	-	-	-
Under 20	17,744	13,813	3,625	281	25	-	-	-	-	-	-	-	-
20	15,611	10,010	4,858	687	53	2	1	-	-	-	-	-	-
21	21,521	12,744	7,087	1,470	203	14	2	-	-	1	-	-	-
22	27,846	15,595	9,405	2,401	389	54	1	1	-	-	-	-	-
23	33,210	17,302	11,689	3,391	716	101	9	2	-	-	-	-	-
24	37,171	18,126	13,461	4,241	1,102	210	25	5	-	-	1	-	-
20-24	135,359	73,777	46,500	12,190	2,463	381	38	8	-	1	1	-	-
25	39,852	18,216	14,906	5,008	1,346	313	49	11	2	-	1	-	-
26	39,893	16,849	15,512	5,470	1,529	416	92	20	4	-	1	-	-
27	38,944	15,598	15,430	5,625	1,593	526	132	29	9	1	-	1	-
28	36,507	13,378	14,822	5,668	1,786	592	195	55	10	1	-	-	-
29	32,918	11,042	13,566	5,684	1,714	594	215	75	21	4	3	-	-
25-29	188,114	75,083	74,236	27,455	7,968	2,441	683	190	46	6	5	1	-
30	28,606	8,836	11,655	5,499	1,663	578	251	82	35	4	3	-	-
31	23,572	6,574	9,690	4,824	1,545	531	250	112	32	10	3	1	-
32	20,029	5,001	8,033	4,514	1,522	509	277	108	41	12	10	2	-
33	16,270	3,526	6,392	3,989	1,391	508	270	95	63	26	8	2	-
34	12,482	2,726	4,434	3,250	1,187	421	268	112	48	23	6	7	-
30-34	100,959	26,663	40,204	22,076	7,308	2,547	1,316	509	219	75	30	12	-
35	10,113	2,065	3,474	2,619	1,132	394	229	114	47	24	7	8	-
36	7,603	1,434	2,507	2,050	883	355	165	108	57	26	9	9	-
37	5,618	1,053	1,714	1,489	720	306	161	84	46	21	13	11	-
38	4,402	771	1,290	1,130	654	233	145	88	41	22	14	14	-
39	3,302	566	894	841	504	231	124	74	30	21	7	10	-
35-39	31,038	5,889	9,879	8,129	3,893	1,519	824	468	221	114	50	52	-
40	1,843	291	449	471	276	147	86	60	28	13	12	8	2
41	1,111	182	220	249	173	112	66	47	34	13	10	5	-
42	691	112	149	151	102	65	28	34	21	17	3	8	1
43	404	53	72	80	53	36	36	33	16	11	8	6	-
44	241	21	23	35	48	23	19	25	16	16	8	7	-
40-44	4,290	659	913	986	652	383	235	199	115	70	41	34	3
45	149	14	11	14	15	15	16	29	14	9	6	6	-
46	92	4	6	7	10	9	11	11	10	9	8	7	-
47	52	1	2	3	10	8	3	7	6	3	2	7	-
48	40	1	3	2	3	4	6	7	4	5	-	5	-
49 and over	96	2	3	6	6	10	14	19	11	11	9	6	-
45 and over	429	22	25	32	44	46	50	73	45	37	25	31	-

Notes: 1. 946 cases in which the age of mother at birth, and 181 cases in which the number of previous liveborn children was not stated,
have been included with the stated cases (for method of distribution see Introduction).
2. The distribution of legitimate live births in the '10-14' and '15 and over' categories is given below.

Number of previous liveborn children

10	11	12	13	14	15	16	17	18
68	39	13	6	4	1	1	0	1

TABLE 4.2 Legitimate live births: previous liveborn children and age of mother (single years of age), 1986
c. remarried women

England and Wales

Age of mother at birth	Number of previous liveborn children												
	Total	0	1	2	3	4	5	6	7	8	9	10-14	15 and over
All ages	41,739	11,036	13,804	9,693	4,567	1,661	628	216	82	30	16	6	-
Under 16	-	-	-	-	-	-	-	-	-	-	-	-	-
16	-	-	-	-	-	-	-	-	-	-	-	-	-
17	4	4	-	-	-	-	-	-	-	-	-	-	-
18	14	6	5	2	1	-	-	-	-	-	-	-	-
19	31	14	11	2	3	1	-	-	-	-	-	-	-
Under 20	49	24	16	4	4	1	-	-	-	-	-	-	-
20	92	35	42	11	4	-	-	-	-	-	-	-	-
21	194	70	92	28	3	1	-	-	-	-	-	-	-
22	412	168	168	57	18	1	-	-	-	-	-	-	-
23	712	272	258	138	32	10	1	1	-	-	-	-	-
24	1,216	373	459	284	71	25	4	-	-	-	-	-	-
20-24	2,626	918	1,019	518	128	37	5	1	-	-	-	-	-
25	1,815	596	664	373	136	44	2	-	-	-	-	-	-
26	2,238	718	772	496	182	60	6	3	-	-	-	1	-
27	2,725	828	965	587	259	64	21	1	-	-	-	-	-
28	3,117	1,048	1,069	634	249	82	25	8	1	1	-	-	-
29	3,314	982	1,152	698	329	107	38	5	3	-	-	-	-
25-29	13,209	4,172	4,622	2,788	1,155	357	92	17	4	1	-	1	-
30	3,536	1,069	1,220	728	354	110	38	11	3	-	3	-	-
31	3,283	926	1,160	712	321	103	40	13	6	1	1	-	-
32	3,223	855	1,109	737	328	115	47	26	4	1	1	-	-
33	2,890	716	989	683	320	129	31	15	5	1	1	-	-
34	2,478	525	861	629	276	121	43	14	5	2	2	-	-
30-34	15,410	4,091	5,339	3,489	1,599	578	199	79	23	·5	8	-	-
35	2,358	503	705	617	331	118	67	12	5	-	-	-	-
36	2,004	391	565	581	282	119	35	19	11	1	-	-	-
37	1,730	295	474	495	285	104	43	22	8	3	-	1	-
38	1,470	265	429	394	226	83	39	19	9	4	1	1	-
39	1,153	173	269	329	209	95	49	18	5	5	-	1	-
35-39	8,715	1,627	2,442	2,416	1,333	519	233	90	38	13	1	3	-
40	724	102	164	193	148	63	32	9	6	2	4	-	-
41	447	49	86	130	86	51	26	11	2	4	2	-	-
42	279	29	56	85	54	31	18	2	1	2	-	1	-
43	155	13	30	38	37	15	10	4	3	3	1	1	-
44	65	6	15	15	13	5	8	1	2	-	-	-	-
40-44	1,669	199	351	461	338	165	94	27	14	11	7	2	-
45	34	5	5	10	7	2	2	1	2	-	-	-	-
46	20	-	8	5	2	2	2	1	-	-	-	-	-
47	5	-	1	2	-	-	1	-	1	-	-	-	-
48	2	-	1	-	1	-	-	-	-	-	-	-	-
49 and over	-	-	-	-	-	-	-	-	-	-	-	-	-
45 and over	61	5	15	17	10	4	5	2	3	-	-	-	-

Notes: 1. 61 cases in which the age of mother at birth, and 3 cases in which the number of previous liveborn children was not stated, have been included with the stated cases (for method of distribution see Introduction).
2. The distribution of legitimate live births in the '10-14' and '15 and over' categories is given below:

Number of previous liveborn children							
10	11	12	13	14	15	16	17
3	1	1	1	-	-	-	-

TABLE 4.3 **Legitimate live and still births: previous liveborn children, age of mother and sex of child, 1986**   **England and Wales**

Age of mother at birth	Sex of child	Number of previous liveborn children												
		Total	0	1	2	3	4	5	6	7	8	9	10-14	15 and over
		Numbers												
All ages	M	267,929	106,836	97,489	41,681	13,817	4,609	1,975	844	368	166	85	58	1
	F	254,344	101,272	92,428	39,569	13,267	4,433	1,837	838	365	168	84	81	2
Under 20	M	9,184	7,157	1,854	154	19	-	-	-	-	-	-	-	-
	F	8,716	6,768	1,803	134	10	1	-	-	-	-	-	-	-
20-24	M	71,137	38,372	24,636	6,556	1,312	228	27	4	-	1	1	-	-
	F	67,516	36,743	23,055	6,207	1,295	194	17	5	-	-	-	-	-
25-29	M	103,791	41,000	40,529	15,682	4,641	1,395	411	99	26	3	4	1	-
	F	98,439	38,673	38,615	14,692	4,530	1,417	372	108	26	4	1	1	-
30-34	M	59,776	15,884	23,398	13,080	4,538	1,630	762	296	112	48	20	8	-
	F	57,174	15,031	22,326	12,625	4,427	1,519	763	298	130	32	18	5	-
35-39	M	20,719	3,947	6,417	5,429	2,786	1,038	561	283	140	65	26	27	-
	F	19,312	3,641	5,972	5,180	2,474	1,017	510	280	121	63	25	29	-
40-44	M	3,073	458	632	756	498	295	180	122	64	32	23	12	1
	F	2,937	407	640	704	500	256	152	110	66	49	26	25	2
45 and over	M	249	18	23	24	23	23	34	40	26	17	11	10	-
	F	250	9	17	27	31	29	23	37	22	20	14	21	-
Ratio: legitimate male births per 1,000 legitimate female births														
All ages		1,053	1,055	1,055	1,053	1,041	1,040	1,075	1,007	1,008	988	1,012	716	500
Under 20		1,054	1,057	1,028	1,149	1,900	-	-	-	-	-	-	-	-
20-24		1,054	1,044	1,069	1,056	1,013	1,175	1,588	800	-	-	-	-	-
25-29		1,054	1,060	1,050	1,067	1,025	984	1,105	917	1,000	750	4,000	1,000	-
30-34		1,046	1,057	1,048	1,036	1,025	1,073	999	993	862	1,500	1,111	1,600	-
35-39		1,073	1,084	1,075	1,048	1,126	1,021	1,100	1,011	1,157	1,032	1,040	931	-
40-44		1,046	1,125	988	1,074	996	1,152	1,184	1,109	970	653	885	480	500
45 and over		996	2,000	1,353	889	742	793	1,478	1,081	1,182	850	786	476	-

Notes: 1. 1,033 cases in which the age of mother at birth, and 191 cases in which the number of previous liveborn children was not stated have been included with the stated cases (for method of distribution see Introduction).
2. The distribution of legitimate births in the '10-14' and '15 and over' categories is given below:

Number of previous liveborn children								
10	11	12	13	14	15	16	17	18
72	41	15	7	4	1	1	0	1

TABLE 5.1 First legitimate live births: duration of marriage and age of mother, 1976-1986
a. all married women

England and Wales

Year	All durations	Duration of current marriage														
		Completed months		Completed years													
		0-7	8-11	0	1	2	3	4	5	6	7	8	9	10-14	15-19	20 and over

Age of mother at birth: All ages

Year	All durations	0-7	8-11	0	1	2	3	4	5	6	7	8	9	10-14	15-19	20 and over
1976	217,211	34,745	16,008	50,753	43,482	36,323	30,031	21,340	14,095	8,358	4,915	2,828	1,698	2,782	528	78
1977	214,573	32,430	15,041	47,471	42,508	35,823	28,800	22,106	14,525	9,228	5,575	3,191	1,932	2,915	437	62
1978	226,586	34,224	16,116	50,340	43,385	36,866	30,404	22,580	16,279	10,379	6,441	3,766	2,268	3,364	449	65
1979	238,890	37,180	17,852	55,032	46,871	36,992	29,984	23,373	16,760	11,367	7,147	4,308	2,711	3,851	436	58
1980	240,975	39,329	18,704	58,033	49,048	36,727	28,401	21,867	15,921	10,940	7,611	4,567	2,912	4,403	486	59
1981	224,290	35,830	17,210	53,040	47,300	36,220	25,250	18,830	14,490	9,920	6,950	4,410	2,750	4,520	550	70
1982	211,862	33,595	16,157	49,752	44,587	34,822	24,341	17,593	12,728	9,066	6,489	4,290	2,910	4,749	480	55
1983	211,753	32,824	16,431	49,255	44,272	34,657	25,877	17,628	12,383	8,689	6,289	4,149	2,896	5,059	544	55
1984	210,421	32,573	16,785	49,358	44,596	33,207	25,084	18,549	12,447	8,373	5,863	4,165	3,027	5,105	600	47
1985	212,017	33,675	17,592	51,267	46,184	33,118	23,575	17,985	12,765	8,408	5,910	3,888	2,890	5,356	612	59
1986	206,943	32,935	17,567	50,502	45,742	32,610	22,798	16,205	12,326	8,465	5,590	3,696	2,650	5,519	782	58

Under 20

Year	All durations	0-7	8-11	0	1	2	3	4	5	6	7	8	9	10-14	15-19	20 and over
1976	30,223	18,592	4,154	22,746	6,231	1,069	163	14	–	–	–	–	–	–	–	–
1977	27,907	16,999	3,866	20,865	5,956	946	127	13	–	–	–	–	–	–	–	–
1978	28,078	16,995	4,092	21,087	5,935	924	119	13	–	–	–	–	–	–	–	–
1979	28,581	17,460	4,179	21,639	5,908	875	148	11	–	–	–	–	–	–	–	–
1980	28,189	17,277	4,147	21,424	5,784	869	106	6	–	–	–	–	–	–	–	–
1981	23,650	14,400	3,500	17,900	5,000	700	50	–	–	–	–	–	–	–	–	–
1982	21,071	12,931	3,097	16,028	4,305	732	100	6	–	–	–	–	–	–	–	–
1983	18,723	11,557	2,825	14,382	3,696	546	93	6	–	–	–	–	–	–	–	–
1984	16,865	10,232	2,735	12,967	3,337	477	76	8	–	–	–	–	–	–	–	–
1985	15,811	9,497	2,599	12,096	3,185	457	70	3	–	–	–	–	–	–	–	–
1986	13,837	8,383	2,283	10,666	2,767	351	48	5	–	–	–	–	–	–	–	–

20-24

Year	All durations	0-7	8-11	0	1	2	3	4	5	6	7	8	9	10-14	15-19	20 and over
1976	85,448	11,688	7,473	19,161	23,814	20,433	13,361	6,130	1,987	470	77	11	4	–	–	–
1977	83,565	10,863	6,997	17,860	23,090	20,159	13,205	6,557	2,083	523	72	14	2	–	–	–
1978	88,446	12,029	7,437	19,466	23,899	20,848	13,918	7,029	2,538	617	109	19	3	–	–	–
1979	94,158	13,718	8,579	22,297	26,079	21,044	13,735	7,352	2,757	728	138	25	3	–	–	–
1980	96,393	15,378	9,198	24,576	27,779	20,651	12,984	6,903	2,673	666	120	37	4	–	–	–
1981	89,460	14,940	8,240	23,180	26,940	19,720	10,880	5,630	2,360	640	90	20	10	–	–	–
1982	84,438	14,063	8,010	22,073	25,288	19,007	10,358	5,153	1,940	489	113	12	5	–	–	–
1983	82,829	13,962	8,229	22,191	24,672	18,304	10,755	4,659	1,710	443	77	17	1	–	–	–
1984	80,585	14,396	8,264	22,660	24,399	16,999	9,891	4,570	1,595	389	68	11	3	–	–	–
1985	78,992	15,162	8,681	23,843	24,341	16,020	8,659	4,259	1,450	353	55	10	2	–	–	–
1986	74,695	14,877	8,570	23,447	23,315	14,918	7,822	3,524	1,264	326	67	10	2	–	–	–

25-29

Year	All durations	0-7	8-11	0	1	2	3	4	5	6	7	8	9	10-14	15-19	20 and over
1976	77,219	3,185	2,978	6,163	9,814	11,888	13,913	13,107	10,330	6,304	3,360	1,460	584	296	–	–
1977	75,384	3,117	2,774	5,891	9,512	11,420	12,696	12,990	10,172	6,772	3,556	1,516	594	265	–	–
1978	78,588	3,501	3,024	6,525	9,305	11,518	13,242	12,759	11,198	7,293	4,130	1,749	608	261	–	–
1979	82,260	3,989	3,375	7,364	10,208	11,411	12,877	13,203	11,366	8,085	4,544	2,099	832	271	–	–
1980	81,554	4,411	3,509	7,920	10,790	11,581	12,201	12,166	10,603	7,806	4,903	2,282	944	358	–	–
1981	77,200	4,200	3,610	7,810	10,770	11,680	11,410	10,620	9,770	7,100	4,550	2,170	860	450	–	–
1982	73,585	4,349	3,350	7,699	10,488	11,434	11,045	10,071	8,500	6,452	4,203	2,192	1,003	498	–	–
1983	75,876	4,794	3,604	8,398	11,151	12,037	11,865	10,335	8,333	6,080	3,956	2,159	1,007	555	–	–
1984	77,208	5,153	3,838	8,991	11,936	11,900	12,018	11,122	8,315	5,687	3,641	2,037	1,055	506	–	–
1985	79,906	6,060	4,218	10,278	13,062	12,647	11,735	10,920	8,629	5,614	3,603	1,900	973	545	–	–
1986	79,255	6,359	4,571	10,930	13,938	12,953	11,558	9,769	8,278	5,623	3,239	1 670	802	495	–	–

30 and over

Year	All durations	0-7	8-11	0	1	2	3	4	5	6	7	8	9	10-14	15-19	20 and over
1976	24,321	1,280	1,403	2,683	3,623	2,933	2,594	2,089	1,778	1,584	1,478	1,357	1,110	2,486	528	78
1977	27,717	1,451	1,404	2,855	3,950	3,298	2,772	2,546	2,270	1,933	1,947	1,661	1,336	2,650	437	62
1978	31,474	1,699	1,563	3,262	4,246	3,576	3,125	2,779	2,543	2,469	2,202	1,998	1,657	3,103	449	65
1979	33,891	2,013	1,719	3,732	4,676	3,662	3,224	2,807	2,637	2,554	2,465	2,184	1,876	3,580	436	58
1980	34,839	2,263	1,850	4,113	4,695	3,626	3,110	2,792	2,645	2,468	2,588	2,248	1,964	4,045	486	59
1981	33,980	2,310	1,860	4,160	4,590	4,120	2,900	2,580	2,360	2,180	2,300	2,220	1,880	4,060	550	70
1982	32,768	2,252	1,700	3,952	4,606	3,649	2,838	2,363	2,288	2,125	2,173	2,086	1,902	4,251	480	55
1983	34,325	2,511	1,773	4,284	4,753	3,770	3,164	2,628	2,340	2,166	2,256	1,973	1,888	4,504	544	55
1984	35,763	2,792	1,948	4,740	4,924	3,831	3,099	2,849	2,537	2,297	2,154	2,117	1,969	4,599	600	47
1985	37,308	2,956	2,094	5,050	5,596	3,994	3,111	2,803	2,686	2,441	2,252	1,978	1,915	4,811	612	59
1986	39,156	3,316	2,143	5,459	5,722	4,388	3,370	2,907	2,784	2,516	2,284	2,016	1,846	5,024	782	58

Note: 1981 live births are based on a 10 per cent sample.

TABLE 5.1 First legitimate live births: duration of marriage and age of mother, 1976-1986
b. women married once only

England and Wales

Year	All durations	Completed months		Completed years													
		0-7	8-11	0	1	2	3	4	5	6	7	8	9	10-14	15-19	20 and over
Age of mother at birth: All ages																	
1976	211,178	33,320	15,209	48,529	41,694	35,373	29,497	21,085	13,974	8,302	4,873	2,802	1,685	2,759	527	78
1977	207,824	30,915	14,183	45,098	40,454	34,811	28,214	21,756	14,352	9,155	5,523	3,160	1,916	2,887	437	61
1978	218,644	32,368	15,079	47,447	41,132	35,600	29,690	22,221	16,078	10,269	6,374	3,733	2,252	3,336	448	64
1979	229,694	34,949	16,630	51,579	44,226	35,659	29,207	22,956	16,514	11,208	7,063	4,281	2,682	3,825	436	58
1980	231,270	36,892	17,419	54,311	46,300	35,282	27,634	21,432	15,664	10,799	7,532	4,514	2,882	4,376	478	66
1981	214,840	33,440	15,910	49,350	45,000	34,860	24,470	18,240	14,180	9,770	6,810	4,360	2,700	4,500	540	70
1982	202,166	31,233	14,934	46,167	41,859	33,294	23,562	17,163	12,462	8,910	6,384	4,238	2,878	4,716	478	55
1983	201,487	30,305	15,168	45,473	41,388	33,126	25,016	17,156	12,093	8,521	6,164	4,094	2,853	5,007	541	55
1984	199,827	29,953	15,363	45,316	41,792	31,656	24,241	18,038	12,140	8,170	5,736	4,092	2,964	5,038	597	47
1985	200,955	30,794	16,183	46,977	43,092	31,675	22,737	17,448	12,429	8,214	5,782	3,820	2,839	5,276	607	59
1986	195,907	30,012	16,174	46,186	42,858	31,094	21,927	15,656	11,999	8,259	5,449	3,625	2,592	5,424	780	58
Under 20																	
1976	30,173	18,557	4,149	22,706	6,223	1,068	163	13								
1977	27,844	16,960	3,856	20,816	5,943	945	127	13								
1978	28,034	16,968	4,087	21,055	5,926	922	119	12								
1979	28,544	17,438	4,175	21,613	5,899	873	148	11								
1980	28,146	17,248	4,141	21,389	5,778	867	106	6								
1981	23,580	14,350	3,480	17,830	5,000	710	50	0								
1982	21,052	12,916	3,096	16,012	4,204	730	100	6								
1983	18,687	11,532	2,820	14,352	3,692	545	92	6								
1984	16,850	10,221	2,733	12,954	3,335	477	76	8								
1985	15,786	9,484	2,595	12,079	3,180	455	69	3								
1986	13,813	8,370	2,278	10,648	2,761	351	48	5								
20-24																	
1976	84,631	11,347	7,333	18,680	23,578	20,366	13,341	6,122	1,985	469	75	11	4			
1977	82,700	10,504	6,848	17,352	22,867	20,090	13,164	6,543	2,076	521	71	14	2			
1978	87,424	11,593	7,260	18,853	23,624	20,762	13,887	7,016	2,535	616	109	19	3			
1979	92,996	13,221	8,361	21,582	25,779	20,949	13,700	7,340	2,754	726	138	25	3			
1980	95,154	14,823	9,014	23,837	27,433	20,547	12,949	6,892	2,669	666	120	37	4			
1981	88,260	14,330	8,020	22,350	26,780	19,560	10,840	5,620	2,350	640	90	20	10			
1982	83,411	13,606	7,832	21,438	25,007	18,933	10,330	5,148	1,936	489	113	12	5			
1983	81,910	13,560	8,073	21,633	24,419	18,225	10,736	4,650	1,709	443	77	17	1			
1984	79,716	13,979	8,112	22,091	24,181	16,934	9,878	4,568	1,593	389	68	11	3			
1985	78,091	14,710	8,540	23,250	24,102	15,977	8,645	4,249	1,448	353	55	10	2			
1986	73,777	14,399	8,411	22,810	23,096	14,878	7,805	3,521	1,263	325	67	10	2			
25-29																	
1976	74,381	2,557	2,597	5,154	8,897	11,383	13,657	13,013	10,298	6,289	3,353	1,459	582	296		
1977	72,297	2,471	2,367	4,838	8,429	10,931	12,431	12,877	10,120	6,757	3,547	1,511	592	264		
1978	75,014	2,673	2,521	5,194	8,197	10,882	12,941	12,644	11,151	7,274	4,120	1,746	604	261		
1979	78,275	3,015	2,815	5,830	8,959	10,764	12,553	13,067	11,305	8,065	4,534	2,098	831	269		
1980	77,373	3,362	2,895	6,257	9,495	10,928	11,898	12,004	10,546	7,781	4,892	2,273	942	357		
1981	73,470	3,280	3,020	6,290	9,590	11,220	11,110	10,420	9,720	7,090	4,540	2,160	860	470		
1982	69,355	3,282	2,784	6,066	9,179	10,734	10,712	9,925	8,432	6,426	4,196	2,189	1,001	495		
1983	71,485	3,673	2,997	6,670	9,754	11,359	11,515	10,198	8,273	6,057	3,941	2,157	1,006	555		
1984	72,770	3,985	3,172	7,157	10,609	11,217	11,699	10,955	8,248	5,662	3,632	2,034	1,053	504		
1985	75,516	4,811	3,583	8,394	11,713	12,041	11,434	10,762	8,570	5,595	3,592	1,899	973	543		
1986	75,083	5,172	3,928	9,100	12,700	12,368	11,283	9,616	8,224	5,599	3,232	1,667	801	493		
30 and over																	
1976	21,993	859	1,130	1,989	2,996	2,556	2,336	1,937	1,691	1,544	1,445	1,332	1,099	2,463	527	78
1977	24,983	980	1,112	2,092	3,215	2,845	2,492	2,323	2,156	1,877	1,905	1,635	1,322	2,623	437	61
1978	28,172	1,134	1,211	2,345	3,384	3,034	2,743	2,549	2,392	2,379	2,145	1,968	1,645	3,075	448	64
1979	29,879	1,275	1,279	2,554	3,589	3,073	2,806	2,538	2,455	2,417	2,391	2,158	1,848	3,556	436	58
1980	30,597	1,459	1,369	2,828	3,594	2,940	2,681	2,530	2,449	2,352	2,520	2,204	1,936	4,019	478	66
1981	29,540	1,490	1,390	2,880	3,630	3,380	2,470	2,210	2,100	2,040	2,180	2,180	1,830	4,030	540	70
1982	28,348	1,429	1,222	2,651	3,469	2,897	2,420	2,084	2,094	1,995	2,075	2,037	1,872	4,221	478	55
1983	29,405	1,540	1,278	2,818	3,523	2,997	2,673	2,302	2,111	2,021	2,146	1,920	1,846	4,452	541	55
1984	30,491	1,768	1,346	3,114	3,667	3,028	2,588	2,507	2,299	2,119	2,036	2,047	1,908	4,534	597	47
1985	31,562	1,789	1,465	3,254	4,097	3,202	2,589	2,434	2,411	2,266	2,135	1,911	1,864	4,733	607	59
1986	33,234	2,071	1,557	3,628	4,301	3,497	2,791	2,514	2,512	2,335	2,150	1,948	1,789	4,931	780	58

Note: 1981 live births are based on a 10 per cent sample.

TABLE 5.1 First legitimate live births: duration of marriage and age of mother, 1976-1986
c. remarried women

England and Wales

Year	All durations	Duration of current marriage															
		Completed months		Completed years													
		0-7	8-11	0	1	2	3	4	5	6	7	8	9	10-14	15-19	20 and over

Age of mother at birth: All ages

Year	All durations	0-7	8-11	0	1	2	3	4	5	6	7	8	9	10-14	15-19	20 and over
1976	6,033	1,425	799	2,224	1,788	950	534	255	121	56	42	26	13	23	1	–
1977	6,749	1,515	858	2,373	2,054	1,012	586	350	173	73	52	31	16	28	–	1
1978	7,942	1,856	1,037	2,893	2,253	1,266	714	359	201	110	67	33	16	28	1	1
1979	9,196	2,231	1,222	3,453	2,645	1,333	777	417	246	159	84	27	29	26	–	–
1980	9,705	2,437	1,285	3,722	2,748	1,445	767	435	257	141	79	53	30	27	1	–
1981	9,450	2,360	1,270	3,630	2,380	1,370	753	421	355	144	90	51	30	29	2	–
1982	9,696	2,362	1,223	3,585	2,728	1,528	779	430	266	156	105	52	32	33	2	–
1983	10,266	2,519	1,263	3,782	2,884	1,531	861	472	290	168	125	55	43	52	3	–
1984	10,594	2,620	1,422	4,042	2,804	1,551	843	511	307	203	127	73	63	67	3	–
1985	11,062	2,881	1,409	4,290	3,092	1,443	838	537	336	194	128	68	51	80	5	–
1986	11,036	2,923	1,393	4,316	2,884	1,516	871	549	327	206	141	71	58	95	2	–

Under 20

Year	All durations	0-7	8-11	0	1	2	3	4	5	6	7	8	9	10-14	15-19	20 and over
1976	50	35	5	40	8	1	–	1	–	–	–	–	–	–	–	–
1977	63	39	10	49	13	1	–	–	–	–	–	–	–	–	–	–
1978	44	27	5	32	9	2	–	1	–	–	–	–	–	–	–	–
1979	37	22	4	26	9	2	–	–	–	–	–	–	–	–	–	–
1980	43	29	6	35	6	2	–	–	–	–	–	–	–	–	–	–
1981	60	40	10	50	10	–	–	–	–	–	–	–	–	–	–	–
1982	19	15	1	16	1	2	–	–	–	–	–	–	–	–	–	–
1983	36	25	5	30	4	1	1	–	–	–	–	–	–	–	–	–
1984	15	11	2	13	2	–	–	–	–	–	–	–	–	–	–	–
1985	25	13	4	17	5	2	1	–	–	–	–	–	–	–	–	–
1986	24	13	5	18	6	–	–	–	–	–	–	–	–	–	–	–

20-24

Year	All durations	0-7	8-11	0	1	2	3	4	5	6	7	8	9	10-14	15-19	20 and over
1976	817	341	140	481	236	67	20	8	2	1	2	–	–	–	–	–
1977	865	359	149	508	223	69	41	14	7	2	1	–	–	–	–	–
1978	1,022	436	177	613	275	86	31	13	3	1	–	–	–	–	–	–
1979	1,162	497	218	715	300	95	35	12	3	2	–	–	–	–	–	–
1980	1,239	555	184	739	346	104	35	11	4	–	–	–	–	–	–	–
1981	1,200	580	210	790	210	150	34	8	4	–	–	–	–	–	–	–
1982	1,027	457	178	635	281	74	28	5	4	–	–	–	–	–	–	–
1983	919	402	156	558	253	79	19	9	1	–	–	–	–	–	–	–
1984	869	417	152	569	218	65	13	2	2	–	–	–	–	–	–	–
1985	901	452	141	593	239	43	14	10	2	–	–	–	–	–	–	–
1986	918	478	159	637	219	40	17	3	1	1	–	–	–	–	–	–

25-29

Year	All durations	0-7	8-11	0	1	2	3	4	5	6	7	8	9	10-14	15-19	20 and over
1976	2,838	628	381	1,009	917	505	256	94	32	15	7	1	2	–	–	–
1977	3,087	646	407	1,053	1,083	489	265	113	52	15	9	5	2	1	–	–
1978	3,574	828	503	1,331	1,108	636	301	115	47	19	10	3	4	–	–	–
1979	1,985	974	560	1,534	1,249	647	324	136	61	20	10	1	1	2	–	–
1980	4,181	1,049	614	1,663	1,295	653	303	162	57	25	11	9	2	1	–	–
1981	3,740	920	590	1,510	1,200	601	283	137	55	23	8	5	2	2	–	–
1982	4,230	1,067	566	1,633	1,309	700	333	146	68	26	7	3	2	3	–	–
1983	4,391	1,121	607	1,728	1,397	678	350	137	60	23	15	2	1	–	–	–
1984	4,438	1,168	666	1,834	1,327	683	319	167	67	25	9	3	2	2	–	–
1985	4,390	1,249	635	1,884	1,349	606	301	158	59	19	11	1	–	2	–	–
1986	4,172	1,187	643	1,830	1,238	585	275	153	54	24	7	3	1	2	–	–

30 and over

Year	All durations	0-7	8-11	0	1	2	3	4	5	6	7	8	9	10-14	15-19	20 and over
1976	2,328	421	273	694	627	377	258	152	87	40	33	25	11	23	1	–
1977	2,734	471	292	763	735	453	280	223	114	56	42	26	14	27	–	1
1978	3,302	565	352	917	861	542	382	230	151	90	57	30	12	28	1	1
1979	4,012	738	440	1,178	1,087	589	418	269	182	137	74	26	28	24	–	–
1980	4,242	804	481	1,285	1,101	686	429	262	196	116	68	44	38	26	1	–
1981	4,450	810	470	1,280	970	739	436	277	200	126	85	47	30	29	2	–
1982	4,420	823	478	1,301	1,137	752	448	279	194	130	98	49	30	30	2	–
1983	4,920	971	495	1,466	1,230	773	491	326	229	145	110	53	42	52	3	–
1984	5,272	1,024	602	1,626	1,257	803	511	342	238	178	118	70	61	65	3	–
1985	5,746	1,167	629	1,796	1,499	792	522	369	275	175	117	67	51	78	5	–
1986	5,922	1,245	586	1,831	1,421	891	579	393	272	181	134	68	57	93	2	–

Note: 1981 live births are based on a 10 per cent sample.

TABLE 5.2   Legitimate live births: duration of marriage   **England and Wales**
                      (0-7 completed months) and age of mother, 1976-1986

Age of mother at birth	1976	1977	1978	1979	1980	1981	1982	1983	1984	1985	1986
All married women											
All ages	40,231	37,884	40,332	44,239	46,851	42,810	40,772	40,166	40,426	41,902	41,250
Under 16	11	8	13	5	6	-	6	5	9	10	2
16	1,449	1,435	1,327	1,144	1,021	780	665	583	452	465	377
17	4,605	4,090	4,015	4,053	3,549	3,000	2,556	2,175	1,831	1,685	1,426
18	6,944	6,227	6,309	6,545	6,543	5,240	4,785	4,308	3,732	3,456	3,052
19	6,035	5,642	5,753	6,189	6,649	5,920	5,365	4,960	4,687	4,394	4,043
Under 20	19,044	17,402	17,417	17,936	17,768	14,950	13,377	12,031	10,711	10,010	8,900
20	4,360	4,128	4,455	5,110	5,583	5,130	4,653	4,552	4,402	4,539	4,237
21	3,100	2,931	3,334	3,661	4,160	4,230	3,851	3,828	3,912	4,128	3,954
22	2,396	2,159	2,443	2,820	3,296	3,220	3,041	3,182	3,331	3,387	3,536
23	1,916	1,746	1,904	2,270	2,514	2,180	2,496	2,557	2,750	3,042	3,056
24	1,477	1,445	1,577	1,787	1,973	2,070	2,034	2,044	2,343	2,537	2,658
20-24	13,249	12,409	13,713	15,648	17,526	16,830	16,075	16,163	16,738	17,633	17,441
25-29	4,930	4,881	5,381	6,144	6,650	6,470	6,430	6,920	7,469	8,549	8,899
30-34	2,032	2,226	2,682	3,147	3,472	3,310	3,325	3,418	· 3,612	3,821	4,009
35-39	770	784	920	1,125	1,189	1,080	1,336	1,361	1,645	1,602	1,669
40 and over	206	182	219	239	246	180	229	273	251	287	332
Women married once only											
All ages	35,383	32,913	34,533	37,448	39,798	36,170	33,994	33,347	33,231	34,328	33,838
Under 16	11	8	13	5	6	-	6	5	9	10	2
16	1,447	1,430	1,325	1,143	1,019	780	665	579	450	465	377
17	4,595	4,083	4,009	4,049	3,537	3,000	2,555	2,172	1,827	1,682	1,424
18	6,930	6,211	6,299	6,540	6,535	5,210	4,778	4,302	3,729	3,453	3,041
19	6,017	5,621	5,739	6,173	6,638	5,910	5,353	4,946	4,679	4,385	4,027
Under 20	19,000	17,353	17,385	17,910	17,735	14,900	13,357	12,004	10,694	9,995	8,871
20	4,297	4,078	4,410	5,068	5,535	5,070	4,627	4,526	4,380	4,507	4,185
21	2,992	2,817	3,219	3,532	4,063	4,060	3,757	3,713	3,822	4,024	3,856
22	2,184	1,970	2,209	2,560	3,021	2,910	2,806	2,984	3,130	3,206	3,321
23	1,620	1,462	1,576	1,881	2,089	1,920	2,172	2,251	2,396	2,727	2,770
24	1,168	1,088	1,178	1,315	1,500	1,530	1,608	1,638	1,941	2,065	2,238
20-24	12,261	11,415	12,592	14,356	16,208	15,490	14,970	15,112	15,669	16,529	16,370
25-29	3,006	2,923	3,162	3,577	4,000	3,950	3,866	4,324	4,719	5,656	6,110
30-34	818	924	1,061	1,230	1,428	1,380	1,356	1,459	1,605	1,611	1,878
35-39	236	249	274	322	357	430	396	378	488	471	530
40 and over	62	49	59	53	70	20	49	70	56	66	79
Remarried women											
All ages	4,848	4,971	5,799	6,791	7,053	6,650	6,778	6,819	7,195	7,574	7,412
Under 16	-	-	-	-	-	-	-	-	-	-	-
16	2	5	2	1	2	-	-	4	2	-	-
17	10	7	6	4	12	10	1	3	4	3	2
18	14	16	10	5	8	30	7	6	3	3	11
19	18	21	14	16	11	10	12	14	8	9	16
Under 20	44	49	32	26	33	50	20	27	17	15	29
20	63	50	45	42	48	60	26	26	22	32	52
21	108	114	115	129	97	170	94	115	90	104	98
22	212	189	234	260	275	310	235	198	201	181	215
23	296	284	328	389	425	260	324	306	354	315	286
24	309	357	399	472	473	540	426	406	402	472	420
20-24	988	994	1,121	1,292	1,318	1,340	1,105	1,051	1,069	1,104	1,071
25-29	1,924	1,958	2,219	2,567	2,650	2,520	2,564	2,596	2,750	2,893	2,789
30-34	1,214	1,302	1,621	1,917	2,044	1,930	1,969	1,959	2,007	2,210	2,131
35-39	534	535	646	803	832	650	940	983	1,157	1,131	1,139
40 and over	144	133	160	186	176	150	180	203	195	221	253

TABLE 5.3 Legitimate live births: duration of current marriage (0-7 completed months) and age of mother, 1986 — England and Wales

Age of mother at birth	Duration of current marriage - completed months								
	0-7	0	1	2	3	4	5	6	7
All married women									
All ages	41,250	1,177	2,219	3,258	5,229	8,483	9,979	6,777	4,128
Under 16	2	1	-	-	1	-	-	-	-
16	377	30	45	57	66	64	63	37	15
17	1,426	58	102	173	234	350	290	172	47
18	3,052	96	199	327	487	717	703	367	156
19	4,043	136	229	359	616	883	981	532	307
Under 20	8,900	321	575	916	1,404	2,014	2,037	1,108	525
20	4,237	82	209	330	612	999	1,026	600	379
21	3,954	78	189	303	497	885	996	633	373
22	3,536	72	157	258	446	799	924	532	348
23	3,056	78	151	201	339	639	782	522	344
24	2,658	61	126	174	327	532	683	455	300
20-24	17,441	371	832	1,266	2,221	3,854	4,411	2,742	1,744
25-29	8,899	257	443	613	969	1,587	2,170	1,738	1,122
30-34	4,009	128	218	310	404	714	927	822	486
35-39	1,669	86	119	131	184	260	371	306	212
40 and over	332	14	32	22	47	54	63	61	39
Women married once only									
All ages	33,838	856	1,700	2,663	4,369	7,252	8,422	5,379	3,197
Under 16	2	1	-	-	1	-	-	-	-
16	377	30	45	57	66	64	63	37	15
17	1,424	58	102	173	234	349	289	172	47
18	3,041	95	197	326	487	715	703	363	155
19	4,027	133	229	355	614	881	981	530	304
Under 20	8,871	317	573	911	1,402	2,009	2,036	1,102	521
20	4,185	80	203	323	601	990	1,017	595	376
21	3,856	70	180	295	480	868	978	615	370
22	3,321	61	145	241	414	751	887	498	324
23	2,770	63	129	173	303	583	731	481	307
24	2,238	45	87	142	271	450	600	390	253
20-24	16,370	319	744	1,174	2,069	3,642	4,213	2,579	1,630
25-29	6,110	144	275	397	646	1,130	1,586	1,190	742
30-34	1,878	49	77	136	185	351	456	396	228
35-39	530	26	25	42	55	104	115	97	66
40 and over	79	1	6	3	12	16	16	15	10
Remarried women									
All ages	7,412	321	519	595	860	1,231	1,557	1,398	931
Under 16	-	-	-	-	-	-	-	-	-
16	-	-	-	-	-	-	-	-	-
17	2	-	-	-	-	1	1	-	-
18	11	1	2	1	-	2	-	4	1
19	16	3	-	4	2	2	-	2	3
Under 20	29	4	2	5	2	5	1	6	4
20	52	2	6	7	11	9	9	5	3
21	98	8	9	8	17	17	18	18	3
22	215	11	12	17	32	48	37	34	24
23	286	15	22	28	36	56	51	41	37
24	420	16	39	32	56	82	83	65	47
20-24	1,071	52	88	92	152	212	198	163	114
25-29	2,789	113	168	216	323	457	584	548	380
30-34	2,131	79	141	174	219	363	471	426	258
35-39	1,139	60	94	89	129	156	256	209	146
40 and over	253	13	26	19	35	38	47	46	29

TABLE 6.1 **Maternities with multiple births: age of mother** **England and Wales**
and legitimacy, 1976-1986
a. numbers

Year	Age of mother at birth							
	All ages	Under 20	20-24	25-29	30-34	35-39	40-44	45 and over
	All maternities							
1976	5,621	360	1,403	2,314	1,121	350	68	5
1977	5,519	301	1,379	2,139	1,278	347	72	3
1978	5,930	327	1,494	2,231	1,393	417	60	8
1979	6,181	348	1,499	2,284	1,551	426	66	7
1980	6,404	345	1,572	2,315	1,609	487	72	4
1982	6,277	336	1,512	2,246	1,532	575	69	7
1983	6,387	312	1,616	2,243	1,559	592	61	4
1984	6,406	282	1,583	2,270	1,518	655	94	4
1985	6,803	320	1,677	2,375	1,628	707	85	11
1986	7,105	372	1,633	2,503	1,754	754	85	4
	Legitimate maternities							
1976	5,146	239	1,284	2,207	1,040	310	64	2
1977	5,037	197	1,240	2,023	1,198	314	62	3
1978	5,412	204	1,349	2,113	1,311	377	50	8
1979	5,609	221	1,331	2,153	1,445	393	59	7
1980	5,742	213	1,357	2,178	1,502	428	61	3
1982	5,471	173	1,245	2,044	1,427	519	56	7
1983	5,535	147	1,309	2,049	1,436	538	53	3
1984	5,494	124	1,259	2,064	1,386	578	79	4
1985	5,622	118	1,249	2,104	1,444	621	76	10
1986	5,755	124	1,164	2,172	1,564	656	71	4
	Illegitimate maternities							
1976	475	121	119	107	81	40	4	3
1977	482	104	139	116	80	33	10	-
1978	518	123	145	118	82	40	10	-
1979	572	127	168	131	106	33	7	-
1980	662	132	215	137	107	59	11	1
1982	806	163	267	202	105	56	13	-
1983	852	165	307	194	123	54	8	1
1984	912	158	324	206	132	77	15	-
1985	1,181	202	428	271	184	86	9	1
1986	1,350	248	469	331	190	98	14	-

Notes: 1. The figures include maternities where stillbirths occurred.
2. Figures for 1981 are not available.

TABLE 6.1 **Maternities with multiple births: age of mother**   **England and Wales**
and legitimacy, 1976-1986
b. rates

Year	Age of mother at birth							
	All ages	Under 20	20-24	25-29	30-34	35-39	40-44	45 and over
	All maternities with multiple births per 1,000 all maternities							
1976	9.6	6.2	7.7	10.5	12.4	13.4	11.2	9.8
1977	9.7	5.5	7.9	10.3	12.7	13.6	12.9	6.5
1978	10.0	5.8	8.2	10.6	12.4	15.0	10.4	15.2
1979	9.7	5.9	7.8	10.3	12.4	13.6	10.9	13.0
1980	9.8	5.7	7.8	10.4	12.5	14.4	11.8	6.3
1982	10.1	6.1	7.9	10.7	12.8	14.8	11.7	10.9
1983	10.2	5.8	8.4	10.5	13.0	14.4	9.8	6.0
1984	10.1	5.2	8.3	10.5	12.5	15.4	14.4	7.1
1985	10.4	5.6	8.7	10.5	13.0	16.1	12.4	18.9
1986	10.8	6.5	8.5	11.0	13.7	16.8	12.1	7.5
	Legitimate maternities with multiple births per 1,000 legitimate maternities							
1976	9.7	6.2	7.7	10.5	12.1	13.0	11.7	4.3
1977	9.8	5.7	7.9	10.2	12.6	13.5	12.6	7.2
1978	10.1	5.9	8.3	10.6	12.3	14.7	9.7	16.7
1979	9.9	6.3	7.8	10.3	12.2	13.7	11.0	14.3
1980	9.9	6.1	7.8	10.4	12.3	13.9	11.4	5.1
1982	10.2	6.5	7.8	10.5	12.8	14.8	10.9	12.0
1983	10.5	6.2	8.5	10.5	13.0	14.6	9.8	4.8
1984	10.5	5.8	8.4	10.5	12.4	15.2	13.9	7.7
1985	10.7	5.9	8.6	10.4	12.7	16.0	12.9	18.8
1986	11.1	7.0	8.5	10.9	13.6	16.7	12.0	8.1
	Illegitimate maternities with multiple births per 1,000 illegitimate maternities							
1976	8.8	6.1	7.1	11.1	17.2	17.8	6.5	62.5
1977	8.7	5.1	8.0	11.9	15.2	14.8	15.2	-
1978	8.5	5.6	7.3	11.3	13.9	17.2	16.6	-
1979	8.2	5.3	7.3	10.7	15.4	12.3	10.3	-
1980	8.6	5.1	8.1	10.2	14.2	19.5	14.4	21.3
1982	9.0	5.7	8.2	12.7	13.0	15.3	16.8	-
1983	8.6	5.4	8.4	10.9	13.4	13.2	10.1	20.4
1984	8.3	4.8	7.9	10.0	13.1	17.0	17.0	-
1985	9.4	5.5	9.0	11.2	16.4	16.9	9.0	20.8
1986	9.6	6.3	8.7	12.0	14.6	17.3	13.1	-

Notes: 1. The figures include maternities where stillbirths occurred.
2. Figures for 1981 are not available.

TABLE 6.2   **Maternities with multiple live and still births: age of mother, legitimacy and sex, 1986**   **England and Wales**

Age of mother at birth	All maternities			All births											
	Total	Legit-imate	Illegit-imate	Total				Legitimate				Illegitimate			
				Live		Still		Live		Still		Live		Still	
				Total	Female only	Total	Female only	Total	Female only	Total	Female only	Total	Female only	Total	Female only
Multiple births (including twin)															
All ages	7,105	5,755	1,350	14,094	7,023	269	115	11,438	5,652	209	92	2,656	1,371	60	23
Under 20	372	124	248	737	398	14	9	248	129	2	2	489	269	12	7
20-24	1,633	1,164	469	3,229	1,615	59	18	2,309	1,154	39	15	920	461	20	3
25-29	2,503	2,172	331	4,964	2,470	93	44	4,314	2,124	77	37	650	346	16	7
30-34	1,754	1,564	190	3,501	1,735	63	34	3,124	1,547	56	29	377	188	7	5
35-39	754	656	98	1,490	721	33	9	1,297	626	29	8	193	95	4	1
40-44	85	71	14	165	79	7	1	138	67	6	1	27	12	1	-
45 and over	4	4	-	8	5	-	-	8	5	-	-	-	-	-	-
Twin only															
All ages	6,969	5,635	1,334	13,683	6,834	255	109	11,071	5,486	199	90	2,612	1,348	56	19
Under 20	365	122	243	716	395	14	9	242	129	2	2	474	266	12	7
20-24	1,613	1,146	467	3,170	1,589	56	18	2,256	1,132	36	15	914	457	20	3
25-29	2,456	2,129	327	4,819	2,396	93	44	4,181	2,059	77	37	638	337	16	7
30-34	1,708	1,522	186	3,359	1,668	57	29	2,990	1,486	54	28	369	182	3	1
35-39	740	643	97	1,452	705	28	8	1,262	611	24	7	190	94	4	1
40-44	83	69	14	159	76	7	1	132	64	6	1	27	12	1	-
45 and over	4	4	-	8	5	-	-	8	5	-	-	-	-	-	-

TABLE 6.3   **Maternities with multiple births: age of mother, legitimacy and type of outcome, 1986**   **England and Wales**

Outcome	All maternities								Illegitimate maternities only							
	All ages	Under 20	20-24	25-29	30-34	35-39	40-44	45 and over	All ages	Under 20	20-24	25-29	30-34	35-39	40-44	45 and over
All multiple births	7,105	372	1,633	2,503	1,754	754	85	4	1,350	248	469	331	190	98	14	-
Twins	6,969	365	1,613	2,456	1,708	740	83	4	1,334	243	467	327	186	97	14	-
2 LM	2,349	117	569	830	560	244	28	1	420	74	167	92	55	29	3	-
1 LM and 1 LF	2,046	83	411	729	553	245	24	1	398	56	109	112	76	36	9	-
2 LF	2,349	153	582	814	547	226	25	2	465	103	172	108	52	29	1	-
1 LM and 1 SM	83	3	29	26	11	12	2	-	23	3	13	4	1	2	-	-
1 LM and 1 SF	22	1	3	8	7	2	1	-	3	1	1	1	-	-	-	-
1 LF and 1 SM	25	-	3	10	5	5	2	-	7	-	2	3	1	-	1	-
1 LF and 1 SF	65	6	11	29	16	3	-	-	13	4	2	6	1	-	-	-
2 SM	18	1	3	6	6	1	1	-	3	1	1	1	-	-	-	-
1 SM and 1 SF	2	-	-	1	-	1	-	-	1	-	-	-	-	1	-	-
2 SF	10	1	2	3	3	1	-	-	1	1	-	-	-	-	-	-
Triplets	123	7	19	43	39	13	2	-	16	5	2	4	4	1	-	-
3 LM	30	4	5	10	8	3	-	-	2	2	-	-	-	-	-	-
2 LM and 1 LF	28	3	3	11	8	2	1	-	5	3	-	1	-	1	-	-
1 LM and 2LF	34	-	6	11	12	4	1	-	4	-	2	1	1	-	-	-
3 LF	21	-	2	11	7	1	-	-	3	-	-	2	1	-	-	-
2 LM and 1 SM	3	-	2	-	-	1	-	-	-	-	-	-	-	-	-	-
1 LM, 1LF and 1 SM	3	-	1	-	1	1	-	-	-	-	-	-	-	-	-	-
1 LM, 1LF and 1 SF	1	-	-	-	1	-	-	-	1	-	-	-	1	-	-	-
1 LF, 1 SM and 1 SF	1	-	-	-	-	1	-	-	-	-	-	-	-	-	-	-
1 LM and 1 SF	1	-	-	-	1	-	-	-	-	-	-	-	-	-	-	-
3 SF	1	-	-	-	1	-	-	-	1	-	-	-	1	-	-	-
Quads and over	13	-	1	4	7	1	-	-	-	-	-	-	-	-	-	-
3 LM and 1 LF	4	-	-	2	2	-	-	-	-	-	-	-	-	-	-	-
2 LM and 2 LF	2	-	-	-	2	-	-	-	-	-	-	-	-	-	-	-
1 LM and 3 LF	3	-	-	2	1	-	-	-	-	-	-	-	-	-	-	-
5 LM	1	-	-	-	1	-	-	-	-	-	-	-	-	-	-	-
3 LF and 1 SM	1	-	-	-	-	1	-	-	-	-	-	-	-	-	-	-
1 LM and 4LF	1	-	1	-	-	-	-	-	-	-	-	-	-	-	-	-
3 LM and 3LF	1	-	-	-	1	-	-	-	-	-	-	-	-	-	-	-

LM - Liveborn male   SM - Stillborn male   LF - Liveborn female   SF - Stillborn female.

TABLE 6.4   Legitimate maternities with multiple births: age of mother and previous liveborn children, 1986   **England and Wales**

Number of previous liveborn children	Age of mother at birth							
	All ages	Under 20	20–24	25–29	30–34	35–39	40–44	45 and over
Numbers								
Total	5,755	124	1,164	2,172	1,564	656	71	4
0	2,169	92	635	861	426	142	13	–
1	2,062	28	384	857	584	199	9	1
2	946	4	115	295	351	164	17	–
3	347	–	27	110	117	79	14	–
4 and over	231	–	3	49	86	72	18	3
Rates: legitimate maternities with multiple births per 1,000 maternities								
Total	11.1	7.0	8.5	10.9	13.6	16.7	12.0	8.1
0	10.5	6.7	8.5	10.9	14.0	19.1	15.3	–
1	11.0	7.7	8.1	10.9	12.9	16.3	7.1	25.6
2	11.8	14.1	9.1	9.8	13.8	15.7	11.8	–
3	13.0	–	10.5	12.1	13.2	15.2	14.2	–
4 and over	14.7	–	6.3	12.8	15.5	17.5	12.9	9.3

Note: The figures include maternities where stillbirths occurred.

TABLE 7.1   Live and still births: area of usual residence and legitimacy, 1986

England and Wales, England, Wales, standard regions, Greater London, metropolitan counties regional health authorities

Area of usual residence	Estimated number of women aged 15-44 (thousands)	Live births Total	Legit-imate	Illegit-imate	Stillbirths Total	Legit-imate	Illegit-imate	Illegitimate live births per 1,000 live births	Stillbirths per 1,000 live and still births	General fertility rate (GFR)	Total period fertility rate (TPFR)
England and Wales	10,903.1	661,018	519,673	141,345	3,549	2,600	949	214	5	60.6	1.77
Outside England and Wales	:	371	326	45	3	3	-	121	8	:	:
England	10,306.9	623,609	490,132	133,477	3,337	2,443	894	214	5	60.5	1.77
Wales	596.2	37,038	29,215	7,823	209	154	55	211	6	62.1	1.82
Standard regions											
North	661.1	40,239	30,430	9,809	223	157	66	244	6	60.9	1.76
Yorkshire and Humberside	1,059.3	65,342	50,201	15,141	373	265	108	232	6	61.7	1.79
East Midlands	858.0	50,306	39,439	10,867	252	194	58	216	5	58.6	1.71
East Anglia	429.3	24,592	20,556	4,036	111	81	30	164	4	57.3	1.67
South East	3,845.2	230,401	184,991	45,410	1,145	863	282	197	5	59.9	1.75
South West	956.0	54,513	45,052	9,461	307	234	73	174	6	57.0	1.69
West Midlands	1,122.7	70,408	55,022	15,386	425	311	114	219	6	62.7	1.84
North West	1,375.2	87,808	64,441	23,367	501	338	163	266	6	63.9	1.86
Metropolitan counties											
Greater London	1,562.2	97,669	73,530	24,139	509	348	161	247	5	62.5	1.78
Greater Manchester	563.0	36,549	26,087	10,462	211	139	72	286	6	64.9	1.87
Merseyside	314.9	20,417	14,134	6,283	111	65	46	308	5	64.8	1.87
South Yorkshire	282.0	17,002	12,971	4,031	112	77	35	237	7	60.3	1.73
Tyne and Wear	242.6	15,200	11,116	4,084	88	61	27	269	6	62.7	1.79
West Midlands	562.4	38,164	28,526	9,638	243	170	73	253	6	67.9	1.96
West Yorkshire	445.4	29,018	22,112	6,906	158	115	43	238	5	65.2	1.88
Regional health authorities											
Northern	661.1	40,239	30,430	9,809	223	157	66	244	6	60.9	1.76
Yorkshire	777.2	48,340	37,230	11,110	261	188	73	230	5	62.2	1.81
Trent	1,008.2	59,284	46,099	13,185	324	240	84	222	5	58.8	1.71
East Anglian	429.3	24,592	20,556	4,036	111	81	30	164	4	57.3	1.67
North West Thames	803.9	48,124	39,504	8,620	230	183	47	179	5	59.9	1.73
North East Thames	845.4	52,959	41,476	11,483	283	197	86	217	5	62.6	1.80
South East Thames	781.3	47,558	35,548	12,010	261	176	85	253	5	60.9	1.78
South West Thames	641.9	36,734	30,569	6,165	171	141	30	168	5	57.2	1.71
Wessex	612.6	35,772	29,758	6,014	187	154	33	168	5	58.4	1.72
Oxford	571.9	33,201	27,845	5,356	147	123	24	161	4	58.1	1.70
South Western	669.1	38,119	31,295	6,824	212	153	59	179	6	57.0	1.68
West Midlands	1,122.7	70,408	55,022	15,386	425	311	114	219	6	62.7	1.84
Mersey	524.4	32,712	24,024	8,688	180	120	60	266	5	62.4	1.82
North Western	857.7	55,567	40,776	14,791	322	219	103	266	6	64.8	1.88

Note: The figures relate to usual area of residence of the mother. Births to mothers usually resident outside England and Wales are included in the total for England and Wales.

TABLE 7.2   Live births: area of usual residence and age of mother, 1986

England and Wales, England, Wales, standard regions, Greater London, metropolitan counties regional health authorities

Area of usual residence	Age of mother at birth							Age of mother at birth						
	All ages	Under 20	20-24	25-29	30-34	35-39	40 and over	All ages	Under 20	20-24	25-29	30-34	35-39	40-44
	Numbers							Rates per 1,000 women in age-group						
England and Wales	661,018	57,406	192,064	229,035	129,487	45,465	7,561	60.6	30.1	92.7	124.0	78.1	24.6	4.8
Outside England and Wales	371	19	99	115	93	36	9	:	:	:	:	:	:	:
England	623,609	53,532	179,981	216,606	123,063	43,263	7,164	60.5	29.8	92.0	123.8	78.3	24.7	4.8
Wales	37,038	3,855	11,984	12,314	6,331	2,166	388	62.1	35.5	103.0	127.2	72.7	21.5	4.5
Standard regions														
North	40,239	4,559	12,842	13,598	6,829	2,103	308	60.9	38.9	101.9	120.7	68.1	19.1	3.3
Yorkshire and Humberside	65,342	7,067	20,845	22,097	11,186	3,495	652	61.7	37.0	102.6	123.7	70.3	19.8	4.3
East Midlands	50,306	4,701	15,407	17,569	9,185	2,979	465	58.6	31.4	95.5	121.5	70.4	20.2	3.7
East Anglia	24,592	1,797	7,343	8,809	4,772	1,633	238	57.3	24.5	92.6	121.5	70.0	22.0	3.9
South East	230,401	15,081	59,336	81,968	51,669	19,225	3,122	59.9	23.3	81.0	123.7	86.8	29.3	5.7
South West	54,513	3,896	15,756	19,722	10,682	3,844	613	57.0	22.7	88.8	124.2	73.7	23.5	4.4
West Midlands	70,408	6,852	21,436	23,617	13,090	4,585	828	62.7	33.9	101.1	125.9	78.4	24.2	5.0
North West	87,808	9,579	27,016	29,226	15,650	5,399	938	63.9	38.7	102.3	125.7	76.2	23.6	4.8
Metropolitan counties														
Greater London	97,669	6,679	24,860	33,331	22,323	8,922	1,554	62.5	27.0	79.0	117.6	91.0	34.4	7.3
Greater Manchester	36,549	4,456	11,471	11,868	6,263	2,112	379	64.9	44.0	104.0	123.7	74.7	22.8	4.8
Merseyside	20,417	2,125	6,157	6,895	3,726	1,301	213	64.8	36.7	100.3	127.2	79.3	25.7	4.9
South Yorkshire	17,002	1,963	5,581	5,678	2,736	886	158	60.3	39.1	101.9	117.4	65.2	19.0	3.9
Tyne and Wear	15,200	1,832	4,867	5,039	2,577	795	90	62.7	42.6	102.6	119.2	70.1	20.2	2.7
West Midlands	38,164	4,171	12,153	12,390	6,664	2,320	466	67.9	40.1	109.4	129.4	81.3	25.6	5.9
West Yorkshire	29,018	3,302	9,244	9,583	4,984	1,556	349	65.2	41.3	107.3	127.0	73.9	21.0	5.6
Regional health authorities														
Northern	40,239	4,559	12,842	13,598	6,829	2,103	308	60.9	38.9	101.9	120.7	68.1	19.1	3.3
Yorkshire	48,340	5,104	15,264	16,419	8,450	2,609	494	62.2	36.3	102.9	126.1	72.1	20.1	4.5
Trent	59,284	5,914	18,661	20,407	10,406	3,348	548	58.8	33.3	97.4	119.5	68.4	19.6	3.8
East Anglian	24,592	1,797	7,343	8,809	4,772	1,633	238	57.3	24.5	92.6	121.5	70.0	22.0	3.9
North West Thames	48,124	2,682	11,484	17,325	11,527	4,375	731	59.9	20.6	73.9	122.1	91.2	32.0	6.5
North East Thames	52,959	3,765	14,433	18,616	11,172	4,218	754	62.6	27.2	87.1	124.9	85.3	29.5	6.4
South East Thames	47,558	3,632	13,470	16,723	9,667	3,508	558	60.9	26.7	90.2	125.4	81.2	26.6	5.0
South West Thames	36,734	1,964	7,856	12,948	9,564	3,862	540	57.2	18.4	67.6	120.4	95.8	33.8	5.6
Wessex	35,772	2,606	10,322	12,955	7,095	2,401	393	58.4	24.0	90.5	126.4	76.2	22.9	4.4
Oxford	33,201	2,233	8,600	12,043	7,413	2,502	410	58.1	22.4	79.6	123.4	83.5	25.7	5.1
South Western	38,119	2,789	11,126	13,764	7,341	2,682	417	57.0	23.5	89.4	124.3	72.2	23.3	4.2
West Midlands	70,408	6,852	21,436	23,617	13,090	4,585	828	62.7	33.9	101.1	125.9	78.4	24.2	5.0
Mersey	32,712	3,179	9,715	11,110	6,206	2,159	343	62.4	33.5	97.2	125.0	79.2	24.8	4.6
North Western	55,567	6,456	17,429	18,272	9,531	3,278	601	64.8	42.0	105.3	126.1	74.4	22.9	4.9

Note: The rates for women of all ages, under 20 and 40 and over are based on women aged 15-44, 15-19 and 40-44 respectively.

TABLE 8.1 Maternities: place of confinement, age of mother and previous liveborn children/legitimacy, 1986

England and Wales

	Place of confinement	Age of mother at birth							
		All ages	Under 20	20-24	25-29	30-34	35-39	40-44	45 and over
Total	Total	657,308	57,394	191,425	227,579	128,357	45,011	7,009	533
	NHS hospital A	14,897	785	4,376	6,046	3,021	638	29	2
	NHS hospital B	628,595	55,987	183,723	216,779	121,808	42,995	6,779	524
	Other hospitals	7,232	272	2,016	2,397	1,685	737	121	4
	At home	6,042	288	1,146	2,180	1,749	608	68	3
	Elsewhere	542	62	164	177	94	33	12	-
All legitimate	Total	516,380	17,774	137,468	200,011	115,334	39,361	5,937	495
	NHS hospital A	12,832	291	3,496	5,622	2,808	586	27	2
	NHS hospital B	491,748	17,232	131,233	190,155	109,345	37,559	5,738	486
	Other hospitals	6,795	180	1,877	2,307	1,623	695	109	4
	At home	4,675	56	777	1,805	1,488	493	53	3
	Elsewhere	330	15	85	122	70	28	10	-
Number of legitimate previous liveborn children:									
0	Total	205,863	13,831	74,464	78,784	30,467	7,440	850	27
	NHS hospital A	2,951	192	1,312	1,208	216	21	2	-
	NHS hospital B	199,582	13,469	71,945	76,407	29,676	7,234	824	27
	Other hospitals	2,952	145	1,098	1,029	493	166	21	-
	At home	344	19	93	134	77	18	3	-
	Elsewhere	34	6	16	6	5	1	-	-
1	Total	187,813	3,629	47,305	78,272	45,117	12,188	1,263	39
	NHS hospital A	6,332	94	1,728	3,012	1,322	170	6	-
	NHS hospital B	176,771	3,469	44,454	73,411	42,544	11,642	1,215	36
	Other hospitals	2,507	31	646	889	656	251	31	3
	At home	2,058	28	438	895	571	117	9	-
	Elsewhere	145	7	39	65	24	8	2	-
2	Total	80,289	284	12,645	30,076	25,348	10,442	1,443	51
	NHS hospital A	2,674	4	378	1,121	945	220	6	-
	NHS hospital B	75,158	265	11,940	28,092	23,551	9,861	1,400	49
	Other hospitals	917	4	118	279	319	172	24	1
	At home	1,452	9	188	548	513	181	12	1
	Elsewhere	88	2	21	36	20	8	1	-
3	Total	26,737	29	2,580	9,061	8,848	5,181	984	54
	NHS hospital A	720	1	74	233	266	136	9	1
	NHS hospital B	25,137	28	2,439	8,560	8,242	4,873	943	52
	Other hospitals	274	-	13	78	106	58	19	-
	At home	573	-	46	180	225	110	11	1
	Elsewhere	33	-	8	10	9	4	2	-
4 and over	Total	15,678	1	474	3,818	5,554	4,110	1,397	324
	NHS hospital A	155	0	4	48	59	39	4	1
	NHS hospital B	15,100	1	455	3,685	5,332	3,949	1,356	322
	Other hospitals	145	0	2	32	49	48	14	0
	At home	248	0	12	48	102	67	18	1
	Elsewhere	30	0	1	5	12	7	5	0
Illegitimate	Total	140,928	39,620	53,957	27,568	13,023	5,650	1,072	38
	NHS hospital A	2,065	494	880	424	213	52	2	-
	NHS hospital B	136,847	38,755	52,490	26,624	12,463	5,436	1,041	38
	Other hospitals	437	92	139	90	62	42	12	-
	At home	1,367	232	369	375	261	115	15	-
	Elsewhere	212	47	79	55	24	5	2	-

Note: For detailed description of the categories - NHS hospital 'A' etc - see Introduction.

TABLE 8.2 Maternities: place of confinement and area of usual residence, 1986

England and Wales, regional health authorities

Place of confinement	Usual residence of mother - regional health authority							
	England and Wales	Wales	Northern	Yorkshire	Trent	East Anglian	North West Thames	North East Thames
Total	657,308	36,901	40,020	48,059	58,936	24,425	47,830	52,616
NHS hospital A	14,897	781	1,413	1,344	1,993	578	9	997
NHS hospital B	628,595	35,735	38,352	45,997	56,370	21,987	46,220	50,498
Other hospitals	7,232	5	10	220	2	1,414	1,165	460
At home	6,042	330	213	451	526	427	409	631
Elsewhere	542	50	32	47	45	19	27	30

	South East Thames	South West Thames	Wessex	Oxford	South Western	West Midlands	Mersey	North Western
Total	47,300	36,454	35,582	32,978	37,917	70,084	32,522	55,320
NHS hospital A	173	10	2,214	1,008	1,733	1,726	1	898
NHS hospital B	46,507	33,927	32,319	30,745	35,667	67,649	32,269	54,038
Other hospitals	65	2,185	698	928	46	5	1	1
At home	515	314	320	267	430	630	232	347
Elsewhere	40	18	31	30	41	74	19	36

Note: For detailed description of the categories - NHS hospital 'A' etc - see Introduction.

TABLE 9.1 Live births: birthplace of mother, 1976-1986 — England and Wales

Birthplace of mother	1976	1981	1982	1983	1984	1985	1986
a. Numbers							
Total	584,270	634,492	625,931	629,134	636,818	656,417	661,018
United Kingdom*	511,212	551,432	544,407	549,435	556,518	575,220	579,322
Total outside United Kingdom	72,354	82,829	81,303	79,536	80,175	81,063	81,591
Irish Republic	11,387	8,262	7,302	6,711	6,428	6,311	6,188
Australia, Canada and New Zealand	2,105	2,313	2,187	2,246	2,321	2,361	2,470
New Commonwealth and Pakistan	41,953	53,165	53,186	52,010	52,445	52,733	52,705
India	12,044	12,402	12,152	11,502	11,102	11,110	10,650
Pakistan	8,173	13,349	13,416	13,423	13,399	13,643	13,559
Bangladesh	1,415	3,079	3,437	3,896	4,067	4,238	4,717
East Africa	4,161	6,610	6,638	6,589	6,959	7,110	7,142
Rest of Africa	2,517	3,519	3,533	3,481	3,472	3,593	3,700
Caribbean	7,171	6,247	5,876	5,307	5,255	4,851	4,674
Far East†	2,379	3,324	3,525	3,482	3,736	3,795	3,934
Mediterranean≠	2,769	2,966	2,993	2,737	2,886	2,802	2,795
Remainder of New Commonwealth	1,324	1,669	1,616	1,593	1,569	1,591	1,534
West Germany	2,131	2,725	6,531	6,400	6,571	3,348	3,463
Other European Community**	4,841	4,085				3,495	3,336
Other Europe (including USSR)	2,378	1,964	1,848	1,793	1,695	1,882	1,950
United States of America	2,212	2,504	2,585	2,688	2,882	3,109	3,136
Rest of the World	5,347	7,811	7,664	7,688	7,833	7,824	8,343
Not stated	704	231	221	163	125	134	105
b. Percentage of all live births							
Total	100.0	100.0	100.0	100.0	100.0	100.0	100.0
United Kingdom*	87.5	86.9	87.0	87.3	87.4	87.6	87.6
Total outside United Kingdom	12.4	13.1	13.0	12.6	12.6	12.3	12.3
Irish Republic	1.9	1.3	1.2	1.1	1.0	1.0	0.9
Australia, Canada and New Zealand	0.4	0.4	0.3	0.4	0.4	0.4	0.4
New Commonwealth and Pakistan	7.2	8.4	8.5	8.3	8.2	8.0	8.0
India	2.1	2.0	1.9	1.8	1.7	1.7	1.6
Pakistan	1.4	2.1	2.1	2.1	2.1	2.1	2.1
Bangladesh	0.2	0.5	0.5	0.6	0.6	0.6	0.7
East Africa	0.7	1.0	1.1	1.0	1.1	1.1	1.1
Rest of Africa	0.4	0.6	0.6	0.6	0.5	0.5	0.6
Caribbean	1.2	1.0	0.9	0.8	0.8	0.7	0.7
Far East†	0.4	0.5	0.6	0.6	0.6	0.6	0.6
Mediterranean≠	0.5	0.5	0.5	0.4	0.5	0.4	0.4
Remainder of New Commonwealth	0.2	0.3	0.3	0.3	0.2	0.2	0.2
West Germany	0.4	0.4	1.0	1.0	1.0	0.5	0.5
Other European Community**	0.8	0.6				0.5	0.5
Other Europe (including USSR)	0.4	0.3	0.3	0.3	0.3	0.3	0.3
United States of America	0.4	0.4	0.4	0.4	0.5	0.5	0.5
Rest of the World	0.9	1.2	1.2	1.2	1.2	1.2	1.3
Not stated	0.1	0.0	0.0	0.0	0.0	0.0	0.0

* Including Isle of Man and Channel Islands.
† Hong Kong, Malaysia and Singapore.
≠ Cyprus, Gibraltar and Malta.
** As constituted in 1986.

TABLE 9.2   Live births: birthplace of mother and area of usual residence, 1986

England and Wales, metropolitan counties, Greater London, London boroughs, selected metropolitan and non-metropolitan districts (where 15% or more of the total live births in 1986 were to mothers born outside the United Kingdom)

Area of usual residence of mother	All live births	Birthplace of mother outside United Kingdom							
		Irish Republic		New Commonwealth and Pakistan		Rest of the World		All outside United Kingdom	
		Number	%	Number	%	Number	%	Number	%
ENGLAND AND WALES	661,018	6,188	1	52,705	8	22,698	3	81,591	12
Greater London	97,669	2,669	3	20,940	21	8,004	8	31,613	32
Inner London	39,454	1,215	3	9,976	25	4,407	11	15,598	40
Camden	2,273	131	6	425	19	474	21	1,030	45
Hackney	3,364	85	3	990	29	381	11	1,456	43
Hammersmith and Fulham	2,036	103	5	319	16	287	14	709	35
Haringey	3,170	126	4	878	28	357	11	1,361	43
Islington	2,492	128	5	471	19	254	10	853	34
Kensington and Chelsea	1,767	60	3	220	12	656	37	936	53
Lambeth	4,092	144	4	983	24	344	8	1,471	36
Lewisham	3,466	83	2	576	17	172	5	831	24
Newham	4,073	44	1	1,640	40	138	3	1,822	45
Southwark	3,563	100	3	767	22	219	6	1,086	30
Tower Hamlets	2,998	42	1	1,388	46	130	4	1,560	52
Wandsworth	3,745	85	2	780	21	355	9	1,220	33
Westminster City†	2,415	84	3	539	22	640	27	1,263	52
Outer London	58,215	1,454	2	10,964	19	3,597	6	16,015	28
Barking and Dagenham	2,071	26	1	132	6	35	2	193	9
Barnet	4,004	123	3	791	20	559	14	1,473	37
Bexley	2,900	27	1	199	7	60	2	286	10
Brent	3,899	259	7	1,709	44	366	9	2,334	60
Bromley	3,423	56	2	187	5	155	5	398	12
Croydon	4,597	79	2	712	15	246	5	1,037	23
Ealing	4,216	174	4	1,454	34	338	8	1,966	47
Enfield	3,539	102	3	687	19	156	4	945	27
Greenwich	3,308	68	2	418	13	139	4	625	19
Harrow	2,756	97	4	813	29	172	6	1,082	39
Havering	2,718	28	1	97	4	48	2	173	6
Hillingdon	3,125	66	2	409	13	137	4	612	20
Hounslow	3,021	58	2	813	27	213	7	1,084	36
Kingston-upon-Thames	1,728	38	2	163	9	161	9	362	21
Merton	2,363	52	2	378	16	207	9	637	27
Redbridge	2,876	64	2	709	25	120	4	893	31
Richmond-upon-Thames	1,958	35	2	131	7	263	13	429	22
Sutton	2,269	24	1	144	6	100	4	268	12
Waltham Forest	3,444	78	2	1,018	30	122	4	1,218	35
Metropolitan districts*									
Greater Manchester	36,549	462	1	3,114	9	713	2	4,289	12
Bolton	3,699	17	0	555	15	49	1	621	17
Manchester	7,055	207	3	871	12	244	3	1,322	19
Oldham	3,260	19	1	550	17	40	1	609	19
Rochdale	3,114	28	1	443	14	37	1	508	16
Merseyside	20,417	127	1	251	1	285	1	663	3
South Yorkshire	17,002	57	0	693	4	263	2	1,013	6
Tyne and Wear	15,200	22	0	410	3	237	2	669	4
West Midlands	38,164	454	1	6,595	17	539	1	7,588	20
Birmingham	15,928	283	2	3,875	24	313	2	4,471	28
Coventry	4,620	83	2	584	13	68	1	735	16
Sandwell	4,323	16	0	729	17	34	1	779	18
Wolverhampton	3,424	18	1	580	17	32	1	630	18
West Yorkshire	29,018	173	1	3,848	13	474	2	4,495	15
Bradford	7,357	26	0	1,860	25	124	2	2,010	27
Kirklees	5,371	34	1	912	17	58	1	1,004	19

* Where 15 per cent or more of the total live births were to mothers born outside the United Kingdom.
† Includes City of London.

TABLE 9.2 - *continued*

Area of usual residence of mother	All live births	Birthplace of mother outside United Kingdom							
		Irish Republic		New Commonwealth and Pakistan		Rest of the World		All outside United Kingdom	
		Number	%	Number	%	Number	%	Number	%
Non-metropolitan districts*									
Bedfordshire	8,059	143	2	1,049	13	313	4	1,505	19
North Bedfordshire	1,748	22	1	227	13	78	4	327	19
Luton	3,130	92	3	742	24	73	2	907	29
Berkshire	10,378	87	1	1,127	11	515	5	1,729	17
Reading	2,121	27	1	225	11	103	5	355	17
Slough	1,715	18	1	601	35	60	3	679	40
Windsor and Maidenhead	1,618	12	1	152	9	113	7	277	17
Buckinghamshire	8,216	81	1	696	8	360	4	1,137	14
Wycombe	2,050	11	1	302	15	89	4	402	20
Cambridgeshire	8,276	33	0	462	6	553	7	1,048	13
Cambridge	1,080	4	0	84	8	115	11	203	19
Peterborough	2,222	16	1	255	11	74	3	345	16
Derbyshire	11,520	53	0	521	5	138	1	712	6
Derby	3,087	29	1	403	13	44	1	476	15
Hertfordshire	12,458	153	1	696	6	437	4	1,286	10
St Albans	1,535	28	2	133	9	89	6	250	16
Watford	1,104	33	3	157	14	42	4	232	21
Lancashire	18,547	88	0	1,733	9	263	1	2,084	11
Blackburn	2,303	6	0	645	28	35	2	686	30
Hyndburn	1,095	3	0	156	14	10	1	169	15
Pendle	1,292	2	0	300	23	10	1	312	24
Preston	1,805	17	1	248	14	32	2	297	16
Leicestershire	11,722	51	0	1,837	16	248	2	2,136	18
Leicester	4,694	20	0	1,542	33	95	2	1,657	35
Oxfordshire	7,052	63	1	318	5	621	9	1,002	14
Cherwell	1,822	10	1	73	4	246	14	329	18
Oxford	1,199	24	2	150	13	124	10	298	25
Suffolk	7,887	26	0	149	2	871	11	1,046	13
Forest Heath	871	2	0	10	1	339	39	351	40
Suffolk Coastal	1,152	2	0	20	2	237	21	259	22
Surrey	11,473	116	1	565	5	720	6	1,401	12
Elmbridge	1,241	14	1	52	4	139	11	205	17
Epsom and Ewell	693	17	2	42	6	54	8	113	16
Woking	1,190	11	1	129	11	93	8	233	20
West Sussex	7,549	54	1	358	5	310	4	722	10
Crawley	1,272	7	1	159	12	41	3	207	16

Where 15 per cent or more of the total live births were to mothers born outside the United Kingdom.

TABLE 9.3 Live births: birthplace of mother and father, 1986 — England and Wales

Birthplace of father	Birthplace of mother					New Commonwealth and Pakistan				
	Total	United Kingdom*	Total outside United Kingdom	Irish Republic	Australia, Canada and New Zealand	Total	India	Pakistan	Bangladesh	East Africa
Total	661,018	579,322	81,591	6,188	2,470	52,705	10,650	13,559	4,717	7,142
United Kingdom*	529,476	506,017	23,371	3,312	1,836	8,457	1,302	528	49	1,018
Total outside United Kingdom	83,588	28,446	55,137	2,374	505	42,488	9,298	12,994	4,662	6,026
Irish Republic	6,166	3,998	2,168	1,903	25	92	14	2	0	16
Australia, Canada and New Zealand	1,809	1,323	486	18	287	48	8	2	0	8
New Commonwealth and Pakistan	55,711	12,730	42,978	245	71	41,443	9,103	12,952	4,659	5,862
India	11,005	2,150	8,855	30	12	8,615	6,544	354	28	1,511
Pakistan	14,045	1,226	12,818	17	1	12,724	130	12,257	12	268
Bangladesh	4,846	166	4,680	3	0	4,658	21	14	4,612	5
East Africa	8,104	1,130	6,974	34	9	6,713	2,291	309	7	3,965
Rest of Africa	3,668	940	2,728	21	8	2,608	10	2	0	34
Caribbean	5,833	3,255	2,578	52	12	2,401	11	2	0	26
Far East†	3,439	1,365	2,072	24	14	1,696	71	8	0	21
Mediterranean≠	3,130	2,066	1,064	27	9	923	1	2	0	4
Remainder of New Commonwealth	1,641	432	1,209	37	6	1,105	24	4	0	28
Other European Community	6,066	4,516	1,549	59	38	163	20	0	0	20
Other Europe (including USSR)	1,443	750	693	12	11	65	3	1	0	3
United States of America	3,324	1,238	2,086	21	27	64	5	0	1	10
Rest of the World	9,069	3,891	5,177	116	46	613	145	37	2	107
Not stated	47,954	44,859	3,083	502	129	1,760	50	37	6	98

Birthplace of father	Birthplace of mother					Other European Community	Other Europe (including USSR)	United States of America	Rest of the World	Not stated
	New Commonwealth and Pakistan - continued									
	Rest of Africa	Caribbean	Far East†	Mediterranean≠	Remainder of New Commonwealth					
Total	3,700	4,674	3,934	2,795	1,534	6,799	1,950	3,136	8,343	105
United Kingdom*	628	1,199	1,753	1,631	349	4,756	1,113	1,057	2,840	88
Total outside United Kingdom	2,655	2,575	2,065	1,063	1,150	1,673	787	1,999	5,311	5
Irish Republic	10	16	18	12	4	57	16	20	55	0
Australia, Canada and New Zealand	9	4	11	4	2	41	17	32	43	0
New Commonwealth and Pakistan	2,569	2,450	1,802	936	1,110	267	85	55	812	3
India	15	9	121	6	27	33	13	8	144	0
Pakistan	6	13	16	5	17	20	4	1	51	1
Bangladesh	0	5	0	0	1	6	3	1	9	0
East Africa	48	17	36	10	30	27	14	8	169	0
Rest of Africa	2,427	117	9	2	7	28	7	7	49	0
Caribbean	63	2,249	17	12	21	41	6	15	51	0
Far East†	6	7	1,550	5	28	50	7	8	273	2
Mediterranean≠	2	9	10	892	3	47	24	6	28	0
Remainder of New Commonwealth	2	24	43	4	976	15	7	1	38	0
Other European Community	11	22	31	44	15	997	71	72	149	1
Other Europe (including USSR)	3	9	4	40	2	37	507	17	44	0
United States of America	4	25	13	3	3	96	19	1,737	122	0
Rest of the World	49	49	186	24	14	178	72	66	4,086	1
Not stated	417	900	116	101	35	370	50	80	192	12

* Including Isle of Man and Channel Islands.
† Hong Kong, Malaysia and Singapore.
≠ Cyprus, Gibraltar and Malta.

TABLE 9.4   Live births: birthplace of mother
             and age of mother, 1986   **England and Wales**

Birthplace of mother	Age of mother at birth								Total period fertility rate (TPFR)
	All ages	Under 20	20-24	25-29	30-34	35-39	40-44	45 and over	
a. Number of live births									
Total*	661,018	57,406	192,064	229,035	129,487	45,465	7,033	528	
United Kingdom†	579,322	53,963	173,173	200,795	108,524	37,226	5,459	182	
Total outside United Kingdom	81,591	3,430	18,856	28,208	20,947	8,231	1,573	346	
New Commonwealth and Pakistan	52,705	2,287	13,073	19,062	12,751	4,334	897	301	
India	10,650	309	3,362	3,959	2,167	703	134	16	
Pakistan and Bangladesh	18,276	1,470	5,424	5,407	3,814	1,423	466	272	
East Africa	7,142	111	1,299	3,117	1,999	558	57	1	
Rest of Africa	3,700	58	724	1,557	938	367	52	4	
Caribbean	4,674	67	458	1,875	1,612	555	101	6	
Far East≠	3,934	151	886	1,488	1,091	300	17	1	
Mediterranean**	2,795	105	702	1,157	574	216	40	1	
Remainder New Commonwealth	1,534	16	218	502	556	212	30	0	
Rest of the World	28,886	1,143	5,783	9,146	8,196	3,897	676	45	
b. Age-specific fertility rates: all live births per 1,000 women in age-group									
Total	61	30	93	124	78	25	4	0	1.8
United Kingdom†	58	30	90	121	74	22	4	0	1.7
Total outside United Kingdom	90	40	130	150	110	50	10	0	2.4
New Commonwealth and Pakistan	100	50	180	160	110	50	10	0	2.9
India	90	60	220	170	80	30	10	0	2.9
Pakistan and Bangladesh	200	120	360	240	190	110	50	30	5.6
East Africa	90	10	90	140	110	40	10	0	2.0
Rest of Africa	120	30	150	170	120	80	20	0	2.8
Caribbean	60	40	100	100	80	40	10	0	1.8
Far East≠	80	20	80	110	120	40	10	0	1.9
Mediterranean**	80	30	120	150	80	30	10	0	2.1
Remainder New Commonwealth	80	10	100	170	120	50	10	0	2.3
Rest of the World	70	30	80	120	100	40	10	0	1.9

Note: The rates for women of all ages, under 20 and 45 and over are based upon the population of women 15-44, 15-19 and 45-49 respectively.
*   Includes 105 births to women whose country of birth was not stated.
†   Including Isle of Man and Channel Islands.
≠   Hong Kong, Malaysia and Singapore.
**   Cyprus, Gibraltar and Malta.

F   **73**

TABLE 9.5   Total period fertility rates by birthplace of mother, 1981-1986   **England and Wales**

Birthplace of mother	1981	1982	1983	1984	1985	1986
Total	1.80	1.76	1.76	1.75	1.78	1.77
United Kingdom*	1.7	1.7	1.7	1.7	1.7	1.7
Total outside United Kingdom	2.5	2.5	2.4	2.5	2.5	2.4
New Commonwealth and Pakistan	2.9	2.9	2.8	2.8	2.9	2.9
India	3.1	3.0	2.8	2.8	2.9	2.9
Pakistan and Bangladesh	6.5	6.3	6.1	5.7	5.6	5.6
East Africa	2.1	2.1	2.0	2.1	2.1	2.0
Rest of Africa	3.4	3.3	3.1	2.9	3.0	2.8
Caribbean	2.0	2.0	1.8	1.8	1.8	1.8
Far East†	1.7	1.9	1.9	2.0	2.0	1.9
Mediterranean≠	2.1	2.2	2.1	2.2	2.2	2.1
Remainder New Commonwealth	2.3	2.3	2.4	2.3	2.3	2.3
Rest of World	2.0	1.9	1.9	2.0	2.0	1.9

* Including Isle of Man and Channel Islands.
† Hong Kong, Malaysia and Singapore.
≠ Cyprus, Gibraltar and Malta.

TABLE 9.6   Live births: birthplace of mother and number
             of previous liveborn children/legitimacy, 1986

England and Wales

Birthplace of mother	Year	All live births (= 100%)	All legitimate births	Number of previous legitimate liveborn children						Illegitimate births
				0	1	2	3	4	5 and over	
Total*	1976	584,270	90.8	37.2	34.8	12.1	4.0	1.4	1.2	9.2
	1981	634,492	87.2	35.3	32.4	13.0	4.1	1.4	1.0	12.8
	1985	656,417	80.8	32.3	29.4	12.6	4.1	1.4	1.0	19.2
	1986	661,018	78.6	31.3	28.6	12.2	4.1	1.4	1.0	21.4
United Kingdom†	1976	511,212	90.8	37.5	35.8	12.0	3.7	1.2	0.8	9.2
	1981	551,432	86.6	35.8	32.9	12.7	3.7	1.1	0.5	13.4
	1985	575,220	79.4	32.6	29.6	12.1	3.6	1.0	0.5	20.6
	1986	579,322	77.1	31.4	28.7	11.8	3.6	1.0	0.5	22.9
Irish Republic	1976	11,387	88.0	28.1	31.0	15.7	7.4	3.1	2.7	12.0
	1981	8,262	85.1	27.6	26.9	16.8	8.2	2.8	2.8	14.9
	1985	6,311	79.8	23.9	25.9	17.2	6.8	3.2	2.7	20.2
	1986	6,188	77.6	23.9	25.2	15.5	7.3	2.8	2.8	22.4
New Commonwealth and Pakistan – Total	1976	41,953	89.6	32.3	25.1	14.1	7.8	4.5	5.7	10.4
	1981	53,165	91.6	29.7	28.3	15.6	8.4	4.6	5.0	8.4
	1985	52,733	91.8	27.5	27.0	16.8	9.3	5.4	5.8	8.2
	1986	52,705	91.6	28.1	26.5	16.5	8.9	5.4	6.1	8.4
India	1976	12,044	98.9	33.6	29.2	17.8	9.5	4.6	4.1	1.1
	1981	12,402	98.8	32.8	36.0	15.7	7.4	3.8	3.1	1.2
	1985	11,110	98.2	30.8	33.4	19.7	8.7	3.2	2.4	1.8
	1986	10,650	98.3	32.4	32.7	19.9	8.0	3.0	2.2	1.7
Pakistan	1976	8,173	99.3	27.2	20.3	16.4	12.6	9.0	13.7	0.7
	1981	13,349	99.5	21.8	22.9	19.6	14.7	9.2	11.2	0.5
	1985	13,643	99.3	20.2	19.2	18.9	16.2	11.6	13.1	0.7
	1986	13,559	99.3	21.9	19.4	18.7	15.1	11.4	12.9	0.7
Bangladesh	1976	1,415	99.4	20.4	17.9	14.7	10.2	9.2	26.9	0.6
	1981	3,079	99.6	17.2	19.5	21.1	16.2	9.4	16.6	0.4
	1985	4,238	99.7	18.6	15.7	16.6	15.2	13.4	20.2	0.3
	1986	4,717	99.7	17.0	17.0	15.7	14.5	13.4	22.1	0.3
East Africa	1976	4,161	97.3	50.8	29.7	11.3	3.7	0.9	0.9	2.7
	1981	6,610	97.6	45.8	34.2	11.5	5.0	0.9	0.2	2.4
	1985	7,110	96.8	38.1	37.4	15.9	4.1	0.9	0.4	3.2
	1986	7,142	96.6	38.9	36.6	15.2	4.3	1.1	0.5	3.4
Rest of Africa	1976	2,517	89.5	33.0	25.0	16.6	7.9	4.4	2.3	10.5
	1981	3,519	87.0	27.8	27.8	17.0	7.0	5.0	2.4	13.0
	1985	3,593	80.6	26.8	25.2	15.8	7.3	3.6	1.9	10.4
	1986	3,700	77.9	28.4	24.1	14.1	6.9	2.8	1.5	22.1
Caribbean	1976	7,171	51.6	15.2	16.6	8.2	4.8	3.3	3.6	48.4
	1981	6,247	50.0	15.4	15.0	10.4	3.8	2.9	2.6	50.0
	1985	4,851	51.4	16.1	17.2	10.9	4.2	1.8	1.2	48.6
	1986	4,674	51.7	15.3	17.7	10.8	4.5	1.9	1.5	48.3
Far East≠	1976	2,379	..	..	..	..	..	..	..	..
	1981	3,324	94.4	43.3	29.8	15.6	4.8	0.9	0.3	5.6
	1985	3,795	91.3	40.4	32.5	13.0	4.1	1.2	0.1	8.7
	1986	3,934	90.0	39.3	31.3	13.8	4.2	1.2	0.3	10.0
Mediterranean**	1976	2,769	95.4	41.2	34.5	14.0	4.1	1.1	0.6	4.6
	1981	2,966	93.2	40.1	33.4	14.8	3.7	1.0	–	6.8
	1985	2,802	90.3	34.0	35.7	14.9	4.5	0.9	0.3	9.7
	1986	2,795	88.7	32.1	33.0	17.3	4.8	1.0	0.6	11.3
Remainder New Commonwealth	1976	1,324	..	..	..	..	..	..	..	..
	1981	1,669	93.2	40.7	41.3	9.0	1.8	0.6	0.0	6.8
	1985	1,591	93.1	37.9	37.7	14.6	2.3	0.4	0.3	6.9
	1986	1,534	93.2	40.5	38.3	11.3	2.2	0.5	0.3	6.8
Rest of the World	1976	19,014	93.8	43.5	34.0	10.9	3.3	1.1	1.1	6.2
	1981	21,402	92.8	41.4	31.9	13.2	3.8	1.4	1.2	7.2
	1985	22,019	89.6	37.6	31.9	13.2	4.3	1.3	1.3	10.4
	1986	22,698	88.6	37.4	31.3	13.0	4.2	1.5	1.3	11.4

*   Including births to women whose country of birth was not stated.
†   Including Isle of Man and Channel Islands.
≠   Hong Kong, Malaysia and Singapore.
** Cyprus, Gibraltar and Malta.

TABLE 10.1 Age-specific fertility rates: calendar years of birth of woman, 1920-1971

Year of birth of woman/female birth cohort	Age of woman – completed years														
	15	16	17	18	19	20	21	22	23	24	25	26	27	28	29
1920	0	3	10	23	40	59	84	104	117	131	119	159	164	136	123
1921	0	3	10	23	40	61	91	109	126	123	158	183	147	134	121
1922	0	3	9	21	39	64	91	113	117	152	181	152	138	129	118
1923	0	2	8	21	40	65	95	108	143	182	159	149	136	129	119
1924	0	2	8	21	42	69	93	123	173	163	153	143	135	127	121
1925	0	2	9	22	43	67	101	147	157	156	147	141	134	131	118
1926	1	3	9	23	44	72	124	142	151	150	148	148	142	133	121
1927	1	3	10	24	45	86	124	138	144	149	148	152	142	134	128
1928	1	3	11	24	54	88	123	134	146	152	155	150	143	143	135
1929	1	4	10	27	59	90	117	132	146	158	156	151	148	148	137
1930	1	3	11	30	60	87	117	138	155	162	161	165	160	154	141
1931	1	3	12	32	58	85	119	143	156	162	169	170	162	153	146
1932	1	3	14	31	57	87	123	142	154	171	175	173	160	156	147
1933	1	4	13	31	58	90	125	146	167	180	183	178	172	166	151
1934	1	3	12	32	61	92	128	157	175	188	190	189	179	173	155
1935	1	3	13	33	61	94	137	162	180	190	198	193	181	173	158
1936	1	3	13	35	63	103	141	167	179	191	201	196	184	174	150
1937	1	3	14	34	70	107	147	168	184	198	206	199	188	167	142
1938	1	3	15	40	75	112	150	174	194	204	210	202	181	162	136
1939	1	4	18	44	79	116	155	180	200	208	213	193	174	154	131
1940	1	5	20	48	83	123	162	189	204	214	208	191	169	152	127
1941	1	5	22	52	91	127	169	193	209	210	201	183	162	144	123
1942	1	6	24	54	91	132	169	192	202	202	193	178	159	139	121
1943	1	7	27	57	95	132	167	187	197	191	187	172	154	139	112
1944	1	8	31	63	98	135	166	183	188	189	180	168	154	128	105
1945	2	11	35	66	103	136	166	176	181	181	178	168	145	121	101
1946	2	12	36	67	103	136	161	172	175	179	178	159	139	119	100
1947	2	12	36	66	99	128	151	158	165	169	159	145	130	111	97
1948	3	13	38	67	102	127	147	161	167	160	153	142	127	114	100
1949	2	13	38	71	101	124	144	155	152	148	144	134	125	113	106
1950	3	14	41	73	101	124	142	141	142	141	137	131	123	118	114
1951	3	15	43	75	102	125	129	130	133	130	131	126	126	127	115
1952	3	16	45	77	104	115	121	126	125	128	129	132	136	129	114
1953	3	17	46	78	97	107	115	118	121	122	133	141	138	125	114
1954	4	17	47	73	89	99	105	111	114	127	139	142	133	122	113
1955	4	18	47	68	83	92	101	107	119	134	144	135	129	123	114
1956	4	19	42	62	76	86	95	110	126	136	138	133	129	124	117
1957	4	18	41	57	70	81	98	115	128	131	133	134	130	127	116
1958	4	16	35	50	63	81	100	116	119	127	132	133	132	124	
1959	4	13	30	46	63	83	102	107	116	124	129	133	128		
1960	3	12	28	45	66	85	96	104	114	122	129	127			
1961	3	11	27	47	66	78	90	102	110	119	124				
1962	3	11	28	47	61	74	86	98	108	115					
1963	3	11	27	42	58	71	83	95	105						
1964	3	11	24	41	55	68	83	93							
1965	3	10	24	39	55	69	81								
1966	2	10	24	40	58	70									
1967	2	10	25	43	59										
1968	3	11	27	45											
1969	3	12	28												
1970	3	12													
1971	3														

Notes: 1. The age-specific fertility rates refer to 'all live births per 1,000 women' at the ages shown.
2. Live births to women aged under 15 are not included in the calculation of the rate for age 15.
3. Figures for the 1920-22 female birth cohorts at the younger ages are estimated; information on births by age of mother at birth was not available before 1938.
4. Figures along a diagonal line represent fertility experience of different female birth cohorts in a particular calendar year; for example, the bottom diagonal represents the fertility experience of women by age in the calendar year 1986.

England and Wales

30	31	32	33	34	35	36	37	38	39	40	41	42	43	44	Year of birth of woman/female birth cohort
109	93	87	76	67	58	52	44	38	32	25	17	13	8	5	1920
109	94	89	75	66	59	52	44	38	31	24	17	13	8	4	1921
108	95	86	73	67	61	52	43	40	32	24	16	13	8	4	1922
112	94	86	77	71	63	53	45	41	32	24	17	13	7	4	1923
109	91	89	78	71	62	55	47	41	32	25	17	11	7	3	1924
108	97	90	78	72	65	56	47	40	32	23	15	11	6	3	1925
113	100	94	80	76	67	58	48	43	31	22	15	10	5	3	1926
119	103	95	85	77	67	57	49	40	29	21	13	9	5	3	1927
123	104	101	86	78	67	59	46	38	28	20	12	8	5	2	1928
125	109	102	86	79	68	55	43	36	26	18	11	7	4	2	1929
136	117	108	91	83	68	54	43	35	24	17	11	7	4	2	1930
134	117	107	91	77	63	51	39	30	21	16	10	6	3	2	1931
132	116	111	88	72	60	47	36	28	20	13	8	5	3	2	1932
137	117	105	85	70	57	44	34	26	18	12	7	4	2	1	1933
140	112	97	79	67	53	42	32	22	15	10	6	4	2	1	1934
134	104	92	73	62	50	39	28	19	13	9	6	4	2	2	1935
128	101	88	70	57	47	34	23	17	12	8	5	4	2	2	1936
121	97	83	66	54	41	29	21	16	11	7	5	4	2	1	1937
117	94	78	64	47	35	25	19	14	11	8	5	4	2	1	1938
112	90	75	56	41	31	24	18	14	10	8	6	4	2	1	1939
108	88	67	50	38	29	23	17	14	11	8	7	4	2	1	1940
107	80	60	46	36	28	22	18	15	12	8	6	4	2	2	1941
96	72	57	43	34	28	23	20	16	12	8	6	4	2	1	1942
89	68	54	43	35	30	25	21	15	10	8	6	4	2		1943
85	66	53	43	37	32	27	21	15	11	8	6	3			1944
83	66	56	47	42	34	26	21	16	12	9	6				1945
85	69	60	54	44	34	28	22	17	13	9					1946
83	73	64	53	41	34	27	22	16	12						1947
92	82	69	56	45	36	29	23	18							1948
99	85	69	55	46	37	31	24								1949
103	85	68	56	47	39	31									1950
100	83	70	58	49	42										1951
100	86	72	62	51											1952
102	88	76	64												1953
103	90	77													1954
106	91														1955
106															1956
															1957
															1958
															1959
															1960
															1961
															1962
															1963
															1964
															1965
															1966
															1967
															1968
															1969
															1970
															1971

TABLE 10.2 Average number of liveborn children by successive ages of women: calendar years of birth of woman, 1920-1971

Year of birth of woman/female birth cohort	16	17	18	19	20	21	22	23	24	25	26	27	28	29	30
1920	0.00	0.00	0.01	0.04	0.08	0.13	0.22	0.32	0.44	0.57	0.69	0.85	1.01	1.15	1.27
1921	0.00	0.00	0.01	0.04	0.08	0.14	0.23	0.34	0.46	0.58	0.74	0.93	1.07	1.21	1.33
1922	0.00	0.00	0.01	0.03	0.07	0.14	0.23	0.34	0.46	0.61	0.79	0.94	1.08	1.21	1.33
1923	0.00	0.00	0.01	0.03	0.07	0.14	0.23	0.34	0.48	0.67	0.82	0.97	1.11	1.24	1.36
1924	0.00	0.00	0.01	0.03	0.07	0.14	0.24	0.36	0.53	0.69	0.85	0.99	1.13	1.25	1.37
1925	0.00	0.00	0.01	0.03	0.08	0.14	0.24	0.39	0.55	0.70	0.85	0.99	1.13	1.26	1.37
1926	0.00	0.00	0.01	0.04	0.08	0.15	0.28	0.42	0.57	0.72	0.87	1.01	1.16	1.29	1.41
1927	0.00	0.00	0.01	0.04	0.08	0.17	0.29	0.43	0.58	0.72	0.87	1.02	1.17	1.30	1.43
1928	0.00	0.00	0.02	0.04	0.09	0.18	0.30	0.44	0.58	0.74	0.89	1.04	1.18	1.33	1.46
1929	0.00	0.00	0.01	0.04	0.10	0.19	0.31	0.44	0.59	0.75	0.90	1.05	1.20	1.35	1.49
1930	0.00	0.00	0.01	0.04	0.10	0.19	0.31	0.45	0.60	0.76	0.93	1.09	1.25	1.41	1.55
1931	0.00	0.00	0.02	0.05	0.11	0.19	0.31	0.45	0.61	0.77	0.94	1.11	1.27	1.42	1.57
1932	0.00	0.00	0.02	0.05	0.11	0.19	0.32	0.46	0.61	0.78	0.96	1.13	1.29	1.45	1.59
1933	0.00	0.00	0.02	0.05	0.11	0.20	0.32	0.47	0.63	0.81	1.00	1.18	1.35	1.51	1.66
1934	0.00	0.00	0.02	0.05	0.11	0.20	0.33	0.49	0.66	0.85	1.04	1.23	1.41	1.58	1.73
1935	0.00	0.00	0.02	0.05	0.11	0.20	0.34	0.50	0.68	0.87	1.07	1.26	1.45	1.62	1.78
1936	0.00	0.00	0.02	0.05	0.12	0.22	0.36	0.53	0.71	0.90	1.10	1.29	1.48	1.65	1.80
1937	0.00	0.00	0.02	0.05	0.12	0.23	0.38	0.54	0.73	0.93	1.13	1.33	1.52	1.69	1.83
1938	0.00	0.00	0.02	0.06	0.13	0.25	0.40	0.57	0.76	0.97	1.18	1.38	1.56	1.72	1.86
1939	0.00	0.00	0.02	0.07	0.14	0.26	0.42	0.60	0.80	1.00	1.22	1.41	1.58	1.74	1.87
1940	0.00	0.01	0.03	0.07	0.16	0.28	0.44	0.63	0.83	1.05	1.26	1.45	1.61	1.77	1.89
1941	0.00	0.01	0.03	0.08	0.17	0.30	0.47	0.66	0.87	1.08	1.28	1.46	1.63	1.77	1.89
1942	0.00	0.01	0.03	0.08	0.18	0.31	0.48	0.67	0.87	1.07	1.27	1.44	1.60	1.74	1.86
1943	0.00	0.01	0.04	0.09	0.19	0.32	0.49	0.67	0.87	1.06	1.25	1.42	1.57	1.71	1.83
1944	0.00	0.01	0.04	0.10	0.20	0.34	0.50	0.69	0.87	1.06	1.24	1.41	1.56	1.69	1.80
1945	0.00	0.01	0.05	0.11	0.22	0.35	0.52	0.69	0.87	1.06	1.23	1.40	1.55	1.67	1.77
1946	0.00	0.01	0.05	0.12	0.22	0.36	0.52	0.69	0.86	1.04	1.22	1.38	1.52	1.64	1.74
1947	0.00	0.01	0.05	0.12	0.22	0.34	0.49	0.65	0.82	0.99	1.14	1.29	1.42	1.53	1.63
1948	0.00	0.02	0.05	0.12	0.22	0.35	0.50	0.66	0.83	0.99	1.14	1.28	1.41	1.52	1.62
1949	0.00	0.02	0.05	0.13	0.23	0.35	0.50	0.65	0.80	0.95	1.09	1.23	1.35	1.47	1.57
1950	0.00	0.02	0.06	0.13	0.23	0.36	0.50	0.64	0.78	0.92	1.06	1.19	1.31	1.43	1.54
1951	0.00	0.02	0.06	0.14	0.24	0.36	0.49	0.62	0.76	0.89	1.02	1.14	1.27	1.40	1.51
1952	0.00	0.02	0.07	0.14	0.25	0.36	0.48	0.61	0.73	0.86	0.99	1.12	1.26	1.39	1.50
1953	0.00	0.02	0.07	0.14	0.24	0.35	0.46	0.58	0.70	0.82	0.96	1.11	1.24	1.36	1.48
1954	0.00	0.02	0.07	0.14	0.23	0.33	0.44	0.55	0.66	0.79	0.93	1.07	1.20	1.32	1.44
1955	0.00	0.02	0.07	0.14	0.22	0.31	0.41	0.52	0.64	0.77	0.92	1.05	1.18	1.31	1.42
1956	0.00	0.02	0.07	0.13	0.20	0.29	0.39	0.50	0.62	0.76	0.90	1.03	1.16	1.28	1.40
1957	0.00	0.02	0.06	0.12	0.19	0.27	0.37	0.49	0.61	0.74	0.88	1.01	1.14	1.27	1.38
1958	0.00	0.02	0.06	0.11	0.17	0.25	0.35	0.47	0.58	0.71	0.84	0.98	1.11	1.23	
1959	0.00	0.02	0.05	0.09	0.16	0.24	0.34	0.45	0.56	0.69	0.82	0.95	1.08		
1960	0.00	0.02	0.04	0.09	0.15	0.24	0.34	0.44	0.55	0.68	0.81	0.93			
1961	0.00	0.02	0.04	0.09	0.16	0.23	0.32	0.42	0.53	0.65	0.78				
1962	0.00	0.01	0.04	0.09	0.15	0.23	0.31	0.41	0.52	0.63					
1963	0.00	0.01	0.04	0.08	0.14	0.21	0.30	0.39	0.50						
1964	0.00	0.01	0.04	0.08	0.13	0.20	0.29	0.38							
1965	0.00	0.01	0.04	0.08	0.13	0.20	0.28								
1966	0.00	0.01	0.04	0.08	0.14	0.21									
1967	0.00	0.01	0.04	0.08	0.14										
1968	0.00	0.01	0.04	0.09											
1969	0.00	0.02	0.04												
1970	0.00	0.02													
1971	0.00														

* Includes births at ages 45 and over achieved up to the end of 1986 by woman born in 1939 and earlier years.

England and Wales

31	32	33	34	35	36	37	38	39	40	41	42	43	44	45*	Year of birth of woman/female birth cohort
1.38	1.47	1.56	1.64	1.70	1.76	1.81	1.86	1.90	1.93	1.95	1.97	1.98	1.99	2.00	1920
1.44	1.53	1.62	1.69	1.76	1.82	1.87	1.92	1.95	1.98	2.01	2.03	2.04	2.05	2.05	1921
1.44	1.53	1.62	1.69	1.76	1.82	1.87	1.91	1.95	1.98	2.01	2.02	2.04	2.05	2.05	1922
1.47	1.56	1.65	1.73	1.80	1.86	1.91	1.96	2.00	2.03	2.05	2.07	2.08	2.09	2.10	1923
1.48	1.57	1.66	1.74	1.81	1.87	1.93	1.98	2.02	2.05	2.07	2.09	2.10	2.11	2.11	1924
1.48	1.58	1.67	1.75	1.82	1.88	1.94	1.99	2.03	2.06	2.08	2.10	2.11	2.11	2.12	1925
1.52	1.62	1.72	1.80	1.87	1.94	2.00	2.05	2.09	2.12	2.14	2.16	2.17	2.17	2.18	1926
1.55	1.65	1.74	1.83	1.91	1.97	2.03	2.08	2.12	2.15	2.17	2.18	2.19	2.19	2.20	1927
1.58	1.69	1.79	1.88	1.95	2.02	2.08	2.13	2.16	2.19	2.21	2.22	2.23	2.24	2.24	1928
1.61	1.72	1.82	1.91	1.99	2.05	2.11	2.15	2.19	2.21	2.23	2.24	2.25	2.25	2.26	1929
1.68	1.80	1.91	2.00	2.08	2.15	2.20	2.25	2.28	2.30	2.32	2.33	2.34	2.34	2.35	1930
1.70	1.82	1.93	2.02	2.10	2.16	2.21	2.25	2.28	2.30	2.32	2.33	2.33	2.34	2.34	1931
1.73	1.84	1.95	2.04	2.11	2.17	2.22	2.26	2.28	2.30	2.32	2.33	2.33	2.33	2.34	1932
1.80	1.92	2.02	2.11	2.18	2.23	2.28	2.31	2.34	2.36	2.37	2.37	2.38	2.38	2.39	1933
1.88	1.99	2.08	2.16	2.23	2.28	2.33	2.36	2.38	2.40	2.41	2.41	2.42	2.42	2.42	1934
1.91	2.01	2.11	2.18	2.24	2.29	2.33	2.36	2.38	2.39	2.40	2.41	2.41	2.41	2.42	1935
1.93	2.03	2.12	2.19	2.25	2.29	2.33	2.35	2.37	2.38	2.39	2.39	2.40	2.40	2.40	1936
1.95	2.05	2.13	2.20	2.25	2.29	2.32	2.34	2.35	2.37	2.37	2.38	2.38	2.38	2.39	1937
1.98	2.07	2.15	2.21	2.26	2.29	2.32	2.34	2.35	2.36	2.37	2.38	2.38	2.38	2.39	1938
1.98	2.07	2.15	2.20	2.24	2.27	2.30	2.32	2.33	2.34	2.35	2.35	2.36	2.36	2.36	1939
2.00	2.09	2.16	2.21	2.24	2.27	2.30	2.31	2.33	2.34	2.35	2.36	2.36	2.36	2.36	1940
2.00	2.08	2.14	2.19	2.22	2.25	2.27	2.29	2.31	2.32	2.32	2.33	2.33	2.34	2.34	1941
1.96	2.03	2.09	2.13	2.16	2.19	2.21	2.23	2.25	2.26	2.27	2.28	2.28	2.28	2.28	1942
1.91	1.98	2.04	2.08	2.12	2.15	2.19	2.21	2.22	2.23	2.23	2.24	2.24			1943
1.88	1.95	2.00	2.04	2.08	2.11	2.14	2.16	2.18	2.19	2.20	2.20				1944
1.85	1.92	1.97	2.02	2.06	2.10	2.12	2.14	2.16	2.17	2.18	2.19				1945
1.82	1.89	1.95	2.00	2.05	2.08	2.11	2.13	2.15	2.16	2.17					1946
1.71	1.78	1.85	1.90	1.94	1.98	2.00	2.02	2.04	2.05						1947
1.71	1.80	1.86	1.92	1.97	2.00	2.03	2.05	2.07							1948
1.67	1.76	1.82	1.88	1.93	1.96	1.99	2.02								1949
1.65	1.73	1.80	1.86	1.91	1.94	1.98									1950
1.61	1.69	1.77	1.82	1.87	1.91										1951
1.60	1.69	1.76	1.82	1.87											1952
1.58	1.67	1.74	1.81												1953
1.54	1.63	1.71													1954
1.53	1.62														1955
1.51															1956
															1957
															1958
															1959
															1960
															1961
															1962
															1963
															1964
															1965
															1966
															1967
															1968
															1969
															1970
															1971

TABLE 10.3 Average number of first liveborn children by successive ages of women: years of birth of woman, 1920-1971

Year of birth of woman/female birth cohort	Age of woman - exact years														
	16	17	18	19	20	21	22	23	24	25	26	27	28	29	30
1920	0.00	0.00	0.01	0.03	0.07	0.11	0.17	0.24	0.32	0.39	0.45	0.53	0.60	0.64	0.67
1921	0.00	0.00	0.01	0.03	0.07	0.11	0.18	0.26	0.34	0.40	0.49	0.58	0.63	0.67	0.70
1922	0.00	0.00	0.01	0.03	0.06	0.11	0.18	0.26	0.33	0.42	0.52	0.58	0.63	0.67	0.70
1923	0.00	0.00	0.01	0.03	0.06	0.12	0.19	0.26	0.35	0.46	0.54	0.59	0.64	0.68	0.71
1924	0.00	0.00	0.01	0.03	0.07	0.12	0.19	0.28	0.39	0.48	0.54	0.60	0.64	0.68	0.71
1925	0.00	0.00	0.01	0.03	0.07	0.12	0.20	0.30	0.40	0.47	0.54	0.59	0.64	0.68	0.71
1926	0.00	0.00	0.01	0.03	0.07	0.13	0.22	0.32	0.40	0.47	0.54	0.59	0.64	0.68	0.71
1927	0.00	0.00	0.01	0.03	0.07	0.14	0.23	0.32	0.40	0.47	0.54	0.60	0.64	0.68	0.72
1928	0.00	0.00	0.01	0.04	0.08	0.15	0.24	0.32	0.40	0.48	0.54	0.60	0.65	0.69	0.73
1929	0.00	0.00	0.01	0.04	0.09	0.16	0.24	0.32	0.40	0.48	0.54	0.60	0.65	0.69	0.73
1930	0.00	0.00	0.01	0.04	0.09	0.16	0.23	0.32	0.41	0.48	0.55	0.62	0.67	0.71	0.75
1931	0.00	0.00	0.01	0.04	0.09	0.15	0.23	0.32	0.41	0.49	0.56	0.62	0.67	0.71	0.75
1932	0.00	0.00	0.02	0.04	0.09	0.15	0.24	0.32	0.41	0.49	0.57	0.63	0.68	0.72	0.75
1933	0.00	0.00	0.02	0.04	0.09	0.16	0.24	0.33	0.42	0.51	0.58	0.64	0.70	0.74	0.77
1934	0.00	0.00	0.02	0.04	0.09	0.16	0.25	0.34	0.44	0.53	0.60	0.66	0.71	0.76	0.79
1935	0.00	0.00	0.02	0.04	0.09	0.16	0.26	0.36	0.45	0.53	0.61	0.67	0.72	0.76	0.79
1936	0.00	0.00	0.02	0.05	0.10	0.17	0.27	0.37	0.46	0.54	0.62	0.68	0.73	0.77	0.80
1937	0.00	0.00	0.02	0.05	0.10	0.18	0.28	0.38	0.47	0.55	0.62	0.68	0.73	0.77	0.80
1938	0.00	0.00	0.02	0.05	0.11	0.19	0.29	0.39	0.48	0.57	0.64	0.70	0.75	0.78	0.81
1939	0.00	0.00	0.02	0.06	0.12	0.20	0.30	0.40	0.50	0.58	0.65	0.71	0.75	0.79	0.81
1940	0.00	0.01	0.02	0.07	0.13	0.22	0.31	0.42	0.51	0.59	0.66	0.72	0.76	0.79	0.82
1941	0.00	0.01	0.03	0.07	0.14	0.23	0.33	0.43	0.52	0.60	0.67	0.73	0.77	0.80	0.82
1942	0.00	0.01	0.03	0.07	0.14	0.23	0.33	0.43	0.52	0.60	0.67	0.72	0.76	0.79	0.82
1943	0.00	0.01	0.03	0.08	0.15	0.24	0.33	0.43	0.52	0.60	0.66	0.71	0.75	0.79	0.81
1944	0.00	0.01	0.04	0.09	0.16	0.25	0.34	0.44	0.53	0.60	0.66	0.71	0.76	0.79	0.82
1945	0.00	0.01	0.04	0.10	0.17	0.26	0.35	0.44	0.53	0.60	0.66	0.71	0.76	0.79	0.82
1946	0.00	0.01	0.05	0.10	0.18	0.26	0.35	0.44	0.52	0.59	0.66	0.71	0.75	0.79	0.82
1947	0.00	0.01	0.05	0.10	0.17	0.25	0.34	0.42	0.49	0.56	0.63	0.68	0.72	0.75	0.78
1948	0.00	0.02	0.05	0.10	0.18	0.26	0.34	0.42	0.49	0.56	0.62	0.67	0.72	0.75	0.78
1949	0.00	0.02	0.05	0.11	0.18	0.26	0.34	0.41	0.48	0.54	0.60	0.65	0.69	0.73	0.76
1950	0.00	0.02	0.05	0.11	0.19	0.26	0.34	0.40	0.47	0.53	0.58	0.63	0.67	0.71	0.75
1951	0.00	0.02	0.06	0.12	0.19	0.26	0.33	0.39	0.45	0.51	0.56	0.61	0.66	0.70	0.73
1952	0.00	0.02	0.06	0.12	0.20	0.26	0.32	0.38	0.44	0.49	0.55	0.60	0.65	0.69	0.72
1953	0.00	0.02	0.06	0.13	0.19	0.26	0.31	0.37	0.42	0.48	0.53	0.59	0.64	0.68	0.71
1954	0.00	0.02	0.06	0.12	0.18	0.24	0.30	0.35	0.40	0.46	0.52	0.57	0.62	0.66	0.69
1955	0.00	0.02	0.06	0.12	0.18	0.23	0.28	0.34	0.39	0.45	0.51	0.56	0.61	0.65	0.68
1956	0.00	0.02	0.06	0.11	0.16	0.22	0.27	0.32	0.38	0.44	0.50	0.55	0.59	0.63	0.67
1957	0.00	0.02	0.06	0.10	0.15	0.20	0.26	0.32	0.38	0.43	0.48	0.54	0.58	0.63	0.66
1958	0.00	0.02	0.05	0.09	0.14	0.19	0.25	0.30	0.36	0.41	0.47	0.52	0.57	0.61	
1959	0.00	0.02	0.04	0.08	0.13	0.18	0.24	0.29	0.35	0.40	0.45	0.50	0.55		
1960	0.00	0.02	0.04	0.08	0.13	0.18	0.24	0.29	0.34	0.39	0.45	0.50			
1961	0.00	0.02	0.04	0.08	0.13	0.18	0.23	0.28	0.33	0.38	0.43				
1962	0.00	0.01	0.04	0.08	0.12	0.17	0.22	0.27	0.32	0.37					
1963	0.00	0.01	0.04	0.07	0.12	0.16	0.21	0.26	0.31						
1964	0.00	0.01	0.04	0.07	0.11	0.16	0.20	0.25							
1965	0.00	0.01	0.03	0.07	0.11	0.16	0.20								
1966	0.00	0.01	0.03	0.07	0.11	0.16									
1967	0.00	0.01	0.04	0.07	0.12										
1968	0.00	0.01	0.04	0.08											
1969	0.00	0.01	0.04												
1970	0.00	0.02													
1971	0.00														

* Includes births at ages 45 and over achieved up to the end of 1985 by woman born in 1939 and earlier years.

England and Wales

31	32	33	34	35	36	37	38	39	40	41	42	43	44	45*	Year of birth of woman/female birth cohort
0.70	0.72	0.73	0.75	0.76	0.76	0.77	0.78	0.78	0.78	0.79	0.79	0.79	0.79	0.79	1920
0.73	0.75	0.76	0.77	0.78	0.79	0.80	0.81	0.81	0.81	0.81	0.82	0.82	0.82	0.82	1921
0.72	0.74	0.76	0.77	0.78	0.79	0.80	0.80	0.81	0.81	0.81	0.81	0.81	0.81	0.81	1922
0.73	0.76	0.77	0.79	0.80	0.81	0.81	0.82	0.82	0.83	0.83	0.83	0.83	0.83	0.83	1923
0.74	0.76	0.77	0.79	0.80	0.81	0.81	0.82	0.82	0.82	0.83	0.83	0.83	0.83	0.83	1924
0.73	0.75	0.77	0.78	0.79	0.80	0.81	0.82	0.82	0.82	0.82	0.83	0.83	0.83	0.83	1925
0.74	0.76	0.78	0.79	0.80	0.81	0.82	0.82	0.83	0.83	0.83	0.83	0.83	0.83	0.83	1926
0.74	0.76	0.78	0.79	0.81	0.81	0.82	0.83	0.83	0.83	0.83	0.84	0.84	0.84	0.84	1927
0.75	0.77	0.79	0.80	0.82	0.82	0.83	0.84	0.84	0.84	0.84	0.84	0.84	0.85	0.85	1928
0.76	0.78	0.79	0.81	0.82	0.82	0.83	0.84	0.84	0.84	0.84	0.84	0.84	0.84	0.84	1929
0.77	0.79	0.81	0.82	0.83	0.84	0.85	0.85	0.86	0.86	0.86	0.86	0.86	0.86	0.86	1930
0.77	0.79	0.81	0.82	0.83	0.84	0.84	0.85	0.85	0.85	0.85	0.86	0.86	0.86	0.86	1931
0.78	0.80	0.81	0.82	0.83	0.84	0.84	0.85	0.85	0.85	0.85	0.86	0.86	0.86	0.86	1932
0.79	0.81	0.83	0.84	0.85	0.85	0.86	0.86	0.87	0.87	0.87	0.87	0.87	0.87	0.87	1933
0.81	0.83	0.84	0.85	0.86	0.87	0.87	0.88	0.88	0.88	0.88	0.88	0.88	0.88	0.88	1934
0.82	0.83	0.85	0.86	0.86	0.87	0.88	0.88	0.88	0.88	0.88	0.88	0.88	0.89	0.89	1935
0.82	0.84	0.85	0.86	0.87	0.87	0.88	0.88	0.88	0.88	0.88	0.88	0.88	0.88	0.89	1936
0.82	0.84	0.85	0.86	0.87	0.87	0.87	0.88	0.88	0.88	0.88	0.88	0.88	0.88	0.88	1937
0.83	0.84	0.86	0.86	0.87	0.88	0.88	0.88	0.88	0.89	0.89	0.89	0.89	0.89	0.89	1938
0.83	0.84	0.86	0.86	0.87	0.88	0.88	0.88	0.88	0.88	0.89	0.89	0.89	0.89	0.89	1939
0.84	0.85	0.86	0.87	0.87	0.88	0.88	0.88	0.89	0.89	0.89	0.89	0.89	0.89	0.89	1940
0.84	0.85	0.86	0.87	0.88	0.88	0.88	0.89	0.89	0.89	0.89	0.89	0.89	0.89	0.89	1941
0.83	0.85	0.86	0.86	0.87	0.87	0.88	0.88	0.88	0.88	0.89	0.89	0.89	0.89	0.89	1942
0.83	0.84	0.85	0.86	0.87	0.87	0.88	0.88	0.88	0.88	0.88	0.88	0.88	0.88		1943
0.84	0.85	0.86	0.87	0.87	0.88	0.88	0.89	0.89	0.89	0.89	0.89	0.89			1944
0.84	0.85	0.86	0.87	0.88	0.88	0.89	0.89	0.89	0.90	0.90	0.90				1945
0.84	0.85	0.87	0.88	0.88	0.89	0.89	0.90	0.90	0.90	0.90					1946
0.80	0.82	0.83	0.84	0.85	0.86	0.86	0.86	0.87	0.87						1947
0.80	0.82	0.84	0.85	0.86	0.86	0.87	0.87	0.87							1948
0.79	0.81	0.82	0.83	0.84	0.85	0.85	0.86								1949
0.77	0.80	0.81	0.82	0.83	0.84	0.84									1950
0.76	0.78	0.79	0.80	0.81	0.82										1951
0.75	0.77	0.78	0.80	0.81											1952
0.74	0.76	0.78	0.79												1953
0.72	0.74	0.76													1954
0.71	0.74														1955
0.70															1956
															1957
															1958
															1959
															1960
															1961
															1962
															1963
															1964
															1965
															1966
															1967
															1968
															1969
															1970
															1971

TABLE 10.4   Components of average family size: calendar years of birth of woman, 1920-1967   **England and Wales**

All ages of mother at birth

Mother's year of birth	All live births	Illegitimate live births	Legitimate live births All	First	Second	Third	Fourth	Fifth and later
1920	2.00	0.13	1.87	0.77	0.55	0.28	0.13	0.15
1921	2.05	0.13	1.93	0.79	0.57	0.29	0.14	0.15
1922	2.05	0.13	1.92	0.79	0.56	0.29	0.14	0.15
1923	2.10	0.13	1.97	0.80	0.58	0.30	0.14	0.15
1924	2.11	0.13	1.98	0.80	0.58	0.30	0.15	0.16
1925	2.12	0.12	2.00	0.80	0.58	0.30	0.15	0.17
1926	2.18	0.12	2.05	0.80	0.60	0.32	0.16	0.17
1927	2.20	0.12	2.08	0.81	0.61	0.32	0.16	0.18
1928	2.24	0.12	2.13	0.82	0.62	0.33	0.17	0.18
1929	2.26	0.11	2.14	0.82	0.63	0.34	0.17	0.18
1930	2.35	0.12	2.23	0.84	0.66	0.36	0.18	0.19
1931	2.34	0.12	2.22	0.84	0.66	0.36	0.18	0.18
1932	2.34	0.12	2.22	0.84	0.66	0.36	0.18	0.18
1933	2.39	0.12	2.26	0.85	0.69	0.37	0.18	0.17
1934	2.42	0.13	2.30	0.86	0.70	0.38	0.18	0.17
1935	2.42	0.13	2.29	0.86	0.71	0.38	0.18	0.16
1936	2.40	0.13	2.27	0.86	0.71	0.38	0.17	0.15
1937	2.39	0.14	2.25	0.85	0.71	0.38	0.17	0.13
1938	2.39	0.14	2.24	0.86	0.72	0.38	0.17	0.12
1939	2.36	0.15	2.21	0.86	0.72	0.37	0.16	0.11
1940	2.36	0.16	2.21	0.86	0.73	0.37	0.15	0.11
1941	2.34	0.16	2.18	0.86	0.73	0.36	0.14	0.09

Under 20

Mother's year of birth	All live births	Illegitimate live births	Legitimate live births All	First	Second	Third	Fourth	Fifth and later
1920	0.08	0.01	0.06	0.06	0.01	0.00		
1921	0.08	0.01	0.06	0.06	0.01	0.00		
1922	0.07	0.01	0.06	0.05	0.01	0.00		
1923	0.07	0.02	0.06	0.05	0.01	0.00		
1924	0.07	0.02	0.06	0.05	0.00	0.00		
1925	0.08	0.02	0.06	0.05	0.00	0.00		
1926	0.08	0.02	0.06	0.05	0.00	0.00		
1927	0.08	0.02	0.06	0.05	0.00	0.00		
1928	0.09	0.02	0.07	0.06	0.01	0.00		
1929	0.10	0.02	0.08	0.07	0.01	0.00		
1930	0.10	0.02	0.09	0.08	0.01	0.00		
1931	0.11	0.02	0.09	0.08	0.01	0.00		
1932	0.11	0.02	0.09	0.08	0.01	0.00		
1933	0.11	0.02	0.09	0.08	0.01	0.00		
1934	0.11	0.02	0.09	0.08	0.01	0.00		
1935	0.11	0.02	0.09	0.08	0.01	0.00		
1936	0.12	0.02	0.10	0.08	0.01	0.00		
1937	0.12	0.02	0.10	0.09	0.01	0.00		
1938	0.13	0.02	0.11	0.10	0.01	0.00		
1939	0.14	0.02	0.12	0.10	0.02	0.00		
1940	0.16	0.03	0.13	0.11	0.02	0.00		
1941	0.17	0.03	0.14	0.12	0.02	0.00		
1942	0.18	0.03	0.14	0.12	0.02	0.00		
1943	0.19	0.03	0.15	0.13	0.02	0.00		
1944	0.20	0.04	0.16	0.13	0.03	0.00		
1945	0.22	0.04	0.17	0.14	0.03	0.00		
1946	0.22	0.05	0.17	0.14	0.03	0.00		
1947	0.22	0.05	0.17	0.13	0.03	0.00		
1948	0.22	0.05	0.17	0.13	0.03	0.00		
1949	0.23	0.06	0.17	0.14	0.03	0.00		
1950	0.23	0.06	0.17	0.14	0.03	0.00		
1951	0.24	0.06	0.18	0.14	0.03	0.00		
1952	0.25	0.06	0.18	0.15	0.03	0.00		
1953	0.24	0.06	0.18	0.14	0.03	0.00		
1954	0.23	0.06	0.17	0.14	0.03	0.00		
1955	0.22	0.06	0.16	0.13	0.03	0.00		
1956	0.20	0.06	0.14	0.12	0.03	0.00		
1957	0.19	0.06	0.13	0.10	0.02	0.00		
1958	0.17	0.06	0.11	0.09	0.02	0.00		
1959	0.16	0.06	0.10	0.08	0.02	0.00		
1960	0.15	0.06	0.09	0.08	0.02	0.00		
1961	0.16	0.06	0.09	0.08	0.02	0.00		
1962	0.15	0.07	0.09	0.07	0.02	0.00		
1963	0.14	0.07	0.07	0.06	0.01	0.00		
1964	0.13	0.07	0.06	0.05	0.01	0.00		
1965	0.13	0.08	0.06	0.05	0.01	0.00		
1966	0.14	0.08	0.05	0.04	0.01	0.00		
1967	0.14	0.09	0.05	0.04	0.01	0.00		

20-24

Mother's year of birth	All live births	Illegitimate live births	Legitimate live births All	First	Second	Third	Fourth	Fifth and later
1920	0.49	0.04	0.45	0.31	0.11	0.03	0.01	0.00
1921	0.51	0.05	0.46	0.32	0.11	0.03	0.01	0.00
1922	0.54	0.05	0.49	0.33	0.12	0.03	0.01	0.00
1923	0.59	0.06	0.54	0.37	0.13	0.03	0.01	0.00
1924	0.62	0.05	0.57	0.39	0.14	0.03	0.01	0.00
1925	0.63	0.05	0.58	0.39	0.15	0.04	0.01	0.00
1926	0.64	0.04	0.60	0.39	0.16	0.04	0.01	0.00
1927	0.64	0.04	0.60	0.39	0.16	0.04	0.01	0.00
1928	0.64	0.03	0.61	0.38	0.17	0.05	0.01	0.00
1929	0.64	0.03	0.61	0.38	0.17	0.05	0.01	0.00
1930	0.66	0.03	0.63	0.38	0.18	0.05	0.01	0.00
1931	0.66	0.03	0.63	0.39	0.18	0.05	0.01	0.00
1932	0.68	0.03	0.64	0.39	0.18	0.05	0.01	0.00
1933	0.71	0.03	0.67	0.41	0.19	0.06	0.01	0.00
1934	0.74	0.04	0.70	0.42	0.20	0.06	0.02	0.00
1935	0.76	0.04	0.72	0.43	0.21	0.06	0.02	0.00
1936	0.78	0.04	0.74	0.43	0.22	0.07	0.02	0.01
1937	0.80	0.04	0.76	0.43	0.23	0.07	0.02	0.01
1938	0.83	0.05	0.79	0.44	0.24	0.08	0.02	0.01
1939	0.86	0.05	0.81	0.44	0.25	0.08	0.02	0.01
1940	0.89	0.06	0.83	0.44	0.27	0.09	0.03	0.01
1941	0.91	0.06	0.84	0.44	0.28	0.09	0.02	0.01
1942	0.90	0.07	0.83	0.44	0.27	0.09	0.02	0.01
1943	0.87	0.06	0.81	0.43	0.27	0.08	0.02	0.01
1944	0.86	0.07	0.79	0.42	0.27	0.08	0.02	0.01
1945	0.84	0.07	0.77	0.41	0.27	0.08	0.02	0.01
1946	0.82	0.07	0.76	0.40	0.26	0.08	0.02	0.00
1947	0.77	0.06	0.71	0.38	0.24	0.07	0.02	0.00
1948	0.76	0.06	0.70	0.37	0.24	0.07	0.02	0.00
1949	0.72	0.06	0.66	0.35	0.23	0.06	0.01	0.00
1950	0.69	0.06	0.63	0.34	0.22	0.06	0.01	0.00
1951	0.65	0.05	0.59	0.31	0.21	0.05	0.01	0.00
1952	0.62	0.05	0.56	0.29	0.21	0.05	0.01	0.00
1953	0.58	0.05	0.53	0.28	0.20	0.04	0.01	0.00
1954	0.56	0.05	0.51	0.27	0.19	0.04	0.01	0.00
1955	0.55	0.05	0.50	0.27	0.18	0.04	0.01	0.00
1956	0.55	0.06	0.50	0.27	0.18	0.04	0.01	0.00
1957	0.55	0.06	0.49	0.26	0.17	0.04	0.01	0.00
1958	0.54	0.07	0.47	0.26	0.17	0.04	0.01	0.00
1959	0.53	0.08	0.45	0.25	0.16	0.04	0.01	0.00
1960	0.52	0.09	0.44	0.24	0.15	0.04	0.01	0.00
1961	0.50	0.09	0.41	0.22	0.14	0.04	0.01	0.00
1962	0.48	0.10	0.38	0.20	0.13	0.03	0.01	0.00

Note: Average family sizes are obtained by summing rates for each single year of age.

TABLE 10.4 - *continued*

25-29

Mother's year of birth	All live births	Illegitimate live births	Legitimate live births All	Birth order First	Second	Third	Fourth	Fifth and later
1920	0.70	0.04	0.66	0.28	0.24	0.10	0.03	0.02
1921	0.74	0.03	0.71	0.30	0.25	0.10	0.04	0.02
1922	0.72	0.03	0.69	0.28	0.25	0.10	0.04	0.02
1923	0.69	0.03	0.66	0.25	0.25	0.11	0.04	0.02
1924	0.68	0.03	0.65	0.24	0.24	0.11	0.04	0.02
1925	0.67	0.02	0.65	0.23	0.24	0.11	0.04	0.03
1926	0.69	0.02	0.67	0.24	0.24	0.11	0.05	0.03
1927	0.70	0.02	0.68	0.25	0.24	0.11	0.05	0.03
1928	0.72	0.02	0.70	0.25	0.25	0.12	0.05	0.03
1929	0.74	0.02	0.72	0.26	0.26	0.12	0.05	0.04
1930	0.78	0.02	0.76	0.26	0.27	0.13	0.05	0.04
1931	0.80	0.03	0.77	0.26	0.28	0.13	0.06	0.04
1932	0.81	0.03	0.79	0.26	0.28	0.14	0.06	0.04
1933	0.85	0.03	0.82	0.26	0.30	0.15	0.06	0.04
1934	0.89	0.03	0.85	0.26	0.31	0.16	0.07	0.05
1935	0.90	0.04	0.87	0.26	0.32	0.17	0.07	0.05
1936	0.91	0.04	0.87	0.25	0.32	0.17	0.07	0.05
1937	0.90	0.04	0.86	0.25	0.32	0.17	0.07	0.05
1938	0.89	0.04	0.85	0.24	0.32	0.17	0.07	0.05
1939	0.87	0.04	0.83	0.23	0.31	0.17	0.07	0.04
1940	0.85	0.04	0.80	0.23	0.31	0.16	0.07	0.04
1941	0.81	0.04	0.77	0.22	0.30	0.16	0.06	0.04
1942	0.79	0.04	0.75	0.22	0.30	0.15	0.06	0.03
1943	0.76	0.04	0.73	0.22	0.29	0.14	0.05	0.03
1944	0.73	0.03	0.70	0.22	0.29	0.13	0.04	0.02
1945	0.71	0.03	0.68	0.23	0.28	0.12	0.04	0.02
1946	0.69	0.03	0.66	0.23	0.28	0.11	0.03	0.01
1947	0.64	0.03	0.62	0.22	0.26	0.09	0.03	0.01
1948	0.64	0.03	0.61	0.23	0.26	0.09	0.02	0.01
1949	0.62	0.03	0.59	0.22	0.25	0.08	0.02	0.01
1950	0.62	0.03	0.59	0.23	0.25	0.08	0.02	0.01
1951	0.63	0.03	0.59	0.23	0.25	0.08	0.02	0.01
1952	0.64	0.04	0.60	0.23	0.25	0.09	0.03	0.01
1953	0.65	0.04	0.61	0.24	0.25	0.09	0.03	0.01
1954	0.65	0.04	0.61	0.24	0.24	0.09	0.03	0.01
1955	0.65	0.05	0.60	0.23	0.24	0.09	0.03	0.01
1956	0.64	0.05	0.59	0.23	0.24	0.09	0.03	0.01
1957	0.64	0.06	0.58	0.22	0.23	0.09	0.03	0.01

30-34

Mother's year of birth	All live births	Illegitimate live births	Legitimate live births All	Birth order First	Second	Third	Fourth	Fifth and later
1920	0.43	0.02	0.41	0.09	0.14	0.09	0.05	0.05
1921	0.43	0.02	0.42	0.09	0.14	0.10	0.05	0.05
1922	0.43	0.02	0.41	0.09	0.13	0.09	0.05	0.05
1923	0.44	0.02	0.42	0.09	0.14	0.09	0.05	0.05
1924	0.44	0.02	0.42	0.09	0.13	0.09	0.05	0.05
1925	0.45	0.02	0.43	0.09	0.14	0.09	0.05	0.06
1926	0.46	0.02	0.45	0.09	0.14	0.10	0.05	0.06
1927	0.48	0.02	0.46	0.09	0.14	0.10	0.06	0.06
1928	0.49	0.02	0.47	0.09	0.15	0.11	0.06	0.07
1929	0.50	0.02	0.48	0.09	0.15	0.11	0.06	0.07
1930	0.53	0.02	0.51	0.09	0.15	0.12	0.07	0.08
1931	0.53	0.02	0.50	0.09	0.15	0.12	0.07	0.08
1932	0.52	0.02	0.49	0.08	0.14	0.12	0.07	0.08
1933	0.51	0.03	0.49	0.08	0.14	0.12	0.07	0.07
1934	0.50	0.02	0.47	0.08	0.14	0.12	0.07	0.07
1935	0.47	0.02	0.44	0.07	0.13	0.11	0.06	0.06
1936	0.44	0.02	0.42	0.07	0.13	0.11	0.06	0.06
1937	0.42	0.02	0.40	0.06	0.12	0.11	0.06	0.05
1938	0.40	0.02	0.38	0.06	0.12	0.10	0.05	0.05
1939	0.37	0.02	0.35	0.06	0.11	0.09	0.05	0.04
1940	0.35	0.02	0.33	0.06	0.11	0.09	0.04	0.03
1941	0.33	0.02	0.31	0.06	0.10	0.08	0.04	0.03
1942	0.30	0.02	0.29	0.06	0.10	0.07	0.03	0.02
1943	0.29	0.02	0.27	0.06	0.10	0.07	0.03	0.02
1944	0.28	0.02	0.27	0.06	0.11	0.06	0.02	0.02
1945	0.29	0.02	0.28	0.06	0.11	0.07	0.02	0.01
1946	0.31	0.02	0.29	0.07	0.12	0.07	0.02	0.01
1947	0.31	0.02	0.30	0.07	0.12	0.07	0.02	0.01
1948	0.34	0.02	0.32	0.08	0.13	0.08	0.03	0.01
1949	0.35	0.02	0.33	0.08	0.13	0.08	0.03	0.01
1950	0.36	0.02	0.34	0.08	0.14	0.08	0.03	0.01
1951	0.36	0.03	0.33	0.08	0.13	0.08	0.03	0.02
1952	0.37	0.03	0.34	0.08	0.14	0.08	0.03	0.02

35 and over

Mother's year of birth	All live births	Illegitimate live births	Legitimate live births All	Birth order First	Second	Third	Fourth	Fifth and later
1920	0.30	0.02	0.28	0.03	0.06	0.06	0.05	0.08
1921	0.29	0.02	0.28	0.03	0.06	0.06	0.05	0.08
1922	0.30	0.02	0.28	0.03	0.06	0.06	0.05	0.08
1923	0.30	0.02	0.28	0.03	0.06	0.06	0.05	0.08
1924	0.30	0.02	0.28	0.03	0.06	0.06	0.05	0.08
1925	0.30	0.02	0.28	0.03	0.06	0.06	0.05	0.08
1926	0.30	0.02	0.29	0.03	0.06	0.06	0.05	0.09
1927	0.29	0.02	0.28	0.03	0.05	0.06	0.05	0.08
1928	0.29	0.02	0.27	0.03	0.05	0.06	0.05	0.08
1929	0.27	0.02	0.25	0.03	0.05	0.06	0.04	0.07
1930	0.26	0.02	0.25	0.03	0.05	0.06	0.04	0.07
1931	0.24	0.02	0.23	0.03	0.04	0.05	0.04	0.06
1932	0.22	0.02	0.21	0.02	0.04	0.05	0.04	0.06
1933	0.21	0.01	0.19	0.02	0.04	0.05	0.03	0.05
1934	0.19	0.01	0.18	0.02	0.04	0.04	0.03	0.05
1935	0.17	0.01	0.16	0.02	0.03	0.04	0.03	0.04
1936	0.16	0.01	0.14	0.02	0.03	0.03	0.02	0.03
1937	0.14	0.01	0.13	0.02	0.03	0.03	0.02	0.03
1938	0.13	0.01	0.12	0.02	0.03	0.03	0.02	0.03
1939	0.12	0.01	0.11	0.02	0.03	0.03	0.02	0.02
1940	0.12	0.01	0.11	0.02	0.03	0.03	0.02	0.02
1941	0.12	0.01	0.11	0.02	0.03	0.03	0.02	0.02

Note: Average family sizes are obtained by summing rates for each single year of age.

TABLE 10.5 Percentage distribution of liveborn children at successive ages of women born in selected years

England and Wales

Age of women (exact years)	Year of birth of women	Number of liveborn children†				
		0	1	2	3	4 or more
20	1920	93.5	5.7	0.8	0.1	0.0
	1925	93.2	6.0	0.8	0.1	0.0
	1930	90.9	7.8	1.1	0.1	0.0
	1935	90.6	8.0	1.3	0.2	0.0
	1940	87.0	10.6	2.1	0.3	0.0
	1945	82.8	13.3	3.4	0.5	0.0
	1950	81.5	14.3	3.8	0.4	0.0
	1955	82.3	13.9	3.5	0.4	0.0
	1960	87.3	10.2	2.2	0.2	0.0
	1965	88.9	9.2	1.7	0.2	0.0
	1966	88.6	9.5	1.7	0.2	0.0
25	1920	60.8	25.7	10.1	2.7	0.7
	1925	52.5	29.8	13.4	3.4	0.8
	1930	51.6	28.2	14.5	4.3	1.4
	1935	46.5	29.4	17.0	5.3	1.9
	1940	40.8	28.1	20.8	7.3	3.1
	1945	40.3	26.8	23.0	7.1	2.6
	1950	47.1	23.6	21.7	5.9	1.8
	1955	54.8	20.6	18.6	4.7	1.3
	1960	60.6	18.4	15.5	4.1	1.4
	1961	61.9	18.1	14.7	4.0	1.4
30	1920	32.8	29.0	24.0	9.3	4.8
	1925	29.4	28.7	25.9	10.4	5.6
	1930	25.4	26.6	28.5	12.0	7.5
	1935	20.6	22.9	31.7	14.9	10.0
	1940	18.2	19.0	34.7	17.5	10.5
	1945	18.2	19.9	39.1	15.5	7.3
	1950	25.2	19.4	37.9	12.5	5.0
	1955	31.6	18.1	34.0	11.3	5.0
	1956	32.9	17.7	33.2	11.0	5.2
35	1920	24.4	23.7	28.2	13.1	10.5
	1925	20.5	24.2	29.7	14.1	11.5
	1930	16.6	20.1	31.6	16.4	15.3
	1935	13.5	16.7	30.0	19.7	17.1
	1940	12.7	13.8	35.8	22.2	15.5
	1945	12.0	14.9	43.0	19.8	10.2
	1950	17.0	14.2	42.1	18.7	8.0
	1951	18.6	14.1	40.8	18.6	7.9
40	1920	21.6	21.8	28.0	14.5	14.1
	1925	17.7	22.2	29.2	15.5	15.4
	1930	14.2	18.3	30.8	17.5	19.2
	1935	11.7	15.3	32.8	20.6	19.7
	1940	11.3	12.7	35.9	23.0	17.1
	1945	10.5	13.5	43.0	21.1	11.9
	1946	9.9	13.9	43.8	21.0	11.4
45*	1920	21.1	21.3	27.6	14.7	15.3
	1925	17.2	21.7	28.9	15.7	16.4
	1930	13.8	18.0	30.7	17.6	19.9
	1935	11.4	15.1	32.7	20.7	20.0
	1940	11.1	12.5	35.9	23.0	17.5
	1941	10.6	12.9	36.8	23.2	16.5

* Includes birth at ages over 45 where possible.
† Estimates including legitimate and illegitimate children (see Introduction, page 2).

TABLE 11.1 Estimated legitimate live births: social class of father, age of mother and previous liveborn children, 1976-1986

England and Wales

thousands

SOCIAL CLASSES I AND II

Year	Number of previous liveborn children				
	Total	0	1	2	3 or more
All ages of mother at birth					
1976	140.6	60.7	56.4	17.1	6.4
1977	142.5	62.1	55.8	18.1	6.5
1978	150.3	65.0	58.0	20.0	7.2
1979	158.0	67.8	60.1	22.2	7.9
1979[1]	161.2	69.3	61.6	22.6	7.8
1980	164.5	69.4	62.4	24.4	8.2
1981	163.3	67.5	63.5	23.6	8.8
1982	158.7	63.8	62.0	23.9	9.0
1983	156.0	64.5	59.8	23.0	8.7
1984	154.8	64.2	57.9	23.7	9.0
1985	158.4	65.3	60.6	23.6	8.8
1986	160.1	66.3	60.3	24.1	9.5
Under 20					
1976	2.3	1.9	0.4	0.0	
1977	1.9	1.7	0.2	0.0	
1978	2.1	1.8	0.3	0.0	
1979	2.0	1.7	0.2	–	
1979[1]	2.0	1.7	0.2	–	
1980	2.3	2.0	0.3	–	
1981	2.1	1.8	0.3	0.0	
1982	1.8	1.5	0.3	0.0	
1983	1.8	1.5	0.3	0.0	
1984	1.6	1.3	0.2	0.0	
1985	1.6	1.3	0.2	0.0	
1986	1.4	1.2	0.2	0.0	
20–24					
1976	25.4	16.8	7.4	1.1	0.2
1977	23.7	15.4	7.1	1.1	0.2
1978	24.5	16.5	6.8	1.0	0.1
1979	24.6	16.2	6.9	1.2	0.2
1979[1]	25.0	16.5	7.0	1.2	0.2
1980	25.5	16.7	7.4	1.2	0.2
1981	25.0	16.2	7.4	1.2	0.2
1982	24.4	15.6	7.4	1.2	0.2
1983	23.2	14.7	7.2	1.2	0.2
1984	22.7	15.0	6.3	1.4	0.1
1985	22.9	14.7	6.8	1.2	0.2
1986	22.2	14.4	6.4	1.2	0.2
25–29					
1976	69.3	31.2	30.3	6.5	1.3
1977	66.2	31.4	27.5	6.1	1.2
1978	66.6	31.4	27.6	6.4	1.3
1979	68.5	33.4	27.1	6.5	1.5
1979[1]	69.9	34.2	27.8	6.5	1.4
1980	68.4	33.0	27.2	6.9	1.3
1981	67.4	31.6	27.9	6.2	1.8
1982	64.0	29.7	26.3	6.5	1.5
1983	61.9	30.0	24.1	6.2	1.5
1984	61.1	29.3	24.0	6.4	1.5
1985	62.1	29.9	24.9	6.0	1.4
1986	63.1	30.6	24.1	6.7	1.7
30 and over					
1976	43.6	10.9	18.3	9.4	5.0
1977	50.6	13.6	21.0	10.9	5.1
1978	57.0	15.3	23.3	12.6	5.8
1979	62.9	16.5	25.8	14.4	6.1
1979[1]	64.2	16.8	26.4	14.9	6.1
1980	68.3	17.8	27.5	16.3	6.7
1981	68.8	17.8	27.9	16.2	6.9
1982	68.5	17.0	28.0	16.2	7.3
1983	69.0	18.3	28.1	15.6	7.0
1984	69.4	18.6	27.5	16.0	7.4
1985	71.8	19.4	28.7	16.4	7.2
1986	73.4	20.1	29.6	16.1	7.6

SOCIAL CLASS IIIN

Year	Number of previous liveborn children				
	Total	0	1	2	3 or more
All ages of mother at birth					
1976	55.5	25.2	21.9	6.3	2.1
1977	53.2	24.4	20.9	5.7	2.3
1978	54.6	25.5	21.0	6.2	1.9
1979	56.9	25.9	21.8	6.8	2.4
1979[1]	60.4	27.4	22.9	7.3	2.7
1980	61.9	28.3	23.1	7.6	2.9
1981	60.4	26.6	23.8	7.4	2.7
1982	58.0	25.2	22.6	7.3	2.8
1983	57.1	25.2	22.0	7.1	2.8
1984	57.6	25.5	21.9	7.4	2.9
1985	56.2	24.9	20.8	7.6	2.9
1986	55.2	24.2	20.9	7.4	2.8
Under 20					
1976	2.2	1.9	0.3	0.0	
1977	1.8	1.4	0.3	0.0	
1978	1.6	1.4	0.2	–	
1979	1.7	1.4	0.3	–	
1979[1]	1.9	1.6	0.3	–	
1980	1.8	1.5	0.2	0.0	
1981	1.8	1.4	0.3	0.0	
1982	1.5	1.3	0.2	0.0	
1983	1.5	1.2	0.2	0.0	
1984	1.4	1.2	0.3	–	
1985	1.2	1.0	0.1	0.0	
1986	1.2	0.9	0.2	0.0	
20–24					
1976	15.0	9.2	4.9	0.8	0.1
1977	13.6	8.9	4.2	0.5	0.1
1978	14.0	8.9	4.3	0.7	0.1
1979	14.5	9.4	4.3	0.8	0.1
1979[1]	15.6	10.1	4.7	0.8	0.1
1980	16.5	10.7	5.1	0.6	0.1
1981	15.9	10.0	5.2	0.6	0.2
1982	15.0	9.2	4.8	0.9	0.1
1983	14.4	9.3	4.3	0.7	0.1
1984	13.9	8.6	4.3	0.9	0.1
1985	13.2	8.3	4.1	0.7	0.1
1986	12.5	7.7	3.9	0.8	0.1
25–29					
1976	25.5	10.9	11.3	2.8	0.5
1977	24.2	10.6	10.5	2.5	0.6
1978	23.7	11.0	10.0	2.1	0.6
1979	24.1	10.9	10.4	2.3	0.5
1979[1]	25.6	11.5	11.0	2.5	0.7
1980	25.6	11.6	10.7	2.6	0.7
1981	24.9	10.9	10.8	2.6	0.6
1982	24.1	10.6	10.3	2.5	0.7
1983	23.7	10.6	9.9	2.3	0.8
1984	24.4	11.0	10.0	2.7	0.8
1985	24.3	11.1	9.6	2.8	0.8
1986	23.9	10.7	9.8	2.8	0.7
30 and over					
1976	12.7	3.1	5.4	2.8	1.4
1977	13.6	3.4	5.9	2.8	1.5
1978	15.3	4.1	6.6	3.4	1.2
1979	16.5	4.1	6.8	3.9	1.8
1979[1]	17.1	4.3	6.9	4.0	1.9
1980	18.0	4.5	7.2	4.4	2.0
1981	17.8	4.2	7.5	4.1	2.0
1982	17.4	4.2	7.4	3.9	1.9
1983	17.6	4.1	7.5	4.1	1.9
1984	17.8	4.8	7.3	3.8	1.9
1985	17.5	4.5	7.0	4.0	2.0
1986	17.6	4.9	6.9	3.8	2.0

Notes: 1. For definition of social classes, see Introduction. Table includes 1976 to 1979 data based on the 1970 classification of occupations, and for 1979 and later years based on the 1980 classification of occupations.
2. For an indication of the standard errors attached to the estimates see Introduction and Appendix Tables 3 and 4.

TABLE 11.1 - *continued*

thousands

Year	Number of previous liveborn children					Year	Number of previous liveborn children				
	Total	0	1	2	3 or more		Total	0	1	2	3 or more

SOCIAL CLASS IIIM / **SOCIAL CLASSES IV AND V**

All ages of mother at birth

Year	Total	0	1	2	3 or more	Year	Total	0	1	2	3 or more
1976	204.8	79.3	79.2	29.4	16.8	1976	110.3	42.9	39.0	15.9	12.6
1977	193.4	76.9	74.4	27.5	14.5	1977	106.4	41.9	37.4	15.6	11.5
1978	202.2	82.2	75.2	29.0	15.9	1978	111.6	45.1	38.2	17.1	11.3
1979	216.7	88.7	78.3	33.2	16.4	1979	119.2	47.7	40.3	18.5	12.7
1979[1]	208.9	85.4	75.4	32.0	16.0	1979[1]	120.5	48.0	40.6	18.8	13.0
1980	212.2	85.8	76.4	33.6	16.3	1980	120.4	47.8	40.4	18.4	13.8
1981	198.2	78.4	73.3	30.6	15.8	1981	111.4	42.2	38.1	18.3	12.8
1982	190.0	72.7	70.7	30.3	16.2	1982	109.3	40.4	38.5	17.5	13.0
1983	188.3	72.8	69.6	29.8	16.1	1983	107.7	39.5	37.1	18.0	13.0
1984	185.5	71.8	68.2	29.3	16.1	1984	106.3	38.5	37.3	17.4	13.1
1985	184.3	71.2	66.9	30.2	15.9	1985	105.9	39.0	35.6	17.7	13.6
1986	179.5	68.8	65.7	28.7	16.3	1986	101.1	37.1	33.8	17.6	12.6

Under 20

Year	Total	0	1	2 and 3 or more	Year	Total	0	1	2 and 3 or more
1976	16.6	13.2	3.1	0.3	1976	14.9	11.5	3.2	0.2
1977	15.2	12.3	2.8	0.2	1977	13.4	10.5	2.6	0.2
1978	14.5	12.0	2.4	0.1	1978	14.2	11.2	2.7	0.2
1979	15.4	12.5	2.5	0.3	1979	14.4	11.4	2.9	0.2
1979[1]	14.4	11.7	2.5	0.2	1979[1]	15.0	11.9	2.9	0.2
1980	14.5	11.6	2.8	0.1	1980	14.6	11.5	2.8	0.3
1981	12.1	9.6	2.4	0.2	1981	12.1	9.1	2.8	0.2
1982	10.5	8.3	2.0	0.2	1982	11.1	8.3	2.5	0.2
1983	9.5	7.6	1.8	0.1	1983	9.1	6.9	2.0	0.2
1984	7.9	6.4	1.4	0.1	1984	8.8	6.6	2.0	0.2
1985	7.5	5.8	1.5	0.2	1985	8.0	6.2	1.7	0.1
1986	6.9	5.4	1.4	0.1	1986	6.8	5.1	1.6	0.1

20-24

Year	Total	0	1	2	3 or more	Year	Total	0	1	2	3 or more
1976	74.5	36.2	29.8	7.0	1.5	1976	43.1	19.1	17.6	5.0	1.4
1977	69.8	35.6	27.1	6.1	1.0	1977	42.6	19.4	16.9	4.8	1.5
1978	73.3	38.4	27.5	5.9	1.4	1978	44.3	20.5	17.2	5.4	1.2
1979	76.7	41.7	27.4	6.4	1.2	1979	47.5	22.6	18.0	5.5	1.4
1979[1]	74.3	40.5	26.5	6.1	1.2	1979[1]	48.4	22.8	18.4	5.8	1.5
1980	75.1	40.8	26.2	7.0	1.1	1980	50.0	23.8	19.0	5.5	1.7
1981	70.5	37.2	25.9	5.9	1.5	1981	46.0	21.0	18.0	5.8	1.3
1982	66.6	34.5	24.7	6.2	1.2	1982	45.5	20.1	18.3	5.6	1.6
1983	64.9	33.8	24.0	5.9	1.2	1983	44.0	20.1	16.8	5.5	1.5
1984	62.3	32.3	22.7	6.0	1.3	1984	42.2	19.3	16.6	4.9	1.4
1985	59.4	31.3	21.0	5.8	1.3	1985	41.2	19.5	15.3	5.1	1.3
1986	55.2	29.2	19.8	4.9	1.3	1986	39.1	18.3	14.3	5.1	1.3

25-29

Year	Total	0	1	2	3 or more	Year	Total	0	1	2	3 or more
1976	75.6	23.2	33.9	12.8	5.8	1976	33.6	9.3	13.3	6.7	4.3
1977	69.7	21.9	31.4	11.7	4.6	1977	31.9	9.1	12.7	6.3	3.8
1978	72.0	24.2	30.6	12.4	4.8	1978	32.5	9.7	12.4	6.5	3.8
1979	76.7	25.9	31.6	14.1	5.1	1979	34.8	9.9	13.2	7.4	4.3
1979[1]	73.9	24.8	30.4	13.7	5.0	1979[1]	34.7	9.7	13.1	7.6	4.3
1980	76.0	25.2	31.5	14.1	5.2	1980	33.5	9.2	12.7	6.8	4.8
1981	70.9	23.5	29.6	12.6	5.2	1981	31.8	8.8	11.6	7.1	4.2
1982	68.7	22.0	29.0	12.2	5.5	1982	32.6	8.8	12.4	6.9	4.4
1983	70.3	23.4	29.2	12.5	5.1	1983	33.8	9.3	12.7	7.2	4.5
1984	70.1	24.5	28.4	11.9	5.2	1984	34.4	9.6	12.9	7.2	4.7
1985	72.2	25.3	29.2	12.7	5.0	1985	35.6	10.1	12.7	7.7	5.1
1986	71.1	24.8	29.0	11.9	5.4	1986	34.6	10.1	12.5	7.3	4.6

30 and over

Year	Total	0	1	2	3 or more	Year	Total	0	1	2	3 or more
1976	38.0	6.7	12.4	9.4	9.6	1976	18.8	3.0	4.9	4.0	6.9
1977	38.7	7.1	13.1	9.6	8.8	1977	18.5	2.9	5.2	4.2	6.2
1978	42.4	7.6	14.7	10.5	9.7	1978	20.7	3.6	5.9	5.0	6.2
1979	47.9	8.6	16.6	12.6	10.1	1979	22.5	3.8	6.3	5.4	7.0
1979[1]	46.3	8.4	16.0	12.1	9.8	1979[1]	22.3	3.6	6.2	5.3	7.2
1980	46.5	8.2	15.9	12.4	10.0	1980	22.3	3.3	5.9	5.7	7.3
1981	44.7	8.1	15.5	11.9	9.2	1981	21.5	3.2	5.7	5.3	7.3
1982	44.2	7.9	15.0	11.8	9.6	1982	20.2	3.1	5.2	4.9	7.0
1983	43.7	7.9	14.7	11.3	9.8	1983	20.8	3.1	5.5	5.1	7.1
1984	45.1	8.5	15.8	11.3	9.5	1984	21.0	3.1	5.8	5.1	7.0
1985	45.2	8.8	15.2	11.6	9.6	1985	21.1	3.2	5.8	4.8	7.2
1986	46.2	9.4	15.5	11.8	9.6	1986	20.6	3.5	5.5	5.0	6.6

Notes: 1. For definition of social classes, see Introduction. Table includes 1976 to 1979 data based on the 1970 classification of occupations, and for 1979 and later years based on the 1980 classification of occupations.
2. For an indication of the standard errors attached to the estimates see Introduction and Appendix Tables 3 and 4.

TABLE 11.1 - *continued*   *thousands*

SOCIAL CLASS: NON-MANUAL

Year	Total	0	1	2	3 or more
All ages of mother at birth					
1976	196.0	85.9	78.3	23.4	8.5
1977	195.7	86.5	76.7	23.8	8.7
1978	204.9	90.4	79.1	26.2	9.1
1979	214.9	93.7	81.9	29.0	10.3
1979[1]	221.5	96.7	84.5	29.9	10.5
1980	226.3	97.8	85.5	32.0	11.1
1981	223.7	94.0	87.2	30.9	11.5
1982	216.7	89.1	84.6	31.2	11.8
1983	213.1	89.7	81.8	30.1	11.5
1984	212.4	89.7	79.8	31.1	11.9
1985	214.6	90.2	81.5	31.2	11.7
1986	215.3	90.5	81.2	31.4	12.3
Under 20					
1976	4.5	3.8	0.7	0.0	
1977	3.7	3.2	0.5	0.0	
1978	3.7	3.2	0.5	0.0	
1979	3.7	3.2	0.6	-	
1979[1]	3.9	3.3	0.6	-	
1980	4.0	3.5	0.5	0.0	
1981	3.9	3.3	0.6	0.0	
1982	3.3	2.7	0.5	0.0	
1983	3.3	2.7	0.5	0.0	
1984	3.0	2.5	0.5	0.0	
1985	2.8	2.4	0.4	0.0	
1986	2.6	2.1	0.4	0.0	
20-24					
1976	40.4	26.0	12.3	1.9	0.3
1977	37.4	24.3	11.3	1.5	0.3
1978	38.5	25.4	11.1	1.7	0.2
1979	39.1	25.6	11.3	2.0	0.3
1979[1]	40.7	26.6	11.7	2.0	0.4
1980	41.9	27.4	12.5	1.8	0.3
1981	40.9	26.2	12.6	1.8	0.3
1982	39.4	24.8	12.1	2.1	0.4
1983	37.7	23.9	11.6	1.9	0.3
1984	36.7	23.6	10.6	2.3	0.3
1985	36.2	22.9	10.9	1.9	0.4
1986	34.6	22.1	10.3	2.0	0.3
25-29					
1976	94.8	42.1	41.6	9.3	1.8
1977	90.4	42.0	38.0	8.6	1.9
1978	90.3	42.5	37.6	8.5	1.8
1979	92.6	44.3	37.5	8.8	2.1
1979[1]	95.6	45.7	38.8	9.0	2.1
1980	94.0	44.6	37.9	9.5	2.0
1981	92.3	42.5	38.7	8.7	2.4
1982	88.1	40.3	36.6	9.0	2.2
1983	85.5	40.6	34.1	8.5	2.3
1984	85.6	40.2	34.0	9.0	2.3
1985	86.4	40.9	34.5	8.8	2.2
1986	87.1	41.3	33.9	9.5	2.4
30 and over					
1976	56.3	14.0	23.8	12.2	6.4
1977	64.2	17.0	26.9	13.7	6.6
1978	72.3	19.3	29.8	16.0	7.1
1979	79.5	20.6	32.6	18.3	7.9
1979[1]	81.4	21.1	33.4	18.9	8.1
1980	86.3	22.3	34.6	20.7	8.7
1981	86.6	22.0	35.4	20.3	8.9
1982	85.9	21.2	35.4	20.1	9.2
1983	86.6	22.4	35.6	19.7	8.9
1984	87.2	23.4	34.7	19.8	9.3
1985	89.3	23.9	35.7	20.4	9.2
1986	91.1	25.0	36.5	20.0	9.5

SOCIAL CLASS: MANUAL

Year	Total	0	1	2	3 or more
All ages of mother at birth					
1976	315.1	122.1	118.2	45.3	29.4
1977	299.8	118.9	111.8	43.1	26.0
1978	313.8	127.3	113.4	46.0	27.1
1979	335.9	136.4	118.6	51.7	29.2
1979[1]	329.3	133.4	116.1	50.9	29.0
1980	332.6	133.7	116.8	52.0	30.2
1981	309.7	120.6	111.5	49.0	28.7
1982	299.3	113.1	109.2	47.9	29.2
1983	296.0	112.2	106.8	47.9	29.2
1984	291.8	110.4	105.6	46.7	29.1
1985	290.2	110.2	102.5	47.9	29.5
1986	280.6	105.9	99.5	46.3	28.8
Under 20					
1976	31.5	24.7	6.3	0.5	
1977	28.6	22.8	5.4	0.4	
1978	28.7	23.2	5.1	0.3	
1979	29.7	23.8	5.4	0.4	
1979[1]	29.5	23.7	5.4	0.4	
1980	29.1	23.2	5.6	0.4	
1981	24.2	18.7	5.1	0.3	
1982	21.5	16.6	4.5	0.4	
1983	18.6	14.5	3.8	0.3	
1984	16.7	13.0	3.4	0.3	
1985	15.5	11.9	3.3	0.3	
1986	13.8	10.5	3.0	0.3	
20-24					
1976	117.6	55.3	47.4	12.0	2.9
1977	112.4	55.0	44.0	10.9	2.5
1978	117.6	58.9	44.7	11.3	2.6
1979	124.2	64.3	45.4	11.9	2.6
1979[1]	122.7	63.3	44.9	11.8	2.6
1980	125.1	64.5	45.2	12.6	2.9
1981	116.5	58.2	43.9	11.7	2.7
1982	112.1	54.7	43.0	11.7	2.7
1983	108.8	53.9	40.8	11.4	2.7
1984	104.5	51.6	39.3	10.9	2.7
1985	100.6	50.8	36.4	10.9	2.6
1986	94.3	47.6	34.0	10.0	2.6
25-29					
1976	109.2	32.5	47.2	19.4	10.0
1977	101.6	31.1	44.0	18.0	8.5
1978	104.5	34.0	43.0	18.9	8.6
1979	111.5	35.8	44.8	21.5	9.4
1979[1]	108.6	35.5	43.6	21.2	9.3
1980	109.6	34.4	44.2	21.0	10.0
1981	102.7	32.4	41.3	19.8	9.3
1982	101.3	30.8	41.5	19.2	9.9
1983	104.0	32.8	41.9	19.8	9.6
1984	104.5	34.2	41.3	19.1	9.9
1985	107.8	35.4	41.9	20.4	10.1
1986	105.7	34.9	41.6	19.2	10.0
30 and over					
1976	56.8	9.6	17.3	13.4	16.5
1977	57.2	10.0	18.4	13.9	15.0
1978	63.1	11.2	20.5	15.5	15.9
1979	70.4	12.5	22.9	17.9	17.1
1979[1]	68.6	12.0	22.2	17.4	17.0
1980	68.8	11.6	21.8	18.1	17.3
1981	66.2	11.3	21.1	17.2	16.6
1982	64.4	11.0	20.2	16.7	16.6
1983	64.6	11.0	20.2	16.4	16.9
1984	66.1	11.6	21.6	16.4	16.5
1985	66.3	12.0	21.0	16.4	16.8
1986	66.8	12.9	21.0	16.8	16.2

Notes: 1. For definition of social classes, see Introduction. Table includes 1976 to 1979 data based on the 1970 classification of occupations, and for 1979 and later years based on the 1980 classification of occupations.
2. For an indication of the standard errors attached to the estimates see Introduction and Appendix Tables 3 and 4.

TABLE 11.1 - continued

thousands

OTHERS

All ages of mother at birth

Year	Total	0	1	2	3 or more
1976	19.3	9.2	7.0	3.0	0.9
1977	18.4	9.2	6.5	1.9	0.8
1978	17.1	8.8	5.7	1.9	0.7
1979	17.8	8.8	6.2	2.0	0.8
1979[1]	17.7	8.7	6.1	2.0	0.8
1980	19.9	9.5	6.9	2.4	1.1
1981	20.1	9.7	7.0	2.5	0.9
1982	20.1	9.7	6.9	2.4	1.1
1983	20.8	9.8	7.1	2.8	1.1
1984	22.2	10.4	7.7	2.8	1.2
1985	25.4	11.6	9.1	3.3	1.4
1986	23.8	10.6	8.5	3.1	1.6

Under 20

Year	Total	0	1	2 / 3 or more
1976	2.2	1.8	0.4	0.0
1977	2.1	1.9	0.2	0.0
1978	1.9	1.7	0.2	0.0
1979	1.7	1.6	0.1	0.0
1979[1]	1.7	1.6	0.2	0.0
1980	1.7	1.5	0.2	0.0
1981	2.1	1.7	0.4	0.0
1982	1.9	1.7	0.2	0.0
1983	1.7	1.5	0.2	0.0
1984	1.7	1.4	0.3	0.0
1985	1.8	1.5	0.3	0.0
1986	1.4	1.2	0.2	0.0

20-24

Year	Total	0	1	2	3 or more
1976	7.5	4.1	2.8	0.5	0.1
1977	7.4	4.3	2.5	0.5	0.1
1978	6.8	4.1	2.3	0.4	0.0
1979	7.0	4.3	2.3	0.4	0.0
1979[1]	7.0	4.3	2.3	0.4	0.0
1980	7.9	4.4	2.9	0.5	0.0
1981	8.3	5.0	2.6	0.6	0.1
1982	8.4	4.9	2.9	0.5	0.1
1983	8.7	5.0	3.0	0.7	0.1
1984	9.2	5.4	2.9	0.7	0.1
1985	9.5	5.3	3.3	0.8	0.2
1986	9.1	5.0	3.2	0.7	0.1

25-29

Year	Total	0	1	2	3 or more
1976	7.0	2.6	3.0	1.1	0.3
1977	6.2	2.3	2.9	0.7	0.2
1978	5.3	2.2	2.1	0.7	0.3
1979	5.7	2.1	2.4	0.9	0.2
1979[1]	5.6	2.1	2.4	0.9	0.2
1980	6.4	2.6	2.4	1.0	0.4
1981	6.4	2.4	2.8	1.0	0.3
1982	6.4	2.5	2.6	1.1	0.3
1983	6.6	2.5	2.7	1.2	0.4
1984	7.3	2.8	3.0	1.2	0.4
1985	9.1	3.5	3.7	1.3	0.5
1986	8.6	3.1	3.4	1.5	0.6

30 and over

Year	Total	0	1	2	3 or more
1976	2.7	0.7	0.8	0.7	0.4
1977	2.7	0.7	0.9	0.6	0.5
1978	3.0	0.9	1.0	0.8	0.3
1979	3.4	0.8	1.3	0.8	0.5
1979[1]	3.3	0.8	1.3	0.7	0.5
1980	3.9	1.0	1.4	0.9	0.7
1981	3.4	0.6	1.3	0.9	0.5
1982	3.3	0.7	1.1	0.9	0.7
1983	3.7	0.9	1.2	1.1	0.6
1984	4.0	0.8	1.5	1.0	0.7
1985	5.0	1.3	1.8	1.1	0.7
1986	4.7	1.3	1.7	0.8	0.9

ALL SOCIAL CLASSES

All ages of mother at birth

Year	Total	0	1	2	3 or more
1976	530.5	217.2	203.6	71.0	38.8
1977	513.9	214.6	195.0	68.8	35.5
1978	535.8	226.6	198.1	74.2	36.9
1979	568.6	238.9	206.7	82.7	40.3
1979[1]	568.6	238.9	206.7	82.7	40.3
1980	578.9	241.0	209.2	86.3	42.4
1981	553.5	224.3	205.7	82.4	41.1
1982	536.1	211.9	200.7	81.4	42.1
1983	529.9	211.8	195.6	80.7	41.8
1984	526.4	210.4	193.1	80.6	42.2
1985	530.2	212.0	193.1	82.4	42.7
1986	519.7	206.9	189.2	80.8	42.7

Under 20

Year	Total	0	1	2 / 3 or more
1976	38.1	30.2	7.4	0.5
1977	34.4	27.9	6.1	0.4
1978	34.3	28.1	5.9	0.3
1979	35.1	28.6	6.2	0.3
1979[1]	35.1	28.6	6.2	0.3
1980	34.9	28.2	6.3	0.4
1981	30.1	23.6	6.1	0.4
1982	26.7	21.1	5.2	0.4
1983	23.6	18.7	4.6	0.3
1984	21.4	16.9	4.2	0.3
1985	20.1	15.8	3.9	0.3
1986	17.8	13.8	3.6	0.3

20-24

Year	Total	0	1	2	3 or more
1976	165.6	85.4	62.5	14.4	3.3
1977	157.2	83.6	57.8	12.9	2.9
1978	162.9	88.4	58.1	13.5	2.9
1979	170.3	94.2	58.9	14.2	3.0
1979[1]	170.3	94.2	58.9	14.2	3.0
1980	174.9	96.4	60.5	14.8	3.2
1981	165.7	89.5	59.0	14.1	3.1
1982	159.9	84.4	58.1	14.2	3.2
1983	155.2	82.8	55.4	13.9	3.1
1984	150.4	80.6	52.8	13.9	3.1
1985	146.3	79.0	50.5	13.6	3.2
1986	138.0	74.7	47.5	12.7	3.1

25-29

Year	Total	0	1	2	3 or more
1976	211.0	77.2	91.8	29.8	12.2
1977	198.2	75.4	84.9	27.3	10.6
1978	200.2	78.6	82.7	28.1	10.7
1979	209.8	82.3	84.7	31.1	11.7
1979[1]	209.8	82.3	84.7	31.1	11.7
1980	210.0	81.6	84.6	31.5	12.4
1981	201.5	77.2	82.7	29.5	12.0
1982	195.8	73.6	80.6	29.2	12.4
1983	196.2	75.9	78.7	29.3	12.3
1984	197.4	77.2	78.3	29.3	12.6
1985	203.3	79.9	80.0	30.5	12.8
1986	201.3	79.3	78.9	30.2	13.0

30 and over

Year	Total	0	1	2	3 or more
1976	115.8	24.3	41.9	26.3	23.2
1977	124.1	27.7	46.2	28.2	22.0
1978	138.4	31.5	51.3	32.3	23.3
1979	153.3	33.9	56.8	37.0	25.5
1979[1]	153.3	33.9	56.8	37.0	25.5
1980	159.1	34.8	57.8	39.7	26.8
1981	156.2	34.0	57.8	38.5	26.0
1982	153.6	32.8	56.8	37.6	26.5
1983	154.9	34.3	57.0	37.2	26.4
1984	157.2	35.8	57.8	37.2	26.5
1985	160.6	37.3	58.5	38.0	26.7
1986	162.6	39.2	59.2	37.6	26.6

Notes: 1. For definition of social classes, see Introduction. Table includes 1976 to 1979 data based on the 1970 classification of occupations, and for 1979 and later years based on the 1980 classification of occupations.
2. For an indication of the standard errors attached to the estimates see Introduction and Appendix Tables 3 and 4.

TABLE 11.2 Estimated pre-maritally conceived first live births to all married women: social class of father and age of mother, 1976-1986

England and Wales

Year	All classes (including 'others')	I and II	IIIN	IIIM	IV and V	Non-manual	Manual	All social classes (including 'others')	I and II	IIIN	IIIM	IV and V	Non-manual	Manual
	a. Number (thousands)							b. As a percentage of first legitimate live births						
All ages of mother at birth														
1976	40.2	5.6	3.2	16.7	12.5	8.8	29.2	18.5	9.3	12.5	21.1	29.1	10.2	23.9
1977	37.9	5.4	2.6	15.8	11.8	8.0	27.6	17.7	8.7	10.7	20.6	28.1	9.3	23.2
1978	40.3	6.0	2.9	16.2	13.0	9.0	29.2	17.8	9.3	11.6	19.7	28.8	9.9	22.9
1979	44.2	6.5	3.2	18.5	13.4	9.8	31.9	18.5	9.7	12.4	20.9	28.2	10.4	23.4
1979[1]	44.2	6.5	3.1	18.4	15.0	9.6	33.4	18.5	9.3	11.4	21.5	31.3	9.9	25.0
1980	46.9	7.2	3.6	18.9	14.9	10.8	33.8	19.4	10.4	12.7	22.0	31.2	11.1	25.3
1981	42.8	7.6	3.6	16.8	12.4	11.2	29.1	19.1	11.3	13.5	21.4	29.4	11.9	24.2
1982	40.8	6.5	3.4	16.3	11.5	9.8	27.7	19.2	10.1	13.3	22.4	28.4	11.0	24.5
1983	40.2	7.5	3.3	16.0	11.3	10.8	27.3	19.0	11.6	13.1	22.0	28.6	12.0	24.3
1984	40.4	7.9	3.5	15.7	11.0	11.4	26.7	19.2	12.3	13.8	21.9	28.5	12.7	24.2
1985	41.9	7.4	3.4	15.8	12.6	10.8	28.5	19.8	11.4	13.5	22.2	32.4	12.0	25.8
1986	41.2	8.1	3.5	16.3	11.0	11.6	27.3	19.9	12.2	14.6	23.7	29.6	12.8	25.8
Under 20														
1976	19.0	1.1	1.3	8.5	7.3	2.4	15.7	63.0	58.6	66.5	64.0	63.4	62.5	63.7
1977	17.4	0.9	0.9	7.9	6.7	1.8	14.6	62.4	51.6	62.4	64.4	63.4	56.5	63.9
1978	17.4	1.1	0.9	7.5	7.1	2.0	14.6	62.0	59.7	63.1	62.8	63.3	61.2	63.1
1979	17.9	1.1	1.0	8.1	6.8	2.1	14.9	62.0	63.3	70.6	65.0	59.5	66.6	62.4
1979[1]	17.9	1.0	0.9	7.7	7.5	2.0	15.2	62.8	60.1	57.1	65.2	63.3	58.7	64.2
1980	17.8	1.0	0.9	7.8	7.2	2.0	15.0	63.0	52.6	60.7	66.9	62.6	56.1	64.7
1981	15.0	1.0	0.9	6.2	5.8	1.9	12.1	63.2	57.0	60.4	65.1	63.8	58.5	64.4
1982	13.4	0.9	0.8	5.6	5.2	1.7	10.8	63.5	62.0	58.8	67.6	62.3	60.5	65.0
1983	12.0	0.9	0.7	5.3	4.4	1.5	9.7	64.3	57.2	54.1	69.6	64.2	55.8	67.0
1984	10.7	0.8	0.8	4.4	4.1	1.6	8.5	63.5	62.2	66.2	69.2	61.7	64.1	65.4
1985	10.0	0.7	0.6	3.8	4.1	1.3	7.9	63.3	55.0	55.1	65.6	66.9	55.1	66.3
1986	8.9	0.6	0.5	3.9	3.3	1.2	7.2	64.3	52.4	57.5	71.7	65.0	54.6	68.4
20-24														
1976	13.2	1.9	1.1	5.7	3.7	3.0	9.4	15.5	11.3	12.2	15.8	19.4	11.6	17.0
1977	12.4	1.5	1.1	5.4	3.5	2.6	8.9	14.8	9.9	12.0	15.3	18.0	10.7	16.3
1978	13.7	1.9	1.0	5.9	4.2	3.0	10.0	15.5	11.7	11.7	15.2	20.2	11.7	17.0
1979	15.6	2.1	1.2	6.9	4.5	3.3	11.4	16.6	12.9	13.0	16.5	19.8	12.9	17.7
1979[1]	15.6	1.7	1.2	7.0	4.9	2.9	12.0	16.6	10.3	11.6	17.4	21.6	10.8	18.9
1980	17.5	2.1	1.5	7.4	5.7	3.6	13.1	18.2	12.8	13.7	18.2	23.9	13.2	20.3
1981	16.8	2.2	1.3	7.3	5.0	3.4	12.3	18.8	13.4	12.8	19.6	23.8	13.2	21.1
1982	16.1	2.3	1.5	6.9	4.5	3.7	11.4	19.0	14.4	16.0	20.0	22.4	15.0	20.9
1983	16.2	2.0	1.5	6.9	4.9	3.5	11.7	19.5	13.6	16.6	20.3	24.3	14.8	21.8
1984	16.7	2.2	1.3	7.0	5.1	3.5	12.1	20.8	14.8	14.9	21.7	26.4	14.8	23.4
1985	17.6	2.5	1.4	7.2	5.5	3.9	12.6	22.3	17.2	17.0	22.9	28.2	17.1	24.7
1986	17.4	2.7	1.7	7.0	5.0	4.4	11.9	23.3	18.6	21.9	23.8	27.2	19.8	25.1
25-29														
1976	4.9	1.5	0.4	1.6	1.0	1.9	2.6	6.4	4.8	3.8	7.0	10.9	4.5	8.1
1977	4.9	1.6	0.4	1.5	1.0	2.0	2.6	6.5	5.1	4.0	7.0	11.1	4.8	8.3
1978	5.4	1.5	0.6	1.6	1.2	2.1	2.9	6.8	4.8	5.3	6.8	12.8	4.9	8.5
1979	6.1	1.7	0.6	2.1	1.3	2.3	3.5	7.5	5.1	5.2	8.2	13.4	5.2	9.7
1979[1]	6.1	2.1	0.6	2.2	1.0	2.7	3.2	7.5	6.1	5.5	8.8	10.4	6.0	9.3
1980	6.7	1.9	0.6	2.4	1.3	2.5	3.8	8.2	5.7	5.1	9.7	14.5	5.6	10.9
1981	6.5	2.3	0.9	2.0	1.1	3.1	3.1	8.4	7.1	8.2	8.4	12.9	7.4	9.6
1982	6.4	1.8	0.6	2.6	1.2	2.4	3.7	8.7	6.1	6.0	11.6	13.3	6.0	12.1
1983	6.9	2.2	0.5	2.5	1.4	2.8	3.9	9.1	7.4	5.2	10.6	15.2	6.8	11.9
1984	7.5	2.3	0.9	2.7	1.2	3.2	3.9	9.7	7.8	8.3	11.1	12.7	7.9	11.5
1985	8.5	2.5	1.0	3.0	1.6	3.5	4.6	10.7	8.4	8.8	11.9	15.8	8.5	13.0
1986	8.9	2.5	0.8	3.4	1.7	3.3	5.2	11.2	8.1	7.9	13.8	17.1	8.0	14.8
30 and over														
1976	3.0	1.2	0.4	0.9	0.5	1.5	1.4	12.4	10.6	11.4	13.3	16.4	10.8	14.2
1977	3.2	1.4	0.2	0.9	0.6	1.6	1.5	11.5	10.1	6.4	12.9	20.6	9.4	15.1
1978	3.8	1.5	0.4	1.2	0.5	2.0	1.7	12.1	10.1	10.1	15.2	13.9	10.1	14.7
1979	4.5	1.7	0.4	1.4	0.9	2.1	2.3	13.3	10.1	9.6	16.4	22.4	10.0	18.2
1979[1]	4.5	1.6	0.4	1.5	0.8	2.0	2.3	13.3	9.6	9.7	17.8	21.6	9.6	19.0
1980	4.9	2.2	0.6	1.3	0.7	2.8	1.9	14.1	12.2	13.6	15.4	20.2	12.5	16.8
1981	4.6	2.1	0.5	1.3	0.4	2.7	1.7	13.4	12.0	12.7	16.0	12.8	12.1	15.1
1982	4.9	2.5	0.5	1.2	0.6	3.0	1.8	14.9	14.7	11.9	15.2	19.3	14.1	16.4
1983	5.1	2.4	0.5	1.4	0.6	3.0	1.9	14.7	13.2	13.3	17.3	18.3	13.2	17.6
1984	5.5	2.6	0.6	1.6	0.6	3.1	2.2	15.4	13.9	11.9	18.6	20.5	13.5	19.1
1985	5.7	2.6	0.5	1.6	0.8	3.1	2.3	15.3	13.3	10.9	18.1	23.4	12.9	19.5
1986	6.0	2.3	0.5	2.1	0.9	2.8	3.0	15.3	11.5	9.8	22.2	26.3	11.2	23.3

Notes: 1. For definition of social classes, see Introduction. Table includes 1976 to 1979 data based on the 1970 classification of occupations, and for 1979 and later years based on the 1980 classification of occupations.
2. For an indication of the standard errors attached to the estimates see Introduction and Appendix Tables 3 and 4.
3. Table includes live births at durations 0-7 completed months from marriage.

TABLE 11.3   **Median intervals from marriage to first birth (according to social class of husband*) and between later births, 1976-1986**

Great Britain,
England and Wales

Median intervals in months

Year	Marriage to first birth					First to second birth	Second to third birth	Third to fourth birth
	All social classes	I and II	IIIN	IIIM	IV and V			
	Women married once only					All women†		
1976	29	39	35	26	19	33	42	43
1977	29	40	36	27	19	34	42	39
1978	31	42	39	28	19	34	43	40
1979	30	42	37	27	19	33	44	39
1980	29	41	37	25	18	32	41	41
1981	28	39	34	26	19	31	40	35
1982	29	40	35	26	19	31	40	36
1983	29	39	34	27	20	31	40	35
1984	29	38	34	27	20	31	40	34
1985	28	37	33	26	18	32	40	34
1986	27	36	32	25	19	32	39	33
	Remarried women							
1976	17	17	18	17	13			
1977	18	18	19	16	17			
1978	18	20	22	17	13			
1979	17	19	19	15	13			
1980	16	19	18	15	11			
1981	17	19	18	15	15			
1982	18	19	19	17	15			
1983	19	20	19	17	17			
1984	18	18	19	18	15			
1985	17	19	20	17	12			
1986	16	17	16	16	14			

* For description of social classes and sample used in calculation see Introduction.
† From a 4 per cent sample of family allowance returns for 1976 to 1977 and child benefit returns for 1978 onwards, covering Great Britain.

TABLE 11.4   **Mean ages of women at legitimate live births (according to social class of husband*) and birth order, 1976-1986**

England and Wales

Year	All social classes	I and II	IIIN	IIIM	IV and V	All social classes	I and II	IIIN	IIIM	IV and V
	All legitimate live births					Second legitimate live birth				
1976	26.7	28.4	27.2	26.1	25.5	26.9	28.8	27.8	26.0	25.3
1977	26.8	28.7	27.5	26.2	25.5	27.1	29.0	28.0	26.7	25.4
1978	27.1	28.9	27.6	26.3	25.5	27.2	29.2	28.2	25.8	25.4
1979	27.1	29.0	27.6	26.4	25.5	27.4	29.3	28.1	26.4	25.3
1980	27.1	29.1	27.6	26.4	25.5	27.4	29.4	28.1	26.6	25.3
1981	27.3	29.3	27.8	26.6	25.7	27.5	29.5	28.3	26.6	25.3
1982	27.4	29.4	27.9	26.8	25.7	27.5	29.6	28.3	26.8	25.3
1983	27.5	29.5	28.0	26.8	26.0	27.6	29.7	28.5	26.8	25.6
1984	27.6	29.6	27.9	27.0	26.1	27.8	29.9	28.4	27.0	25.7
1985	27.8	29.7	28.1	27.1	26.1	27.9	29.8	28.5	27.1	25.9
1986	27.9	29.8	28.3	27.3	26.3	28.0	30.1	28.6	27.2	26.0
	First legitimate live birth					Third legitimate live birth				
1976	24.9	26.9	25.7	24.1	23.1	28.9	30.8	29.8	28.3	27.5
1977	25.0	27.2	25.9	24.2	23.2	29.1	30.9	30.2	28.4	27.6
1978	25.1	27.4	26.2	24.3	23.3	29.3	30.2	30.2	28.7	27.6
1979	25.2	27.4	25.4	24.3	23.1	29.4	31.3	30.2	28.8	27.5
1980	25.2	27.5	26.0	24.4	23.1	29.5	31.5	30.6	28.7	27.7
1981	25.4	27.6	26.1	24.5	23.4	29.6	31.7	30.6	29.0	27.7
1982	25.5	27.8	26.2	24.7	23.4	29.6	31.8	30.4	29.0	27.6
1983	25.6	27.9	26.2	24.8	23.7	29.7	32.0	31.0	29.1	27.9
1984	25.8	27.8	26.4	25.1	23.8	29.7	31.8	30.3	29.0	27.8
1985	26.0	28.0	26.5	25.2	24.0	29.8	32.1	30.6	29.0	27.7
1986	26.2	28.1	26.8	25.4	24.2	29.8	32.1	30.4	29.3	27.9

* For description of social classes and sample used in calculation see Introduction.

TABLE 11.5 **Jointly registered illegitimate live births:**
social class of father and age of mother, 1976-1986

Age of mother at birth	Year	All social classes (including 'others')	Social class of father					
			I and II	IIIN	IIIM	IV and V	Non-manual	Manual
All ages	1976	27.4	3.6	1.6	12.7	8.6	5.2	21.3
	1977	29.3	4.3	1.4	12.9	9.9	5.7	22.8
	1978	32.8	4.8	1.9	14.8	10.2	6.8	24.9
	1979	38.3	5.5	2.3	17.0	12.5	7.8	29.5
	1980	44.2	5.9	2.7	19.6	14.7	8.6	34.3
	1981	47.1	6.2	3.0	20.6	15.6	9.2	36.2
	1982	53.4	7.2	3.5	22.6	18.1	10.7	40.7
	1983	60.8	8.2	3.7	25.4	21.0	11.9	46.4
	1984	69.9	9.2	4.6	29.3	23.5	13.8	52.8
	1985	81.8	10.7	5.0	34.6	27.4	15.7	62.0
	1986	93.5	13.3	5.8	38.3	31.8	19.1	70.0
Under 20	1976	7.2	0.4	0.3	3.3	2.9	0.7	6.1
	1977	7.8	0.4	0.3	3.4	3.4	0.7	6.8
	1978	8.9	0.6	0.4	3.9	3.5	1.0	7.4
	1979	10.3	0.5	0.5	4.6	4.2	1.0	8.8
	1980	11.8	0.6	0.5	5.2	5.0	1.1	10.3
	1981	12.8	0.7	0.7	5.3	5.5	1.3	10.7
	1982	14.3	0.8	0.8	5.6	6.2	1.5	11.9
	1983	16.1	0.9	0.8	6.3	6.9	1.7	13.2
	1984	18.2	1.0	1.0	7.2	7.6	2.0	14.8
	1985	21.0	1.0	1.1	8.3	8.9	2.2	17.2
	1986	23.2	1.4	1.2	8.5	10.6	2.6	19.1
20-24	1976	8.6	0.8	0.5	4.2	2.8	1.3	7.0
	1977	9.3	1.1	0.4	4.4	3.2	1.4	7.6
	1978	10.9	1.3	0.7	5.3	3.2	2.0	8.5
	1979	12.7	1.3	0.7	6.0	4.3	2.0	10.4
	1980	15.3	1.8	0.9	6.7	5.4	2.7	12.1
	1981	16.8	1.8	1.1	7.9	5.5	2.9	13.4
	1982	19.4	2.0	1.1	8.7	6.9	3.1	15.6
	1983	22.6	2.2	1.4	9.8	8.3	3.6	18.2
	1984	26.2	2.6	1.5	11.6	9.4	4.1	21.0
	1985	31.3	2.8	1.8	14.1	11.2	4.6	25.3
	1986	36.2	4.0	2.1	15.6	12.7	6.1	28.3
25-29	1976	6.3	1.1	0.5	3.0	1.5	1.5	4.5
	1977	6.4	1.2	0.4	2.8	1.8	1.7	4.6
	1978	6.9	1.4	0.4	3.0	2.0	1.8	4.9
	1979	8.1	1.5	0.6	3.4	2.4	2.2	5.8
	1980	8.9	1.6	0.7	4.2	2.2	2.3	6.4
	1981	9.5	1.6	0.7	4.3	2.6	2.3	6.9
	1982	10.7	1.9	0.8	4.7	3.0	2.7	7.7
	1983	12.1	2.4	0.8	5.2	3.4	3.2	8.6
	1984	14.2	2.4	1.1	6.0	4.2	3.6	10.2
	1985	16.9	2.8	1.2	7.4	4.8	4.0	12.2
	1986	19.5	3.6	1.4	8.1	5.6	5.0	13.8
30 and over	1976	5.3	1.3	0.3	2.2	1.4	1.6	3.6
	1977	5.7	1.6	0.3	2.3	1.4	1.9	3.7
	1978	6.2	1.6	0.5	2.6	1.4	2.1	4.0
	1979	7.2	2.1	0.5	3.0	1.5	2.6	4.5
	1980	8.1	1.9	0.6	3.4	2.0	2.5	5.4
	1981	8.0	2.1	0.5	3.2	2.0	2.6	5.2
	1982	9.0	2.5	0.8	3.6	1.9	3.3	5.5
	1983	10.1	2.8	0.6	4.1	2.3	3.4	6.4
	1984	11.2	3.2	0.9	4.5	2.3	4.1	6.8
	1985	12.7	4.1	0.9	4.8	2.6	5.0	7.3
	1986	14.7	4.3	1.1	6.0	2.9	5.4	8.9

Notes: 1. For definition of social classes, see Introduction. Table includes 1976 to 1979 data based on the 1970 classification of
occupations, and for 1980 and later years on the 1980 classification of occupations.
2. For indication of the standard errors attached to the estimates see Introduction and Appendix Tables 3 and 4.

TABLE 12.1 All conceptions: proportions to women in different age-groups (a) inside and outside marriage and (b) leading to maternities or abortions (under the 1967 Act), 1975-1985

England and Wales

Residents

Age of woman at conception and year of conception	Total number of conceptions (000s)	Percentage of all conceptions (a) Inside marriage	(a) Outside marriage	(b) Leading to maternities	(b) Terminated by abortion	Age of woman at conception and year of conception	Total number of conceptions (000s)	Percentage of all conceptions (a) Inside marriage	(a) Outside marriage	(b) Leading to maternities	(b) Terminated by abortion
All ages						**25-29**					
1975	693.3	76.8	23.2	84.7	15.3	1975	227.9	90.2	9.8	91.0	9.0
1976	671.6	76.8	23.2	84.5	15.5	1976	223.7	89.9	10.1	91.1	8.9
1977	686.4	76.2	23.8	84.8	15.2	1977	218.9	89.5	10.5	91.4	8.6
1978	747.9	75.4	24.6	84.5	15.5	1978	232.9	88.6	11.4	91.2	8.8
1979	774.1	73.7	26.3	83.8	16.2	1979	234.8	87.7	12.3	90.8	9.2
1980	765.0	72.7	27.3	83.5	16.5	1980	229.1	86.9	13.1	90.6	9.4
1981	752.3	71.5	28.5	82.9	17.1	1981	221.8	85.8	14.2	90.3	9.7
1982	755.3	70.0	30.0	83.0	17.0	1982	225.0	84.6	15.4	90.2	9.8
1983	753.4	68.6	31.4	83.0	17.0	1983	226.3	83.8	16.2	90.3	9.7
1984	790.1	66.7	33.3	82.7	17.3	1984	238.6	82.2	17.8	90.0	10.0
1985	797.2	64.4	35.6	82.1	17.9	1985	242.6	80.2	19.8	89.2	10.8
Under 16						**30-34**					
1975	9.2	0.4	99.6	47.9	52.1	1975	88.3	88.5	11.5	82.9	17.1
1976	9.2	0.4	99.6	46.8	53.2	1976	91.3	88.7	11.3	83.7	16.3
1977	9.0	0.4	99.6	46.9	53.1	1977	103.4	88.4	11.6	84.7	15.3
1978	9.1	0.4	99.6	48.5	51.5	1978	121.4	88.4	11.6	85.2	14.8
1979	9.1	0.5	99.5	44.8	55.2	1979	128.1	87.4	12.6	85.1	14.9
1980	8.6	0.4	99.6	45.9	54.1	1980	126.9	87.0	13.0	85.1	14.9
1981	8.6	0.6	99.4	43.1	56.9	1981	126.2	86.3	13.7	85.3	14.7
1982	9.0	0.4	99.6	43.1	56.9	1982	121.9	85.6	14.4	85.7	14.3
1983	9.4	0.3	99.7	43.2	56.8	1983	120.9	84.7	15.3	86.2	13.8
1984	9.6	0.5	99.5	44.3	55.7	1984	126.0	83.8	16.2	86.5	13.5
1985	9.4	0.3	99.7	44.3	55.7	1985	127.8	82.7	17.3	86.6	13.4
Under 20						**35-39**					
1975	112.0	32.0	68.0	73.5	26.5	1975	33.5	85.2	14.8	67.1	32.9
1976	105.7	30.9	69.1	71.9	28.1	1976	31.5	84.6	15.4	66.8	33.2
1977	107.2	29.6	70.4	71.7	28.3	1977	31.9	84.1	15.9	67.5	32.5
1978	114.6	28.3	71.7	71.4	28.6	1978	35.8	83.1	16.9	67.4	32.6
1979	120.9	26.6	73.4	69.7	30.3	1979	38.6	82.8	17.2	68.1	31.9
1980	117.2	25.3	74.7	69.0	31.0	1980	39.3	82.8	17.2	68.7	31.3
1981	115.2	24.1	75.9	68.1	31.9	1981	40.9	80.7	19.3	69.2	30.8
1982	113.9	21.2	78.8	67.6	32.4	1982	44.2	81.1	18.9	70.8	29.2
1983	112.4	19.0	81.0	66.8	33.2	1983	46.4	80.5	19.5	72.3	27.7
1984	118.2	17.2	82.8	66.6	33.4	1984	48.5	79.5	20.5	73.4	26.6
1985	119.3	15.3	84.7	66.2	33.8	1985	48.8	78.7	21.3	74.0	26.0
20-24						**40 and over**					
1975	221.8	79.5	20.5	88.7	11.3	1975	10.0	84.9	15.1	48.9	51.1
1976	210.0	79.4	20.6	88.5	11.5	1976	9.3	84.9	15.1	47.3	52.7
1977	215.2	78.5	21.5	88.8	11.2	1977	9.8	83.3	16.7	48.3	51.7
1978	233.3	77.0	23.0	88.1	11.9	1978	9.9	81.7	18.3	46.6	53.4
1979	241.6	74.7	25.3	87.3	12.7	1979	10.1	80.6	19.4	46.7	53.3
1980	242.0	72.9	27.1	86.7	13.3	1980	10.4	80.1	19.9	47.8	52.2
1981	238.1	71.2	28.8	85.8	14.2	1981	10.0	78.8	20.1	48.7	51.3
1982	240.7	69.1	30.9	85.7	14.3	1982	9.6	79.3	20.7	49.8	50.2
1983	237.9	66.8	33.2	85.3	14.7	1983	9.5	78.5	21.5	52.7	47.3
1984	249.1	63.7	36.3	84.6	15.4	1984	9.7	77.5	22.5	53.0	47.0
1985	249.2	60.0	40.0	83.1	16.9	1985	9.6	76.0	24.0	53.1	46.9

TABLE 12.2   All conceptions: numbers and rates to women in different age-groups leading to maternities or abortions (under the 1967 Act), 1975-1985

Residents

Age of woman at conception and year of conception	Number of conceptions (thousands)			Conception rates per 1,000 women in age-group			Age of woman at conception and year of conception	Number of conceptions (thousands)			Conception rates per 1,000 women in age-group		
	Total conceptions	Conceptions leading to maternities	Conceptions terminated by abortion	Total conceptions	Conceptions leading to maternities	Conceptions terminated by abortion		Total conceptions	Conceptions leading to maternities	Conceptions terminated by abortion	Total conceptions	Conceptions leading to maternities	Conceptions terminated by abortion
All ages*							**25-29**						
1975	693.3	587.0	106.4	72.4	61.3	11.1	1975	227.9	207.5	20.4	122.9	111.9	11.0
1976	671.6	567.5	104.1	69.4	58.6	10.8	1976	223.7	203.9	19.9	120.4	109.7	10.7
1977	686.4	581.8	104.5	70.1	59.4	10.7	1977	218.9	200.1	18.9	123.7	113.1	10.7
1978	747.9	632.0	116.0	75.3	63.6	11.7	1978	232.9	212.4	20.6	135.6	123.6	12.0
1979	774.1	648.5	125.6	76.8	64.4	12.5	1979	234.8	213.3	21.5	138.7	126.0	12.7
1980	765.0	638.5	126.5	74.8	62.5	12.4	1980	229.1	207.7	21.4	137.0	124.1	12.8
1981	752.3	623.9	128.4	72.7	60.3	12.4	1981	221.8	200.3	21.6	132.7	119.8	12.9
1982	755.3	626.8	128.5	72.3	60.0	12.3	1982	225.0	203.0	22.0	134.2	121.0	13.1
1983	753.4	625.0	128.3	71.4	59.3	12.2	1983	226.3	204.3	22.0	133.7	120.7	13.0
1984	790.1	653.8	136.3	74.2	61.4	12.8	1984	238.6	214.7	23.9	138.1	124.3	13.8
1985	797.2	654.3	142.9	74.1	60.8	13.3	1985	242.6	216.5	26.2	136.1	121.4	14.7
Under 16†							**30-34**						
1975	9.2	4.4	4.8	8.1	3.9	4.2	1975	88.3	73.2	15.1	57.9	48.0	9.9
1976	9.2	4.3	4.9	7.9	3.7	4.2	1976	91.3	76.5	14.9	57.5	48.2	9.4
1977	9.0	4.2	4.8	7.6	3.6	4.0	1977	103.4	87.6	15.8	60.0	50.9	9.2
1978	9.1	4.4	4.7	7.6	3.7	3.9	1978	121.4	103.5	17.9	67.8	57.8	10.0
1979	9.1	4.1	5.0	7.5	3.4	4.2	1979	128.1	109.0	19.0	70.3	59.8	10.5
1980	8.6	3.9	4.6	7.2	3.3	3.9	1980	126.9	108.0	18.9	68.9	58.6	10.3
1981	8.6	3.7	4.9	7.3	3.1	4.1	1981	126.2	107.6	18.6	68.4	58.3	10.1
1982	9.0	3.9	5.1	7.8	3.4	4.4	1982	121.9	104.5	17.5	69.7	59.8	10.0
1983	9.4	4.0	5.3	8.3	3.6	4.7	1983	120.9	104.2	16.7	71.4	61.6	9.9
1984	9.6	4.3	5.4	8.6	3.8	4.8	1984	126.0	109.0	17.0	75.6	65.4	10.2
1985	9.4	4.2	5.2	8.6	3.8	4.8	1985	127.8	110.6	17.2	77.4	67.0	10.4
Under 20≠							**35-39**						
1975	112.0	82.3	29.7	64.1	47.2	17.0	1975	33.5	22.5	11.0	23.6	15.9	7.8
1976	105.7	76.0	29.7	58.7	42.2	16.5	1976	31.5	21.0	10.5	22.5	15.0	7.5
1977	107.2	76.9	30.3	57.9	41.5	16.3	1977	31.9	21.5	10.3	22.7	15.3	7.4
1978	114.6	81.9	32.7	60.2	43.0	17.2	1978	35.8	24.1	11.7	25.0	16.8	8.1
1979	120.9	84.3	36.6	61.9	43.2	18.8	1979	38.6	26.3	12.3	26.2	17.8	8.3
1980	117.2	80.9	36.4	58.7	40.5	18.2	1980	39.3	27.0	12.3	25.9	17.8	8.1
1981	115.2	78.4	36.7	57.1	38.9	18.2	1981	40.9	27.3	12.6	25.9	17.3	8.0
1982	113.9	77.0	36.9	56.4	38.1	18.3	1982	44.2	31.3	12.9	25.8	18.3	7.5
1983	112.4	75.0	37.4	56.0	37.4	18.6	1983	46.4	33.6	12.8	26.0	18.8	7.2
1984	118.2	78.8	39.5	59.9	39.9	20.0	1984	48.5	35.6	12.9	26.7	19.6	7.1
1985	119.3	78.9	40.3	61.7	40.8	20.9	1985	48.8	36.1	12.7	26.5	19.6	6.9
20-24							**40 and over****						
1975	221.8	196.6	25.1	133.0	118.0	15.1	1975	10.0	4.9	5.1	7.2	3.5	3.7
1976	210.0	185.8	24.3	126.0	111.4	14.5	1976	9.3	4.4	4.9	6.8	3.2	3.6
1977	215.2	191.0	24.2	127.8	113.5	14.4	1977	9.8	4.8	5.1	7.2	3.5	3.7
1978	233.3	205.5	27.8	136.6	120.3	16.3	1978	9.9	4.6	5.3	7.2	3.3	3.8
1979	241.6	210.9	30.7	139.2	121.5	17.7	1979	10.1	4.7	5.4	7.2	3.4	3.9
1980	242.0	209.9	32.1	135.3	117.4	17.9	1980	10.4	5.0	5.4	7.4	3.5	3.9
1981	238.1	204.3	33.8	128.9	110.6	18.3	1981	10.0	4.7	5.1	7.2	3.4	3.7
1982	240.7	206.3	34.4	127.1	108.9	18.2	1982	9.6	4.8	4.8	6.8	3.4	3.4
1983	237.9	203.0	34.9	122.1	104.2	17.9	1983	9.5	5.0	4.5	6.7	3.5	3.2
1984	249.1	210.6	38.5	124.2	105.0	19.2	1984	9.7	5.1	4.5	6.6	3.5	3.1
1985	249.2	207.2	42.0	121.4	100.9	20.5	1985	9.6	5.1	4.5	6.4	3.4	3.0

* Rates per 1,000 women aged 15-44.
† Rates per 1,000 women aged 13-15.
≠ Rates per 1,000 women aged 15-19.
** Rates per 1,000 women aged 40-44.

TABLE 12.3 All teenage conceptions: numbers and rates at single years of age leading to maternities or abortions (under the 1967 Act), 1975-1985

England and Wales

Residents

Age of woman at conception and year of conception	Number of conceptions			Conception rates per 1,000 women in age-group/age		
	Total conceptions	Conceptions leading to maternities	Conceptions terminated by abortion	Total conceptions	Conceptions leading to maternities	Conceptions terminated by abortion
Under 16*						
1975	9,181	4,394	4,787	8.1	3.9	4.2
1976	9,191	4,298	4,893	7.9	3.7	4.2
1977	8,993	4,216	4,777	7.6	3.6	4.0
1978	9,103	4,412	4,691	7.6	3.7	3.9
1979	9,108	4,079	5,029	7.5	3.4	4.2
1980	8,580	3,935	4,645	7.2	3.3	3.9
1981	8,561	3,694	4,867	7.3	3.1	4.1
1982	8,999	3,875	5,124	7.8	3.4	4.4
1983	9,369	4,046	5,323	8.3	3.6	4.7
1984	9,649	4,278	5,371	8.6	3.8	4.8
1985	9,406	4,169	5,237	8.6	3.8	4.8
Under 14†						
1975	401	159	242	1.0	0.4	0.6
1976	377	153	224	1.0	0.4	0.6
1977	376	138	238	0.9	0.3	0.6
1978	395	163	232	1.0	0.4	0.6
1979	381	144	237	1.0	0.4	0.6
1980	352	125	227	0.9	0.3	0.6
1981	435	171	264	1.1	0.4	0.7
1982	428	138	290	1.1	0.4	0.8
1983	367	148	219	1.0	0.4	0.6
1984	378	151	227	1.0	0.4	0.6
1985	325	139	186	0.9	0.4	0.5
14						
1975	1,919	837	1,082	5.0	2.2	2.8
1976	1,898	782	1,116	4.9	2.0	2.9
1977	1,916	792	1,124	4.9	2.0	2.9
1978	1,822	810	1,012	4.5	2.0	2.5
1979	1,904	760	1,144	4.7	1.9	2.8
1980	1,714	669	1,045	4.3	1.7	2.6
1981	1,817	684	1,133	4.6	1.7	2.9
1982	1,868	702	1,166	4.9	1.8	3.1
1983	2,034	790	1,244	5.4	2.1	3.3
1984	2,018	794	1,244	5.5	2.2	3.4
1985	2,063	836	1,227	5.5	2.2	3.3
15						
1975	6,861	3,398	3,463	18.8	9.3	9.5
1976	6,916	3,363	3,553	18.2	8.8	9.3
1977	6,711	3,296	3,415	17.2	8.5	8.8
1978	6,886	3,439	3,447	17.5	8.7	8.7
1979	6,823	3,175	3,648	16.8	7.8	9.0
1980	6,513	3,140	3,373	16.0	7.7	8.3
1981	6,309	2,839	3,470	15.8	7.1	8.7
1982	6,703	3,035	3,668	17.1	7.7	9.3
1983	6,968	3,108	3,860	18.3	8.2	10.1
1984	7,253	3,333	3,920	19.1	8.8	10.3
1985	7,018	3,194	3,824	19.1	8.7	10.4

Age of woman at conception and year of conception	Number of conceptions			Conception rates per 1,000 women in age-group/age		
	Total conceptions	Conceptions leading to maternities	Conceptions terminated by abortion	Total conceptions	Conceptions leading to maternities	Conceptions terminated by abortion
16						
1975	15,278	9,447	5,831	42.8	26.5	16.3
1976	14,567	8,761	5,806	39.7	23.9	15.8
1977	14,940	8,895	6,045	39.1	23.3	15.8
1978	15,770	9,422	6,348	40.3	24.1	16.2
1979	16,106	9,307	6,799	40.6	23.5	17.2
1980	15,210	8,600	6,610	37.4	21.2	16.3
1981	15,410	8,782	6,628	37.7	21.5	16.2
1982	15,030	8,331	6,699	37.6	20.9	16.8
1983	15,229	8,431	6,798	38.7	21.5	17.3
1984	15,995	8,842	7,153	41.9	23.2	18.7
1985	16,146	9,107	7,039	42.4	23.9	18.5
17						
1975	23,349	16,747	6,602	66.9	48.0	18.9
1976	21,681	15,165	6,516	60.5	42.3	18.2
1977	21,757	15,154	6,603	59.1	41.2	17.9
1978	23,518	16,256	7,262	61.2	42.3	18.9
1979	24,868	16,694	8,174	63.3	42.5	20.8
1980	23,894	15,791	8,103	60.0	39.6	20.3
1981	23,179	14,990	8,189	56.8	36.7	20.1
1982	22,964	15,049	7,915	55.8	36.6	19.2
1983	22,575	14,452	8,123	56.0	35.9	20.2
1984	24,209	15,642	8,567	61.4	39.6	21.7
1985	24,619	15,922	8,697	64.2	41.5	22.7
18						
1975	29,952	23,555	6,397	88.0	69.2	18.8
1976	27,563	21,114	6,449	78.5	60.1	18.4
1977	28,270	21,522	6,748	78.6	59.8	18.8
1978	30,344	22,842	7,502	81.9	61.7	20.3
1979	32,752	24,206	8,546	84.8	62.7	22.1
1980	32,093	23,378	8,715	81.2	59.2	22.1
1981	30,564	21,894	8,670	76.2	54.6	21.6
1982	30,325	21,769	8,556	74.0	53.1	20.9
1983	29,860	21,196	8,664	72.2	51.2	20.9
1984	31,382	22,302	9,080	77.9	55.3	22.5
1985	31,939	22,235	9,704	80.7	56.2	24.5
19						
1975	34,216	28,177	6,039	102.5	84.4	18.1
1976	32,652	26,617	6,035	95.3	77.7	17.6
1977	33,424	27,303	6,121	94.7	77.4	17.3
1978	35,872	28,953	6,919	99.1	80.0	19.1
1979	38,110	30,015	8,095	102.4	80.6	21.7
1980	37,475	29,187	8,288	96.4	75.1	21.3
1981	37,458	29,087	8,371	94.0	73.0	21.0
1982	36,614	27,961	8,653	90.1	68.8	21.3
1983	35,318	26,872	8,446	84.8	64.5	20.3
1984	36,993	27,691	9,302	89.3	66.9	22.5
1985	37,157	27,489	9,668	91.7	67.9	23.9

* Rates per 1,000 women aged 13-15.
† Rates per 1,000 women aged 13.

TABLE 12.4 Conceptions inside marriage: proportions to women in different age-groups leading to maternities or abortions (under the 1967 Act), 1975-1985

Age of woman at conception and year of conception	Total number of conceptions inside marriage (000s)	Percentage of conceptions inside marriage				Age of woman at conception and year of conception	Total number of conceptions inside marriage (000s)	Percentage of conceptions inside marriage			
		All marriages	First marriage	Second or later marriage	Terminated by abortion			All marriages	First marriage	Second or later marriage	Terminated by abortion
All ages						**30-34**					
1975	532.8	91.9	88.0	4.0	8.1	1975	78.1	86.0	77.9	8.1	14.0
1976	515.9	92.0	87.6	4.4	8.0	1976	81.0	86.8	78.1	8.8	13.2
1977	523.0	92.3	87.6	4.7	7.7	1977	91.4	88.0	78.9	9.0	12.0
1978	563.8	92.3	87.1	5.2	7.7	1978	107.4	88.6	78.8	9.8	11.4
1979	570.6	92.2	86.8	5.4	7.8	1979	112.0	88.6	78.6	10.0	11.4
1980	556.4	92.2	86.6	5.6	7.8	1980	110.4	88.9	78.8	10.2	11.1
1981	538.0	92.1	86.2	5.9	7.9	1981	109.0	89.1	78.5	10.6	10.9
1982	528.6	92.4	86.3	6.1	7.6	1982	104.4	89.5	78.2	11.3	10.5
1983	517.0	92.6	86.3	6.3	7.4	1983	102.4	90.2	78.7	11.6	9.8
1984	526.8	92.7	86.2	6.5	7.3	1984	105.7	90.7	79.0	11.7	9.3
1985	513.7	92.6	86.1	6.6	7.4	1985	105.7	90.9	79.2	11.7	9.1
Under 20						**35-39**					
1975	35.9	96.9	96.7	0.3	3.1	1975	28.5	69.1	59.7	9.4	30.9
1976	32.6	96.6	96.2	0.3	3.4	1976	26.7	69.2	59.2	10.1	30.8
1977	31.7	96.9	96.7	0.2	3.1	1977	26.8	70.3	59.5	10.8	29.7
1978	32.4	96.6	96.4	0.2	3.4	1978	29.7	70.6	58.4	12.2	29.4
1979	32.2	96.5	96.2	0.2	3.5	1979	32.0	71.7	59.3	12.4	28.3
1980	29.7	96.4	96.1	0.3	3.6	1980	32.6	72.6	59.8	12.8	27.4
1981	27.7	96.2	96.0	0.2	3.8	1981	33.0	72.1	59.2	12.9	27.2
1982	24.1	96.2	96.0	0.2	3.8	1982	35.9	75.1	61.1	14.0	24.9
1983	21.3	96.6	96.4	0.2	3.4	1983	37.3	76.6	61.8	14.8	23.4
1984	20.4	96.1	96.0	0.1	3.9	1984	38.6	77.7	61.8	15.9	22.3
1985	18.3	96.1	95.9	0.2	3.9	1985	38.4	78.4	61.9	16.4	21.6
20-24						**40 and over**					
1975	176.3	96.4	94.9	1.5	3.6	1975	8.5	49.4	42.9	6.6	50.6
1976	166.7	96.2	94.6	1.7	3.8	1976	7.9	47.9	40.9	7.0	52.1
1977	169.0	96.4	94.7	1.8	3.6	1977	8.2	49.6	42.2	7.4	50.4
1978	179.7	96.3	94.5	1.8	3.7	1978	8.1	48.8	40.6	8.2	51.2
1979	180.4	96.1	94.3	1.8	3.9	1979	8.1	49.1	40.5	8.6	50.9
1980	176.3	96.2	94.4	1.8	3.8	1980	8.3	50.7	40.8	9.8	49.6
1981	169.6	96.0	94.1	1.9	4.0	1981	7.9	51.2	41.9	9.2	49.1
1982	166.2	96.2	94.5	1.7	3.8	1982	7.6	52.6	42.4	10.3	47.4
1983	158.8	96.2	94.6	1.6	3.8	1983	7.4	56.0	44.5	11.4	44.0
1984	158.6	96.1	94.5	1.7	3.9	1984	7.5	56.6	44.6	12.0	43.4
1985	149.4	95.8	94.2	1.6	4.2	1985	7.3	57.0	44.0	13.0	43.0
25-29											
1975	205.5	94.4	90.4	4.3	5.6						
1976	201.1	94.6	89.9	4.7	5.4						
1977	195.9	94.9	89.9	5.0	5.1						
1978	206.4	94.9	89.6	5.3	5.1						
1979	205.9	94.8	89.2	5.6	5.2						
1980	199.1	94.9	89.0	5.9	5.1						
1981	190.2	94.9	88.8	6.0	5.1						
1982	190.4	95.0	88.8	6.2	5.0						
1983	189.7	95.0	88.8	6.2	5.0						
1984	196.0	95.1	88.9	6.2	4.9						
1985	194.7	94.9	88.9	6.0	5.1						

TABLE 12.5 Conceptions outside marriage: proportion to women in different age-groups leading to maternities or abortions (under the 1967 Act), 1975-1985

England and Wales

Residents

Age of woman at conception and year of conception	Total number of conceptions outside marriage (000s)	Percentage of conceptions outside marriage				
		Leading to maternities				Terminated by abortion
		Illegitimate			Legitimate	
		Total	Sole*	Joint†		
All ages						
1975	160.6	34.0	17.0	17.0	26.5	39.5
1976	155.7	34.7	16.6	18.1	24.9	40.4
1977	163.4	36.1	16.7	19.3	24.5	39.4
1978	184.2	36.4	16.5	19.9	24.2	39.4
1979	203.5	36.9	16.2	20.7	23.4	39.7
1980	208.6	38.4	16.1	22.3	21.6	40.0
1981	214.3	40.5	16.7	23.7	19.3	40.2
1982	226.7	42.7	16.8	25.9	18.3	38.9
1983	236.4	44.6	16.8	27.9	17.3	38.1
1984	263.4	46.6	16.6	30.0	16.2	37.2
1985	283.5	48.1	16.5	31.5	14.9	37.0
Under 16						
1975	9.1	37.9	27.4	10.5	9.8	52.3
1976	9.2	36.7	25.3	11.5	9.8	53.4
1977	9.0	38.1	25.7	12.4	8.6	53.3
1978	9.1	39.3	25.3	14.0	8.9	51.7
1979	9.1	37.8	24.4	13.4	6.9	55.4
1980	8.5	39.5	24.6	14.8	6.2	54.3
1981	8.5	37.9	23.8	14.1	4.9	57.1
1982	9.0	39.0	23.8	15.2	3.9	57.1
1983	9.3	39.9	24.1	15.7	3.3	56.9
1984	9.6	41.3	23.9	17.4	2.9	55.9
1985	9.4	41.9	23.6	18.3	2.3	55.8
Under 20						
1975	76.1	31.1	19.7	11.5	31.3	37.5
1976	73.1	31.9	19.3	12.6	29.0	39.1
1977	75.5	33.3	19.5	13.9	27.8	38.8
1978	82.2	34.3	19.4	14.8	27.3	38.5
1979	88.8	34.4	18.8	15.6	25.6	40.0
1980	87.6	36.7	18.6	18.1	23.0	40.3
1981	87.4	38.9	19.4	19.5	20.3	40.8
1982	89.8	41.6	19.6	22.0	18.3	40.1
1983	91.0	43.7	19.5	24.3	16.0	40.2
1984	97.9	46.1	19.5	26.6	14.4	39.5
1985	101.0	48.2	19.6	28.6	12.6	39.2
20-24						
1975	45.5	33.8	15.7	18.1	25.1	41.1
1976	43.4	34.9	15.5	19.4	23.6	41.5
1977	46.2	36.6	15.8	20.9	24.1	39.3
1978	53.6	36.8	15.6	21.1	23.8	39.5
1979	61.1	37.7	15.6	22.1	23.7	38.7
1980	65.7	39.1	15.9	23.2	22.3	38.6
1981	68.5	40.8	16.0	24.8	19.8	39.4
1982	74.5	43.0	16.2	26.8	19.3	37.7
1983	79.1	44.8	16.3	28.6	18.7	36.5
1984	90.4	46.4	15.8	30.7	17.8	35.8
1985	99.8	47.7	15.7	32.0	16.5	35.9
25-29						
1975	22.3	39.4	13.8	25.6	20.4	40.2
1976	22.6	39.5	13.1	26.4	20.5	40.1
1977	23.0	40.8	13.5	27.3	21.1	38.2
1978	26.5	41.1	13.4	27.6	21.3	37.6
1979	28.9	41.5	13.8	27.8	20.9	37.5
1980	30.0	41.1	12.7	28.3	21.1	37.8
1981	31.6	44.2	15.2	29.1	18.3	37.4
1982	34.6	45.6	14.5	31.1	18.5	36.0
1983	36.7	47.3	14.7	32.6	18.4	34.3
1984	42.6	49.0	14.6	34.4	17.5	33.5
1985	48.0	49.5	14.7	34.8	16.6	33.9
30-34						
1975	10.2	41.6	12.8	28.8	17.3	41.0
1976	10.3	41.4	12.3	29.2	17.9	40.7
1977	12.0	41.8	12.0	29.8	18.3	39.9
1978	14.1	40.4	12.0	28.5	19.3	40.3
1979	16.1	41.3	11.8	29.5	19.4	39.3
1980	16.5	41.9	12.5	29.4	17.4	40.7
1981	17.3	42.1	12.2	29.9	18.8	39.1
1982	17.6	45.3	13.2	32.0	17.6	37.2
1983	18.5	46.5	12.7	33.7	17.2	36.3
1984	20.4	48.1	13.4	34.7	16.8	35.1
1985	22.1	49.8	13.3	36.5	15.9	34.2
35-39						
1975	4.9	41.0	13.7	27.3	14.9	44.1
1976	4.8	39.2	12.6	26.6	14.0	46.8
1977	5.1	37.9	12.4	25.5	15.1	47.0
1978	6.0	36.3	11.3	25.0	15.1	48.6
1979	6.6	36.4	11.1	25.3	14.6	49.0
1980	6.7	34.9	10.7	24.1	14.9	50.1
1981	7.5	39.0	11.7	27.3	12.5	48.5
1982	8.3	38.5	11.4	27.1	13.9	47.6
1983	9.1	40.3	11.7	28.6	14.5	45.1
1984	9.9	42.8	11.7	31.2	13.9	43.3
1985	10.4	44.6	12.1	32.5	13.4	42.0
40 and over						
1975	1.5	34.6	12.6	22.0	11.3	54.1
1976	1.4	33.9	11.3	22.6	9.9	56.2
1977	1.6	32.0	11.3	20.7	10.3	57.7
1978	1.8	27.2	10.0	17.2	9.8	63.0
1979	2.0	27.4	10.6	16.8	8.9	63.7
1980	2.1	30.5	10.6	19.7	7.1	62.6
1981	2.0	29.9	7.7	22.1	7.7	62.6
1982	2.0	30.7	10.5	20.2	8.3	61.0
1983	2.0	31.5	10.7	20.7	9.1	59.4
1984	2.2	30.7	9.6	21.1	9.9	59.4
1985	2.3	31.8	9.4	22.4	9.2	59.0

* Conceptions leading to illegitimate births registered by the mother alone.
† Conceptions leading to illegitimate births registered by both parents.

TABLE 12.6 Conceptions inside marriage: numbers and rates to women in different age-groups leading to maternities or abortions (under the 1967 Act), 1975-1985

England and Wales

Residents

Age of woman at conception and year of conception	Numbers of conceptions (thousands)					Conception rates per 1,000 married women in age-group/age				
	Total conceptions inside marriage	Conceptions leading to live or still maternities during			Conceptions terminated by abortion	Total conceptions inside marriage	Conceptions leading to live or still maternities during			Conceptions terminated by abortion
		All marriages	First marriage	Second or later marriage			All marriages	First marriage	Second or later marriage	
All ages* 1975	532.8	489.8	468.6	21.2	43.0	86.3	76.3	73.0	3.3	6.7
1976	515.9	474.8	452.1	22.7	41.2	80.7	74.3	70.7	3.5	6.4
1977	523.0	482.8	458.3	24.5	40.2	82.3	75.9	72.1	3.9	6.3
1978	563.8	520.3	491.2	29.1	43.5	89.2	82.3	77.7	4.6	6.9
1979	570.6	525.8	495.0	30.8	44.8	90.5	83.4	78.5	4.9	7.1
1980	556.4	513.2	482.0	31.2	43.1	88.6	81.7	76.7	5.0	6.9
1981	538.0	495.7	463.9	31.8	42.3	86.3	79.5	74.4	5.1	6.8
1982	528.6	488.3	456.0	32.3	40.3	85.7	79.2	73.9	5.2	6.5
1983	517.0	478.8	446.1	32.6	38.3	84.6	78.4	73.0	5.3	6.3
1984	526.8	488.5	454.2	34.2	38.3	86.7	80.4	74.8	5.6	6.3
1985	513.7	475.8	442.1	33.7	37.9	85.0	78.8	73.2	5.6	6.3
Under 16† 1975	0.0	0.0	0.0	–	0.0	:	:	:	:	:
1976	0.0	0.0	0.0	–	0.0	:	:	:	:	:
1977	0.0	0.0	0.0	–	0.0	:	:	:	:	:
1978	0.0	0.0	0.0	–	0.0	:	:	:	:	:
1979	0.0	0.0	0.0	–	0.0	:	:	:	:	:
1980	0.0	0.0	0.0	–	0.0	:	:	:	:	:
1981	0.1	0.0	0.0	–	0.0	:	:	:	:	:
1982	0.0	0.0	0.0	–	0.0	:	:	:	:	:
1983	0.0	0.0	0.0	–	0.0	:	:	:	:	:
1984	0.0	0.0	0.0	0.0	0.0	:	:	:	:	:
1985	0.0	0.0	0.0	–	0.0	:	:	:	:	:
16 1975	0.8	0.8	0.8	0.0	0.0	290.7	278.6	277.5	1.1	12.1
1976	0.8	0.7	0.7	0.0	0.0	313.6	298.4	298.0	0.4	15.0
1977	0.8	0.7	0.7	0.0	0.0	310.0	297.6	296.4	1.2	12.4
1978	0.8	0.8	0.8	0.0	0.0	334.6	313.8	312.9	0.8	20.8
1979	0.8	0.7	0.7	0.0	0.0	329.6	310.9	310.0	0.9	18.7
1980	0.6	0.6	0.6	–	0.0	303.0	282.0	282.0	–	21.0
1981	0.6	0.5	0.5	0.0	0.0	373.3	342.0	341.3	0.7	31.3
1982	0.5	0.5	0.5	–	0.0	370.0	347.7	347.7	–	22.3
1983	0.4	0.4	0.4	0.0	0.0	409.1	392.7	391.8	0.9	16.4
1984	0.5	0.4	0.4	0.0	0.0	479.0	448.0	446.0	2.0	31.0
1985	0.5	0.4	0.4	0.0	0.0	459.0	425.0	422.0	3.0	34.0
17 1975	4.0	3.9	3.9	0.0	0.1	285.2	275.4	274.4	1.0	9.8
1976	3.4	3.3	3.3	0.0	0.1	285.1	274.0	273.1	0.9	11.1
1977	3.4	3.2	3.2	0.0	0.1	302.8	292.3	291.9	0.4	10.5
1978	3.5	3.4	3.4	0.0	0.1	324.7	311.3	310.9	0.4	13.4
1979	3.3	3.2	3.2	0.0	0.1	315.7	302.1	301.5	0.6	13.6
1980	3.0	2.9	2.9	0.0	0.1	316.3	301.4	300.2	1.1	14.9
1981	2.7	2.5	2.5	–	0.1	340.3	323.9	323.8	0.0	16.4
1982	2.3	2.2	2.1	0.0	0.1	308.9	294.8	294.0	0.8	14.1
1983	2.0	1.9	1.9	0.0	0.1	325.4	312.8	312.6	0.2	12.6
1984	2.0	1.9	1.9	0.0	0.1	375.5	358.9	358.5	0.4	16.6
1985	1.8	1.7	1.7	0.0	0.1	386.1	365.2	364.3	0.9	20.9
18 1975	11.7	11.3	11.3	0.0	0.4	281.0	272.1	271.4	0.7	8.9
1976	10.2	9.8	9.8	0.0	0.4	275.1	265.6	264.8	0.9	9.5
1977	9.8	9.5	9.5	0.0	0.3	298.7	289.4	288.8	0.5	9.3
1978	10.0	9.7	9.7	0.0	0.3	326.4	316.1	315.5	0.6	10.3
1979	10.1	9.7	9.7	0.0	0.3	330.0	319.0	318.4	0.5	11.0
1980	9.3	9.0	8.9	0.0	0.3	317.5	306.2	305.4	0.8	11.3
1981	8.2	7.9	7.9	0.0	0.3	317.8	306.5	306.1	0.4	11.3
1982	7.0	6.8	6.8	0.0	0.2	322.7	311.6	311.2	0.4	11.1
1983	6.3	6.1	6.1	0.0	0.2	317.3	306.8	306.4	0.4	10.5
1984	6.0	5.8	5.8	0.0	0.2	354.8	341.8	341.2	0.6	13.0
1985	5.3	5.1	5.1	0.0	0.2	352.6	340.0	339.5	0.5	12.6
19 1975	19.3	18.7	18.7	0.0	0.5	237.8	231.0	230.4	0.6	6.8
1976	18.1	17.5	17.5	0.1	0.6	233.2	225.6	224.8	0.8	7.7
1977	17.8	17.3	17.3	0.0	0.5	252.1	244.6	244.1	0.6	7.4
1978	18.1	17.5	17.4	0.0	0.6	278.1	279.8	268.4	0.7	8.9
1979	18.0	17.4	17.3	0.0	0.6	288.3	278.5	277.8	0.7	9.8
1980	16.7	16.1	16.1	0.1	0.5	271.0	262.1	261.2	0.9	8.9
1981	16.3	15.7	15.7	0.0	0.6	281.7	271.6	271.0	0.6	10.2
1982	14.3	13.8	13.8	0.0	0.5	285.4	274.7	274.1	0.6	10.8
1983	12.6	12.2	12.2	0.0	0.4	277.9	268.9	268.2	0.7	9.0
1984	11.8	11.4	11.4	0.0	0.4	296.9	285.8	285.5	0.3	11.1
1985	10.7	10.3	10.3	0.0	0.4	303.5	292.5	291.7	0.8	10.9

* Rates per 1,000 married women aged 15-44.
† Rates per 1,000 married women aged 13-15.

TABLE 12.6 - *continued*

Age of woman at conception and year of conception	Numbers of conceptions (thousands)					Conception rates per 1,000 married women in age-group				
	Total conceptions inside marriage	Conceptions leading to live or still maternities during			Conceptions terminated by abortion	Total conceptions inside marriage	Conceptions leading to live or still maternities during			Conceptions terminated by abortion
		All marriages	First marriage	Second or later marriage			All marriages	First marriage	Second or later marriage	
Under 20* 1975	35.9	34.8	34.7	0.1	1.1	256.8	249.0	248.3	0.7	7.9
1976	32.6	31.5	31.4	0.1	1.1	251.9	243.2	242.4	0.8	8.7
1977	31.7	30.7	30.7	0.1	1.0	270.4	262.0	261.4	0.6	8.4
1978	32.4	31.3	31.3	0.1	1.1	297.9	287.9	287.2	0.7	10.1
1979	32.2	31.0	31.0	0.1	1.1	304.4	293.6	292.9	0.6	10.8
1980	29.7	28.6	28.5	0.1	1.1	289.5	279.0	278.2	0.9	10.4
1981	27.7	26.7	26.6	0.0	1.1	298.7	287.3	286.8	0.5	11.4
1982	24.1	23.2	23.2	0.0	0.9	299.4	288.0	287.5	0.6	11.4
1983	21.3	20.6	20.6	0.0	0.7	297.6	287.5	287.0	0.5	10.1
1984	20.4	19.6	19.5	0.0	0.8	322.7	310.3	309.8	0.4	12.5
1985	18.3	17.6	17.5	0.0	0.7	326.7	314.0	313.3	0.8	12.7
20-24 1975	176.3	169.8	167.2	2.6	6.4	186.2	179.4	176.7	2.8	6.8
1976	166.7	160.4	157.6	2.8	6.3	180.3	173.5	170.5	3.0	6.8
1977	169.0	163.0	160.0	3.0	6.0	187.5	180.8	177.5	3.3	6.7
1978	179.7	173.0	169.8	3.2	6.7	206.4	198.8	195.0	3.7	7.6
1979	180.4	173.4	170.1	3.3	7.0	213.6	205.3	201.4	3.9	8.3
1980	176.3	169.6	166.4	3.1	6.7	212.5	204.4	200.6	3.8	8.1
1981	169.6	162.8	159.6	3.2	6.8	209.1	200.7	196.7	4.0	8.4
1982	166.2	159.9	157.0	2.9	6.3	212.5	204.4	200.8	3.6	8.1
1983	158.8	152.7	150.2	2.6	6.1	210.6	202.5	199.1	3.4	8.0
1984	158.6	152.5	149.9	2.6	6.1	217.5	209.1	205.5	3.6	8.4
1985	149.4	143.2	140.8	2.4	6.2	214.0	205.1	201.7	3.4	8.9
25-29 1975	205.5	194.1	185.2	8.9	11.4	134.0	126.6	120.8	5.8	7.4
1976	201.1	190.3	180.8	9.5	10.8	132.1	125.0	118.8	6.2	7.1
1977	195.8	185.8	176.1	9.8	10.1	137.3	130.2	123.4	6.8	7.1
1978	206.4	195.8	184.9	10.9	10.6	151.8	144.0	136.0	8.0	7.8
1979	205.9	195.2	183.7	11.5	10.7	156.4	148.3	139.5	8.8	8.1
1980	199.1	189.0	177.3	11.7	10.1	156.0	148.1	138.9	9.2	7.9
1981	190.2	180.5	169.0	11.5	9.8	152.6	144.7	135.5	9.2	7.8
1982	190.4	180.9	169.0	11.8	9.6	155.6	147.8	138.1	9.7	7.8
1983	189.7	180.2	168.4	11.8	9.4	157.2	149.4	139.6	9.8	7.8
1984	196.0	186.4	174.2	12.2	9.7	163.4	155.3	145.2	10.2	8.1
1985	194.7	184.8	173.1	11.6	9.9	161.8	153.6	143.9	9.7	8.2
30-34 1975	78.1	67.2	60.8	6.3	10.9	58.3	50.2	45.4	4.7	8.2
1976	81.0	70.3	63.2	7.1	10.7	58.4	50.7	45.6	5.1	7.7
1977	91.4	80.4	72.1	8.2	11.0	61.2	53.8	48.3	5.5	7.4
1978	107.4	95.1	84.6	10.5	12.3	69.6	61.6	54.8	6.8	7.9
1979	112.0	99.3	88.0	11.2	12.7	71.9	63.7	56.5	7.2	8.2
1980	110.4	98.2	86.9	11.2	12.2	70.8	62.9	55.8	7.2	7.8
1981	109.0	97.1	85.6	11.5	11.8	70.6	62.9	55.4	7.5	7.7
1982	104.4	93.4	81.6	11.8	10.9	72.4	64.8	56.7	8.2	7.6
1983	102.4	92.4	80.6	11.9	10.0	74.6	67.3	58.7	8.6	7.3
1984	105.7	95.8	83.4	12.4	9.8	79.2	71.8	62.5	9.3	7.4
1985	105.7	96.1	83.7	12.3	9.6	81.1	73.7	64.2	9.5	7.4
35-39 1975	28.5	19.7	17.0	2.7	8.8	22.8	15.7	13.6	2.1	7.0
1976	26.7	18.5	15.8	2.7	8.2	21.6	15.0	12.8	2.2	6.6
1977	26.8	18.8	16.0	2.9	8.0	21.8	15.3	13.0	2.3	6.5
1978	29.7	21.0	17.4	3.6	8.7	23.8	16.8	13.9	2.9	7.0
1979	32.0	22.9	19.0	4.0	9.1	25.0	17.9	14.8	3.1	7.1
1980	32.6	23.6	19.5	4.2	8.9	24.9	18.1	14.9	3.2	6.8
1981	33.0	23.8	19.6	4.3	9.0	24.5	17.6	14.5	3.2	6.7
1982	35.9	26.9	21.9	5.0	8.9	24.6	18.5	15.0	3.5	6.1
1983	37.3	28.6	23.1	5.5	8.7	24.8	19.0	15.3	3.7	5.8
1984	38.6	30.0	23.8	6.1	8.6	25.4	19.7	15.7	4.0	5.7
1985	38.4	30.1	23.8	6.3	8.3	25.1	19.7	15.6	4.1	5.4
40 and over† 1975	8.5	4.2	3.6	0.6	4.3	7.2	3.5	3.0	0.5	3.5
1976	7.9	3.8	3.2	0.6	4.1	6.8	3.2	2.7	0.5	3.4
1977	8.2	4.0	3.4	0.6	4.1	7.2	3.4	2.9	0.5	3.5
1978	8.1	3.9	3.3	0.7	4.1	7.2	3.3	2.7	0.6	3.5
1979	8.1	4.0	3.3	0.7	4.1	7.2	3.3	2.7	0.6	3.4
1980	8.3	4.2	3.4	0.8	4.1	7.4	3.5	2.8	0.7	3.4
1981	7.9	4.0	3.3	0.7	3.9	7.2	3.4	2.8	0.6	3.2
1982	7.6	4.0	3.2	0.8	3.6	6.8	3.4	2.7	0.7	3.0
1983	7.4	4.2	3.3	0.8	3.3	6.7	3.5	2.8	0.7	2.7
1984	7.5	4.2	3.3	0.9	3.2	6.1	3.5	2.7	0.7	2.7
1985	7.3	4.2	3.2	0.9	3.1	5.8	3.3	2.6	0.8	2.5

* Rates per 1,000 married women aged 15-19.
† Rates per 1,000 married women aged 40-44.

TABLE 12.7   Conceptions outside marriage: numbers and rates to women in different age-groups leading to maternities or abortions (under the 1967 Act), 1975-1985

England and Wales

Residents

Age of woman at conception and year of conception		Numbers of conceptions (thousands)						Conception rates per 1,000 unmarried women in age-group/age					
		Total conceptions outside marriage	Conceptions leading to live or still maternities				Conceptions terminated by abortion	Total conceptions outside marriage	Conceptions leading to live or still maternities				Conceptions terminated by abortion
			Total	Illegit-imate	Legitimate following marriage after conception				Total	Illegit-imate	Legitimate following marriage after conception		
					All marriages	First marriage					All marriages	First marriage	
All ages*	1975	160.6	97.1	54.6	42.5	37.6	63.4	50.8	30.7	17.3	13.4	11.9	20.0
	1976	155.7	92.7	54.0	38.7	33.7	62.9	47.3	28.2	16.4	11.8	10.2	19.1
	1977	163.4	99.1	58.9	40.1	34.6	64.4	47.5	28.8	17.1	11.7	10.0	18.7
	1978	184.2	111.7	67.1	44.6	37.8	72.5	51.1	31.0	18.6	12.4	10.5	20.1
	1979	203.5	122.7	75.2	47.5	40.3	80.8	54.0	32.6	19.9	12.6	10.7	21.4
	1980	208.6	125.2	80.1	45.1	38.1	83.4	52.9	31.8	20.3	11.4	9.7	21.2
	1981	214.3	128.2	86.7	41.4	34.6	86.1	52.0	31.1	21.1	10.1	8.4	20.9
	1982	226.7	138.5	96.9	41.6	34.5	88.2	53.0	32.4	22.6	9.7	8.1	20.6
	1983	236.4	146.3	105.5	40.8	33.6	90.1	53.3	33.0	23.8	9.2	7.6	20.3
	1984	263.4	165.3	122.7	42.6	35.0	98.0	57.5	36.1	26.8	9.3	7.6	21.4
	1985	283.5	178.6	136.3	42.2	34.6	105.0	60.0	37.8	28.9	8.9	7.3	22.2
Under 16†	1975	9.1	4.4	3.5	0.9	0.9	4.8	8.1	3.8	3.0	0.8	0.8	4.2
	1976	9.2	4.3	3.4	0.9	0.9	4.9	7.9	3.7	2.9	0.8	0.8	4.2
	1977	9.0	4.2	3.4	0.8	0.8	4.8	7.6	3.5	2.9	0.6	0.6	4.0
	1978	9.1	4.4	3.6	0.8	0.8	4.7	7.5	3.6	3.0	0.7	0.7	3.9
	1979	9.1	4.0	3.4	0.6	0.6	5.0	7.5	3.4	2.8	0.5	0.5	4.2
	1980	8.5	3.9	3.4	0.5	0.5	4.6	7.1	3.3	2.8	0.4	0.4	3.9
	1981	8.5	3.6	3.2	0.4	0.4	4.9	7.2	3.1	2.7	0.4	0.4	4.1
	1982	9.0	3.8	3.5	0.4	0.3	5.1	7.8	3.3	3.0	0.3	0.3	4.4
	1983	9.3	4.0	3.7	0.3	0.3	5.3	8.3	3.6	3.3	0.3	0.3	4.7
	1984	9.6	4.2	4.0	0.3	0.3	5.4	8.6	3.8	3.5	0.2	0.2	4.8
	1985	9.4	4.1	3.9	0.2	0.2	5.2	8.6	3.8	3.6	0.2	0.2	4.8
16	1975	14.5	8.7	4.5	4.1	4.1	5.8	40.9	24.5	12.8	11.7	11.6	16.4
	1976	13.8	8.0	4.5	3.5	3.5	5.8	37.8	22.0	12.3	9.7	9.7	15.8
	1977	14.2	8.2	4.7	3.4	3.4	6.0	37.3	21.5	12.5	9.0	8.9	15.8
	1978	15.0	8.7	5.3	3.4	3.4	6.3	38.5	22.3	13.5	8.8	8.8	16.2
	1979	15.3	8.6	5.5	3.1	3.1	6.8	38.9	21.8	13.9	7.9	7.9	17.1
	1980	14.6	8.0	5.7	2.4	2.4	6.6	36.1	19.8	14.0	5.9	5.9	16.2
	1981	14.8	8.3	6.1	2.2	2.2	6.6	36.5	20.3	14.9	5.4	5.4	16.2
	1982	14.5	7.9	6.0	1.9	1.9	6.7	36.5	19.8	15.0	4.7	4.7	16.8
	1983	14.8	8.0	6.5	1.5	1.5	6.8	37.7	20.4	16.6	3.8	3.8	17.3
	1984	15.5	8.4	7.0	1.4	1.4	7.1	40.8	22.1	18.4	3.6	3.6	18.7
	1985	15.7	8.7	7.4	1.3	1.3	7.0	41.3	22.9	19.5	3.4	3.3	18.4
17	1975	19.3	12.8	5.7	7.1	7.1	6.5	57.6	38.3	17.1	21.2	21.1	19.3
	1976	18.2	11.8	5.7	6.2	6.2	6.4	52.7	34.2	16.2	18.0	17.9	18.4
	1977	18.4	11.9	6.0	5.9	5.9	6.5	51.5	33.3	16.8	16.6	16.6	18.2
	1978	20.0	12.9	6.6	6.3	6.3	7.1	53.5	34.4	17.7	16.8	16.8	19.1
	1979	21.5	13.5	7.3	6.2	6.2	8.0	56.3	35.3	19.2	16.1	16.1	21.0
	1980	20.9	12.9	7.7	5.2	5.2	8.0	53.6	33.2	19.8	13.3	13.3	20.5
	1981	20.5	12.5	7.8	4.7	4.7	8.1	51.3	31.1	19.5	11.6	11.6	20.1
	1982	20.7	12.9	8.8	4.1	4.0	7.8	51.2	31.9	21.9	10.0	10.0	19.3
	1983	20.6	12.5	9.1	3.5	3.5	8.0	51.9	31.6	22.9	8.8	8.8	20.3
	1984	22.2	13.7	10.5	3.2	3.2	8.5	57.1	35.3	27.0	8.3	8.3	21.8
	1985	22.8	14.2	11.5	2.7	2.7	8.6	60.3	37.6	30.3	7.2	7.2	22.7
18	1975	18.2	12.2	5.4	6.8	6.8	6.0	61.0	40.9	18.1	22.8	22.7	20.2
	1976	17.4	11.3	5.3	6.0	6.0	6.1	53.3	35.9	17.9	19.1	19.0	19.4
	1977	18.4	12.0	5.9	6.1	6.1	6.4	56.4	36.7	18.0	18.7	18.7	19.7
	1978	20.4	13.2	6.7	6.5	6.4	7.2	59.9	38.8	19.8	19.0	19.0	21.2
	1979	22.7	14.5	7.5	6.9	6.9	8.2	63.8	40.7	21.2	19.5	19.4	23.1
	1980	22.8	14.4	8.1	6.3	5.7	8.4	62.3	39.4	22.2	17.1	17.1	22.9
	1981	22.4	14.0	8.6	5.4	5.1	8.4	59.7	37.4	23.0	14.4	14.3	22.3
	1982	23.3	15.0	9.7	5.2	5.2	8.3	60.0	38.6	25.1	13.5	13.5	21.4
	1983	23.6	15.1	10.5	4.7	4.7	8.5	59.8	38.4	26.6	11.8	11.8	21.5
	1984	25.4	16.5	12.0	4.5	4.5	8.9	65.7	42.7	31.0	11.8	11.7	22.9
	1985	26.6	17.1	13.0	4.1	4.1	9.5	70.0	45.0	34.1	10.8	10.8	25.0
19	1975	15.0	9.5	4.6	4.9	4.9	5.5	59.2	37.5	18.0	19.4	19.3	21.7
	1976	14.5	9.1	4.5	4.5	4.5	5.4	54.8	34.3	17.1	17.1	16.9	20.5
	1977	15.6	10.0	5.2	4.8	4.8	5.6	55.2	35.4	18.3	17.0	16.8	19.8
	1978	17.8	11.5	6.0	5.4	5.4	6.3	59.9	38.6	20.3	15.3	18.3	21.3
	1979	20.2	12.7	6.8	5.9	5.9	7.5	65.0	40.8	21.8	19.0	19.5	24.2
	1980	20.8	13.0	7.3	5.7	5.7	7.7	63.6	39.9	22.3	17.6	17.9	23.7
	1981	21.2	13.4	8.3	5.1	5.1	7.8	62.2	39.3	24.4	14.9	14.8	22.8
	1982	22.3	14.2	9.3	4.9	4.9	8.1	62.5	39.8	26.1	13.7	13.6	22.8
	1983	22.7	14.7	10.0	4.6	4.6	8.0	61.3	39.6	27.1	12.5	12.5	21.7
	1984	25.2	16.3	11.7	4.7	4.7	8.9	67.2	43.6	31.1	12.5	12.4	23.7
	1985	26.4	17.2	12.8	4.3	4.3	9.3	71.5	46.4	34.7	11.7	11.6	25.1

* Rates per 1,000 unmarried women aged 15-44.
† Rates per 1,000 unmarried women aged 13-15.

TABLE 12.7 - *continued*

Age of woman at conception and year of conception	Numbers of conceptions (thousands)						Conception rates per 1,000 unmarried women in age-group					
	Total conceptions outside marriage	Conceptions leading to live or still maternities				Conceptions terminated by abortion	Total conceptions outside marriage	Conceptions leading to live or still maternities				Conceptions terminated by abortion
		Total	Illegitimate	Legitimate following marriage after conception				Total	Illegitimate	Legitimate following marriage after conception		
				All marriages	First marriage					All marriages	First marriage	
Under 20* 1975	76.1	47.5	23.7	23.9	23.8	28.6	47.4	29.6	14.7	14.8	14.8	17.8
1976	73.1	44.5	23.3	21.2	21.1	28.6	43.7	26.6	14.0	12.7	12.6	17.1
1977	75.5	46.2	25.2	21.0	21.0	29.3	43.5	26.6	14.5	12.1	12.1	16.9
1978	82.2	50.5	28.1	22.4	22.3	31.6	45.8	28.2	15.7	12.5	12.4	17.6
1979	88.8	53.3	30.5	22.7	22.7	35.5	48.1	28.8	16.5	12.3	12.3	19.2
1980	87.6	52.3	32.2	20.1	20.0	35.3	46.2	27.6	17.0	10.6	10.6	18.6
1981	87.4	51.8	34.0	17.7	17.7	35.7	45.5	26.9	17.7	9.2	9.2	18.6
1982	89.8	53.8	37.3	16.4	16.4	36.0	46.3	27.7	19.3	8.5	8.4	18.6
1983	91.0	54.4	39.8	14.6	14.6	36.6	47.0	28.1	20.6	7.5	7.5	18.9
1984	97.9	59.2	45.1	14.1	14.1	38.7	51.2	31.0	23.6	7.4	7.4	20.3
1985	101.0	61.4	48.7	12.7	12.6	39.6	53.8	32.7	25.9	6.8	6.7	21.1
20-24 1975	45.5	26.8	15.4	11.4	10.2	18.7	63.2	37.2	21.4	15.8	14.1	26.0
1976	43.4	25.4	15.1	10.2	9.0	18.0	58.4	34.2	20.4	13.8	12.1	24.2
1977	46.2	28.0	16.9	11.1	9.7	18.2	59.1	35.8	21.6	14.2	12.4	23.2
1978	53.6	32.5	19.7	12.7	11.1	21.2	64.0	38.8	23.5	15.2	13.3	25.3
1979	61.1	37.5	23.0	14.5	12.8	23.6	68.6	42.1	25.8	16.2	14.3	26.5
1980	65.7	40.4	25.7	14.7	12.9	25.3	68.5	42.1	26.8	15.3	13.5	26.4
1981	68.5	41.5	27.9	13.6	12.1	27.0	66.1	40.1	27.0	13.1	11.6	26.1
1982	74.5	46.4	32.0	14.4	12.9	28.1	67.0	41.7	28.8	12.9	11.6	25.3
1983	79.1	50.2	35.5	14.8	13.3	28.9	66.2	42.0	29.7	12.4	11.1	24.2
1984	90.4	58.1	42.0	16.1	14.6	32.4	71.9	45.5	32.9	12.6	11.4	25.4
1985	99.8	64.0	47.5	16.4	14.9	35.8	73.7	47.2	35.1	12.1	11.0	26.4
25-29 1975	22.3	13.4	8.8	4.6	2.7	9.0	69.7	41.7	27.5	14.2	8.3	28.0
1976	22.6	13.6	8.9	4.6	2.6	9.1	67.2	40.3	26.5	13.8	7.8	26.9
1977	23.0	14.2	9.4	4.8	2.7	8.8	67.2	41.5	27.4	14.2	7.9	25.6
1978	26.5	16.5	10.9	5.6	3.1	10.0	74.0	46.1	30.4	15.7	8.6	27.8
1979	28.9	18.0	12.0	6.1	3.4	10.8	76.8	48.0	31.9	16.1	8.9	28.8
1980	30.0	18.6	12.3	6.3	3.6	11.4	75.6	47.0	31.0	16.0	9.0	28.6
1981	31.6	19.8	14.0	5.8	3.3	11.8	74.5	46.6	32.9	13.7	7.9	27.9
1982	34.6	22.1	15.8	6.4	3.7	12.4	76.2	48.8	34.7	14.1	8.1	27.4
1983	36.7	24.1	17.3	6.7	4.0	12.6	75.3	49.5	35.6	13.9	8.2	25.8
1984	42.6	28.3	20.9	7.5	4.6	14.3	80.7	53.7	39.5	14.1	8.6	27.0
1985	48.0	31.7	23.7	8.0	5.1	16.2	82.8	54.7	41.0	13.8	8.8	28.1
30-34 1975	10.2	6.0	4.2	1.8	0.7	4.2	55.1	32.5	22.9	9.6	3.8	22.6
1976	10.3	6.1	4.3	1.8	0.7	4.2	51.7	30.6	21.4	9.2	3.6	21.0
1977	12.0	7.2	5.0	2.2	0.9	4.8	52.6	31.6	21.9	9.6	3.9	21.0
1978	14.1	8.4	5.7	2.7	1.0	5.7	56.6	33.8	22.9	10.9	3.9	22.8
1979	16.1	9.8	6.6	3.1	1.2	6.3	60.9	36.9	25.1	11.8	4.6	23.9
1980	16.5	9.8	6.9	2.9	1.1	6.7	58.3	34.6	24.4	10.1	4.0	23.7
1981	17.3	10.5	7.3	3.2	1.3	6.8	57.1	34.8	24.1	10.7	4.3	22.3
1982	17.6	11.0	7.9	3.1	1.2	6.5	57.1	35.9	25.8	10.0	3.9	21.2
1983	18.5	11.8	8.6	3.2	1.3	6.7	58.0	36.9	26.9	10.0	4.2	21.1
1984	20.4	13.2	9.8	3.4	1.4	7.1	61.2	39.7	29.4	10.3	4.2	21.5
1985	22.1	14.5	11.0	3.5	1.5	7.6	63.6	41.9	31.7	10.1	4.4	21.8
35-39 1975	4.9	2.8	2.0	0.7	0.2	2.2	30.4	17.0	12.5	4.5	1.4	13.4
1976	4.8	2.6	1.9	0.7	0.2	2.3	29.0	15.4	11.4	4.0	1.3	13.6
1977	5.1	2.7	1.9	0.8	0.2	2.4	29.1	15.4	11.0	4.4	1.3	13.7
1978	6.0	3.1	2.2	0.9	0.2	2.9	32.7	16.8	11.9	4.9	1.4	15.9
1979	6.6	3.4	2.4	1.0	0.3	3.2	33.6	17.2	12.2	4.9	1.3	16.5
1980	6.7	3.4	2.4	1.0	0.4	3.4	32.2	16.0	11.2	4.8	1.9	16.1
1981	7.5	3.8	2.9	0.9	0.2	3.6	32.6	16.8	12.7	4.1	1.0	15.8
1982	8.3	4.4	3.2	1.2	0.3	4.0	32.5	17.0	12.5	4.5	1.2	15.5
1983	9.1	5.0	3.7	1.3	0.4	4.1	32.4	17.8	13.1	4.7	1.4	14.6
1984	9.9	5.6	4.3	1.4	0.4	4.3	33.4	18.9	14.3	4.6	1.3	14.5
1985	10.4	6.0	4.6	1.4	0.4	4.4	33.0	19.1	14.7	4.4	1.3	13.9
40 and over† 1975	1.5	0.7	0.5	0.2	0.1	0.8	8.9	4.1	3.1	1.0	0.3	4.8
1976	1.4	0.6	0.5	0.1	0.1	0.8	8.2	3.6	2.8	0.8	0.2	4.6
1977	1.6	0.7	0.5	0.2	0.0	0.9	9.3	4.0	3.0	1.0	0.4	5.4
1978	1.8	0.7	0.5	0.2	0.0	1.1	9.8	3.6	2.7	1.0	0.2	6.2
1979	2.0	0.7	0.5	0.2	0.0	1.2	10.2	3.7	2.8	0.9	0.2	6.5
1980	2.1	0.8	0.6	0.1	0.0	1.3	10.4	3.9	3.2	0.7	0.2	6.5
1981	2.0	0.8	0.6	0.2	0.0	1.3	9.8	3.7	2.9	0.8	0.1	6.2
1982	2.0	0.8	0.6	0.2	0.0	1.2	9.4	3.7	2.9	0.8	0.2	5.7
1983	2.0	0.8	0.6	0.2	0.0	1.2	9.2	3.7	2.9	0.8	0.2	5.4
1984	2.2	0.9	0.7	0.2	0.0	1.3	9.2	3.7	2.8	0.9	0.2	5.5
1985	2.3	0.9	0.7	0.2	0.0	1.4	9.2	3.8	2.9	0.8	0.2	5.4

* Rates per 1,000 unmarried women aged 15-19.
† Rates per 1,000 unmarried women aged 40-44.

TABLE 12.8   All conceptions and conceptions outside marriage: proportions leading to maternities or abortions (under the 1967 Act) to women resident in standard regions and metropolitan counties of England and Wales, 1985

England and Wales

Area of usual residence	Total number of conceptions (000s)	Percentage of all conceptions		Percentage of all conceptions		Total number of conceptions outside marriage (000s)	Percentage of conceptions outside marriage				
							Leading to maternities				Terminated by abortion under the 1967 Act
		Inside marriage	Outside marriage	Maternities	Terminated by abortion under the 1967 Act		Illegitimate			Legitimate following marriage	
							Total	Sole*	Joint†		
a. All women											
England and Wales	797.2	64.4	35.6	82.1	17.9	283.5	48.1	16.5	31.5	14.9	37.0
England	753.9	64.4	35.6	81.9	18.1	268.2	48.0	16.4	31.6	14.6	37.4
Wales	43.3	64.6	35.4	84.6	15.4	15.4	49.0	18.7	30.3	19.8	31.2
Standard regions											
Northern	46.1	63.6	36.4	86.9	13.1	16.8	55.9	20.0	35.9	17.4	26.7
Yorkshire and Humberside	76.3	63.8	36.2	84.8	15.2	27.6	52.5	18.3	34.2	16.7	30.7
East Midlands	58.4	66.5	33.5	85.5	14.5	19.6	53.5	17.4	36.0	15.5	31.0
East Anglia	28.6	70.8	29.2	84.6	15.4	8.4	46.4	14.3	32.2	17.1	36.4
South East	290.9	64.1	35.9	78.2	21.8	104.4	42.1	13.7	28.4	12.9	45.0
South West	64.0	68.8	31.2	84.6	15.4	20.0	46.2	15.9	30.3	17.4	36.3
West Midlands	85.6	64.8	35.2	81.8	18.2	30.1	49.1	17.0	32.1	14.3	36.6
North West	104.2	60.2	39.8	83.8	16.2	41.4	54.7	20.5	34.2	14.4	31.0
Metropolitan counties											
Greater London	133.2	57.4	42.6	72.5	27.5	56.8	41.1	13.6	27.5	9.9	49.0
Greater Manchester	43.6	58.6	41.4	83.7	16.3	18.1	56.1	19.6	36.5	13.7	30.2
Merseyside	24.4	56.5	43.5	83.0	17.0	10.6	56.9	24.2	32.7	11.9	31.2
South Yorkshire	20.1	62.0	38.0	83.6	16.4	7.6	50.6	18.3	32.2	17.9	31.5
Tyne and Wear	17.6	60.3	39.7	86.3	13.7	7.0	56.7	20.6	36.1	16.8	26.5
West Midlands	47.1	62.0	38.0	80.7	19.3	17.9	52.0	18.9	33.1	11.8	36.2
West Yorkshire	33.7	63.6	36.4	85.1	14.9	12.3	53.6	18.7	34.9	16.4	30.0
b. Women aged under 20											
England and Wales	119.3	15.3	84.7	66.2	33.8	101.0	48.2	19.6	28.6	12.6	39.2
England	112.0	15.3	84.7	65.8	34.2	94.8	48.1	19.5	28.6	12.2	39.7
Wales	7.3	15.2	84.8	72.1	27.9	6.2	49.8	21.8	28.0	17.9	32.3
Standard regions											
Northern	8.1	13.3	86.7	74.8	25.2	7.0	56.5	22.8	33.7	14.9	28.6
Yorkshire and Humberside	13.1	16.6	83.4	71.7	28.3	11.0	52.8	21.3	31.6	13.9	33.3
East Midlands	9.2	16.2	83.8	70.1	29.9	7.7	51.9	20.1	31.8	13.0	35.0
East Anglia	3.9	18.6	81.4	64.8	35.2	3.2	43.5	16.6	27.0	14.2	42.3
South East	36.8	15.3	84.7	58.3	41.7	31.2	41.2	16.6	24.6	10.6	48.2
South West	8.7	15.8	84.2	63.5	36.5	7.3	43.9	17.6	26.3	13.4	42.7
West Midlands	14.1	17.1	82.9	65.9	34.1	11.7	47.2	19.0	28.1	12.3	40.5
North West	18.0	12.6	87.4	71.7	28.3	15.8	56.4	24.0	32.4	11.7	31.9
Metropolitan counties											
Greater London	16.8	15.4	84.6	56.9	43.1	14.2	42.3	16.8	25.5	8.0	49.7
Greater Manchester	8.0	13.0	87.0	73.1	26.9	7.0	58.3	23.3	35.0	11.3	30.4
Merseyside	4.0	8.4	91.6	71.0	29.0	3.7	59.9	28.8	31.1	8.6	31.5
South Yorkshire	3.7	15.6	84.4	70.6	29.4	3.1	50.5	21.0	29.4	15.4	34.2
Tyne and Wear	3.2	12.6	87.4	75.6	24.4	2.8	58.3	23.2	35.1	14.2	27.5
West Midlands	8.3	18.7	81.3	67.7	32.3	6.8	50.6	20.7	29.9	10.4	39.0
West Yorkshire	5.9	18.8	81.2	74.1	25.9	4.8	55.2	22.2	33.0	13.5	31.2

* Conceptions leading to illegitimate births registered by the mother alone.
† Conceptions leading to illegitimate births registered by both parents.

TABLE 12.9 Numbers and rates of conceptions to women resident in standard regions, metropolitan counties and regional health authorities of England and Wales, 1985

England and Wales

Area of women's usual residence	All conceptions				Conceptions at ages under 20				Conceptions at ages under 16			
	Number (000s)	Rates per 1,000 women aged 15-44			Number (000s)	Rates per 1,000 women aged 15-19			Number	Rates per 1,000 women aged 13-15		
		Total	Maternities	Abortions*		Total	Maternities	Abortions*		Total	Maternities	Abortions*
England and Wales	797.2	74.1	60.8	13.3	119.3	61.7	40.8	20.9	9,406	8.6	3.8	4.8
England	753.9	74.1	60.7	13.4	112.0	61.4	40.4	21.0	8,829	8.6	3.8	4.8
Wales	43.3	73.5	62.2	11.3	7.3	66.4	47.9	18.6	577	9.2	4.9	4.3
Standard regions												
Northern	46.1	70.1	60.9	9.2	8.1	67.9	50.8	17.1	683	10.0	5.4	4.7
Yorkshire and Humberside	76.3	72.7	61.6	11.1	13.1	67.7	48.6	19.1	1,046	9.5	4.6	4.9
East Midlands	58.4	69.1	59.0	10.0	9.2	60.3	42.3	18.0	848	9.7	4.6	5.1
East Anglia	28.6	68.2	57.7	10.5	3.9	52.5	34.1	18.5	348	8.3	3.0	5.3
South East	290.9	76.8	60.1	16.7	36.8	56.5	32.9	23.6	2,665	7.4	2.9	4.5
South West	64.0	68.3	57.8	10.5	8.7	50.5	32.1	18.4	702	7.4	2.5	4.9
West Midlands	85.6	76.8	62.8	13.9	14.1	68.3	45.0	23.3	1,184	10.0	4.0	6.0
North West	104.2	76.3	64.0	12.4	18.0	71.6	51.3	20.3	1,353	9.4	4.9	4.5
Metropolitan counties												
Greater London	133.2	86.4	62.6	23.8	16.8	67.5	38.4	29.1	1,071	8.0	3.4	4.6
Greater Manchester	43.6	78.2	65.5	12.8	8.0	77.9	57.0	20.9	645	11.1	5.8	5.3
Merseyside	24.4	77.2	64.0	13.2	4.0	67.5	47.9	19.6	245	7.3	4.2	3.1
South Yorkshire	20.1	71.5	59.8	11.7	3.7	71.6	50.6	21.0	326	11.2	5.2	6.1
Tyne and Wear	17.6	72.9	63.0	10.0	3.2	72.8	55.0	17.8	246	10.0	5.7	4.3
West Midlands	47.1	84.1	67.8	16.2	8.3	78.4	53.1	25.3	669	11.1	4.8	6.3
West Yorkshire	33.7	76.6	65.2	13.4	5.9	72.6	53.8	18.8	442	9.5	5.2	4.3
Regional health authorities												
Northern	46.1	70.1	60.9	9.2	8.1	67.9	50.8	17.1	683	10.0	5.4	4.7
Yorkshire	56.2	73.1	62.3	10.8	9.5	66.3	47.8	18.4	720	8.9	4.4	4.5
Trent	69.1	69.3	58.9	10.4	11.4	63.0	44.4	18.7	1,039	10.1	4.9	5.3
East Anglian	28.6	68.2	57.7	10.5	3.9	52.5	34.1	18.5	348	8.1	2.9	5.2
North West Thames	63.2	79.4	60.1	19.3	7.1	54.3	29.6	24.7	436	6.1	2.2	3.8
North East Thames	69.3	83.1	62.7	20.4	9.3	66.7	38.7	28.0	646	8.3	3.3	5.0
South East Thames	59.4	77.2	60.8	16.4	8.3	60.1	37.3	22.8	612	8.1	3.6	4.6
South West Thames	46.0	72.5	57.2	15.3	5.2	48.0	25.6	22.5	399	6.6	2.4	4.2
Wessex	41.8	69.5	58.4	11.1	5.8	53.2	32.8	20.4	501	8.3	2.6	5.6
Oxford	39.3	70.5	58.9	11.6	5.0	50.1	31.7	18.4	411	7.4	3.2	4.2
South Western	44.7	68.2	58.0	10.2	6.2	51.4	33.4	18.0	491	7.4	2.7	4.7
West Midlands	85.6	76.8	62.8	13.9	14.1	68.3	45.0	23.3	1,184	10.0	4.0	6.0
Mersey	38.8	74.3	62.0	12.3	6.3	64.5	45.0	19.5	423	7.6	4.1	3.6
North Western	65.9	77.6	65.2	12.4	11.9	76.1	55.3	20.8	936	10.5	5.4	5.1

* Legal terminations under the 1967 Abortion Act.

APPENDIX TABLE 1 Estimated population: sex and age, 1976-1986   **England and Wales**

thousands

	Age	Year										
		1976	1977	1978	1979	1980	1981	1982	1983	1984	1985	1986
PERSONS	All ages	49,459.2	49,440.4	49,442.5	49,508.2	49,603.0	49,634.3	49,501.4	49,653.7	49,763.6	49,923.5	50,075.4
MALES	All ages	24,089.1	24,076.2	24,067.3	24,113.1	24,155.5	24,160.1	24,142.6	24,175.9	24,244.2	24,330.0	24,403.5
FEMALES	All ages	25,370.1	25,364.2	25,375.2	25,395.1	25,447.5	25,474.2	24,458.8	25,477.8	25,519.4	25,593.5	25,671.9
	15-44	9,678.2	9,794.7	9,929.4	10,073.6	10,222.3	10,352.0	10,446.3	10,546.2	10,652.3	10,764.5	10,903.1
	15-19	1,799.6	1,852.9	1,902.6	1,952.9	1,996.3	2,015.4	2,020.2	2,007.0	1,973.2	1,932.0	1,906.7
	20-24	1,667.1	1,683.3	1,708.1	1,736.0	1,788.5	1,847.3	1,893.7	1,948.1	2,005.2	2,052.3	2,072.2
	25-29	1,858.9	1,769.3	1,717.8	1,692.7	1,672.9	1,671.4	1,677.1	1,693.2	1,727.9	1,782.4	1,847.0
	30-34	1,588.0	1,721.5	1,792.1	1,821.8	1,842.8	1,845.8	1,748.4	1,692.5	1,667.0	1,650.6	1,658.3
	35-39	1,401.4	1,405.2	1,432.4	1,474.5	1,516.6	1,579.4	1,711.2	1,784.1	1,817.2	1,842.0	1,848.7
	40-44	1,363.2	1,362.5	1,376.4	1,395.7	1,405.2	1,392.7	1,395.7	1,421.3	1,461.8	1,505.2	1,570.1
	45-49	1,441.7	1,424.4	1,405.3	1,381.3	1,363.4	1,352.7	1,352.2	1,366.1	1,384.6	1,393.9	1,382.0

APPENDIX TABLE 2 Estimated female population:
age and marital condition, 1976-1986   **England and Wales**

thousands

	Age	Year										
		1976	1977	1978	1979	1980	1981	1982	1983	1984	1985	1986
Married	15-44	6,390.4	6,356.6	6,323.7	6,305.7	6,281.0	6,234.0	6,166.5	6,108.6	6,072.3	6,041.4	6,019.0
	15-19	129.4	117.3	108.9	105.7	102.5	92.8	80.6	71.7	63.1	55.9	49.3
	20-24	924.5	901.2	870.7	844.5	829.7	811.1	782.1	754.1	729.4	698.2	657.6
	25-29	1,522.2	1,426.8	1,359.7	1,316.6	1,276.0	1,247.1	1,223.7	1,206.4	1,200.0	1,203.3	1,204.4
	30-34	1,387.7	1,493.5	1,543.6	1,557.3	1,559.7	1,543.5	1,440.9	1,373.2	1,334.3	1,303.2	1,291.7
	35-39	1,234.3	1,231.1	1,247.7	1,277.5	1,307.1	1,350.9	1,455.0	1,504.5	1,519.7	1,526.4	1,516.3
	40-44	1,192.3	1,186.7	1,193.1	1,204.1	1,206.0	1,188.6	1,184.2	1,198.7	1,225.8	1,254.4	1,299.7
	45-49	1,233.4	1,216.3	1,195.8	1,172.0	1,153.2	1,140.0	1,134.5	1,140.9	1,150.8	1,152.7	1,136.9
Single, widowed and divorced	15-44	3,287.8	3,438.1	3,605.7	3,767.9	3,941.3	4,118.0	4,279.8	4,437.6	4,580.0	4,723.1	4,884.0
	15-19	1,670.2	1,735.6	1,793.7	1,847.2	1,893.8	1,922.6	1,939.6	1,935.3	1,910.1	1,876.1	1,857.4
	20-24	742.6	782.1	837.4	891.5	958.8	1,036.2	1,111.6	1,194.0	1,275.8	1,354.1	1,414.6
	25-28	336.7	342.5	358.1	376.1	396.9	424.3	453.4	486.8	527.9	579.1	642.6
	30-34	200.3	228.0	248.5	264.5	283.1	302.3	307.5	319.3	332.7	347.4	366.6
	35-39	167.1	174.1	184.7	197.0	209.5	228.5	256.2	279.6	297.5	315.6	332.4
	40-44	170.9	175.8	183.3	191.6	199.2	204.1	211.5	222.6	236.0	250.8	270.4
	45-49	208.3	208.1	209.5	209.3	210.2	212.7	217.7	225.2	233.8	241.2	245.1

APPENDIX TABLE 3 Approximate standard errors for estimated numbers in section 11   **England and Wales**

Estimated number* (thousands)	Standard error (thousands)	Standard error as a percentage of estimated number
	Sample (1 in 10)	Sample (1 in 10)
0.5	0.07	14.0
1.0	0.09	9.0
5.0	0.21	4.2
10.0	0.30	3.0
20.0	0.42	2.1
30.0	0.50	1.7
40.0	0.58	1.4
50.0	0.64	1.3
60.0	0.69	1.2
70.0	0.74	1.1
80.0	0.78	1.0
90.0	0.82	0.9
100.0	0.86	0.9
150.0	0.99	0.7
200.0	1.07	0.5
250.0	1.10	0.4
300.0	1.10	0.4

* Numbers relate to those estimated in section 11 (social class) of this volume.

APPENDIX TABLE 4 Approximate standard errors for estimated percentages in section 11   **England and Wales**

Estimated number* on which percentage is based (thousands)	Percentages					
	5 or 95	10 or 90	20 or 80	30 or 70	40 or 60	50
(a) 1 in 10 sample (1976 to 1986)						
0.5	2.9	4.0	5.4	6.1	6.6	6.7
1.0	2.1	2.8	3.8	4.3	4.6	4.7
5.0	0.9	1.3	1.7	1.9	2.1	2.1
10.0	0.7	0.9	1.2	1.4	1.5	1.5
20.0	0.5	0.6	0.8	1.0	1.0	1.1
30.0	0.4	0.5	0.7	0.8	0.8	0.9
40.0	0.3	0.4	0.6	0.7	0.7	0.8
50.0	0.3	0.4	0.5	0.6	0.7	0.7
60.0	0.3	0.4	0.5	0.6	0.6	0.6
70.0	0.2	0.3	0.5	0.5	0.6	0.6
80.0	0.2	0.3	0.4	0.5	0.5	0.5
90.0	0.2	0.3	0.4	0.5	0.5	0.5
100.0	0.2	0.3	0.4	0.4	0.5	0.5
150.0	0.2	0.2	0.3	0.4	0.4	0.4
200.0	0.1	0.2	0.3	0.3	0.3	0.3
250.0	0.1	0.2	0.2	0.3	0.3	0.3
300.0	0.1	0.2	0.2	0.3	0.3	0.3

* Numbers relate to those estimated in section 11 (social class) of this volume.

SP(T)160 8/85

DRAFT OF PARTICULARS OF LIVE BIRTH TO BE REGISTERED

Reg Dist.	District & SD. Nos.		Entry No.
Sub Dist.	Date of registration		**A**

CHILD

1. Date and place of birth

   (date) ....

2. Name and surname — 3. Sex

FATHER

4. Name and surname

5. Place of birth

6. Occupation

MOTHER

7. Name and surname

8. Place of birth

9. (a) Maiden surname
   (b) Surname at marriage if different from maiden surname

10. Usual address (if different from place of child's birth)

INFORMANT

11. Name and surname (if not the mother or father)

12. Qualification

13. Usual address (if different from that in 10 above)

Signature of registration officer by whom the above particulars were obtained

Signature of registrar registering birth on declaration

SPECIMEN

L

N

grams

Edit Control

POSTCODE

LIVE BIRTH

District & SD. Nos.		Entry No.
Date of registration		

CONFIDENTIAL PARTICULARS

The particulars below, required under the Population (Statistics) Acts, will not be entered in the register. This information will be confidential and used only for the preparation of statistics by the Registrar General.

1. Where the father's name is entered in register:
   Father's date of birth

DAY	MONTH	YEAR

2. In all cases:
   Mother's date of birth

DAY	MONTH	YEAR

3. Where the child is of legitimate birth:
   (i) Date of marriage

DAY	MONTH	YEAR

   (ii) Has the mother been married more than once?   *YES   NO

   (iii) Mother's previous children (excluding birth or births now being registered) by her present husband and any former husband

   (a) Number born alive (including any who have died)

   (b) Number still-born

X Is this birth one of twins, triplets, etc   *YES   NO

If YES, complete (a) and (b)

*(a) Total number of births at this maternity

1   2   3   4   5   6

	Live births	Still-births
(vi)		
	(b) Entry No. of births	(b) Entry No. of births
(vii)		

G(a) Father

(i)   (ii)

(iii)   (iv)

H(a)* See cover for Employment Status codes
1   2   3   4   5

(va)

G(b) Mother

H(b)* See cover for Employment Status codes
1   2   3   4   5

(vb)

* Ring as appropriate

FORM 309

APPENDIX B Birth records: form of entry in register

NHS Number	**BIRTH**	Entry No.

Registration district

Administrative area

Sub-district

CHILD
1. Date and place of birth

2. Name and surname	3. Sex

FATHER
4. Name and surname
5. Place of birth
6. Occupation

MOTHER
7. Name and surname
8. Place of birth

9.(a) Maiden surname	(b) Surname at marriage if different from maiden surname

10. Usual address
(if different from
place of child's birth)

INFORMANT

11. Name and surname (if not the mother or father)	12. Qualification

13. Usual address (if different from that in 10 above)

14. I certify that the particulars entered above are true to the best of my knowledge and belief

.... Signature
....of informant

15. Date of registration	16. Signature of registrar

17. Name given
after registration,
and surname

SPECIMEN

Printed in the United Kingdom by Her Majesty's Stationery Office, Edinburgh Press
Dd 290851 C9 12/87 (252339)

**HMSO
BOOKS**

HMSO publications are available from:

HMSO Publications Centre
(Mail and telephone orders only)
PO Box 276, London, SW8 5DT
Telephone orders (01) 622 3316
General enquiries (01) 211 5656
(queuing system in operation for both numbers)

HMSO Bookshops
49 High Holborn, London, WC1V 6HB   (01) 211 5656 (Counter service only)
258 Broad Street, Birmingham, B1 2HE   (021) 643 3740
Southey House, 33 Wine Street, Bristol, BS1 2BQ   (0272) 264306
9–21 Princess Street, Manchester, M60 8AS   (061) 834 7201
80 Chichester Street, Belfast, BT1 4JY   (0232) 238451
71 Lothian Road, Edinburgh, EH3 9AZ   (031) 228 4181

HMSO's Accredited Agents
(see Yellow Pages)

And through good booksellers

ISBN 0 11 691216 2

KS2 English

CGP
– books
like no others!

Really
Important Stuff

The Revision Guide

CGP

Handwriting
Book 2

How to do well in primary handwriting

Primary Handwriting — Book 2
To do well in primary handwriting you should:

- Make sure that **all** your words are joined up using the right joining lines **all the time**.
- Make sure all your ascenders, (letters that go up, like - d, t, h, l, f, k, b) and descenders (letters that go down, like - q, y, p, g and j), are the same size.
- Make sure all of your ascenders and descenders stand up straight and don't slant.

Are you going to Handwriting Heaven or Handwriting Hell?

Contents

Published by Coordination Group Publications Ltd

Contributors:
Taissa Csáky, Chris Dennett, Chris Fenton, Tim Major, Kate Redmond, Katherine Reed

ISBN 1 84146 196 2

Groovy website: www.cgpbooks.co.uk
Jolly bits of clipart from CorelDRAW
Printed by Elanders Hindson, Newcastle upon Tyne.